ARIZONA
1970

Troopers West

This book is a limited edition.
Copy No 514 of 1000 copies.

Troopers West

Military & Indian Affairs on the American Frontier

Edited by Ray Brandes
Illustrated by De Grazia

FRONTIER HERITAGE PRESS SAN DIEGO, CALIFORNIA 92109
1970

Contents

v

Illustrations

My Frisky Horse

Apache Guide

Taos Rabbit Hunt

A Ride Home

Stampede

Mud House and Indians

Apache Hunter

One Little World

Maps

Introduction

Troopers West is an anthology by writers of Western American history whose interests have deep roots in the interpretation of military and Indian affairs. Each of these writings carries a message about conflict. The shock of the military theme is demonstrated through the arrowhead and the bullet, but the less dramatic story is that of cultural conflict.

As northern Europeans pressed hard from the east to cross the prairies and deserts of this land, and as southern Europeans—the sons of Iberia—pushed northward out of Mexico, the American Indian stood before them as a challenging foe.

The new peoples to this continent had their thirst quenched in the miracles which opened before them. For here stood the open space and free land, the abundance of timber, water, and minerals. Here came the freedoms sought by emigrants from a worn out European landscape —freedoms which shone through as hopeful signals overshadowing the warning omens.

The newcomers held but three views by which to deal with the native: to push him out of the way, to enslave him, or to exterminate him. All three viewpoints were eventually applied. The prejudices of the frontiersmen loomed large in the continental view that the "savage" was uncivilized, to be treated as a child, but by treatying he could be nurtured in the ways of western civilization.

Each tribe had its own traits, distinct cultural assemblages, and economic pursuits. Each group claimed recognizable boundaries, and made treaties and war with Indian neighbors, not unlike the Europeans. Only the Europeans interested enough, however, made the distinctions which considered that not all Indians were alike.

The tide of migration took the frontiersmen across the land following the lines of least resistance geographically. This push to the West overrode and then engulfed the First Americans, culminating in the reservation system.

The close of the 19th century marked an end to the military conflicts. The warrior no longer moved between confinement and open space. He could no longer draw his arrow to preserve some way of life. The Apache Gia-nah-tah who had shouted in 1863,

"Give us weapons and turn us loose, we will fight you again," was now silent. That kind of warfare had ended, but the cultural conflicts continued. With nearly three-quarters of this 20th century gone by, the Indian seems to be further than ever from his goals.

The accounts in this volume are emphatic—reflecting viewpoints of historians who see the several sides of those tragic eras of our past when the troopers and the warriors met in mortal combat. If these give more insight and meaning for the past then we have served an end—to help man understand man—and to not repeat the mistakes of the past.

—Ray Brandes

The U.S. flag spelled out "help" when this photo was taken of the Osage Dance and War Dancers at the Osage Agency, Oklahoma. Credit the *Eleventh Census of the United States*, 1890.

Mrs. Eve Ball, who calls herself a "teacher gone wrong," has lived in Ruidoso, New Mexico, for twenty-two years. She has become friends with, and has interviewed a number of Apaches. Over the years some of her informants have passed away, so that the heritage being preserved by Mrs. Ball will be more and more invaluable to the Mescaleros. For the past two years she has taught a most successful seminar on Apache culture at the College of Artesia. Her most recent book, *In the Days of Victorio*, was published by the University of Arizona Press.

Ray Brandes is Chairman, Department of History, University of San Diego. He holds a doctorate from the University of Arizona. During WWII he served in the European Theatre of Operations, and left the Army with the rank of Master Sergeant. He is a member of Phi Alpha Theta, The Western History Association, and a founder of the San Diego Corral of the Westerners. His next work is a biography of the Apache Mangas Coloradas.

Richard Dillon is Sutro Librarian and head of the historical and rare book collection of the Sutro Library in San Francisco. He holds a Master of Arts degree in history, and a Bachelors of Library Science, both from the University of California. Holder of a number of fellowships or research grants, he is currently working on a history of Hudson's Bay Co., in California titled Siskiyou Trail. During WWII he served as a combat infantryman in the ETO; wounded in action in 1944, he received the Purple Heart.

Greta S. Ezell holds a degree from the University of Arizona with a major in archaeology. As an associate consultant to the Gila-Pima-Maricopa Indian community (for land claims) she has researched the history, geography, natural resources, and cultural history of the Southwestern desert dwellers. Among her publications is "Thematic Changes in Yuman Warfare," with Henry F. Dobyns, Alden W. Jones and Paul H. Ezell in, *Cultural Stability and Cultural Change*, Proceedings of the 1957 Annual Spring Meeting of the American Ethnological Society.

Paul H. Ezell, born in Carbon County, Wyoming, obtained his Ph.D. from the University of Arizona. He has taken part in numerous "digs" in archaeological sites in the Southwest and from 1951, has been a research anthropologist for the Gila-Pima-Maricopa Indian community. Since 1956 he has been with the Department of Anthropology at San Diego State College. Since 1966 he has supervised the excavations programs at the Royal Presidio of San Diego. Among his publications is the *Hispanic Acculturation of the Gila River Pimas*, published by the American Anthropological Assn.

James R. Moriarty III, is with the department of history at the University of San Diego. He formerly served as an associate specialist in oceanography at the University of California. He attended Wayne State University, where he received his BA majoring in geology. He obtained his MA with emphasis on anthropology from San Diego State College, and is a doctoral candidate at United States International University. During WWII he served as an infantry sergeant in the U.S. Army, and was awarded the Bronze Star, the Bronze Arrowhead and for wounds, the Order of the Purple Heart with Star.

William Reed, born in Oklahoma, moved with his parents to Phoenix, where he was raised on a small ranch. In 1946 he enlisted in the U.S. Navy, and as a "mustang" officer had duty for several years in Turkey, in Europe and the Far East, when he worked for the Naval Security Group and other intelligence organizations. Holder of a Master's Degree in History from the University of San Diego, his most recent book of 1969, *Olaf Wieghorst*, a biography of the noted western artist, was selected as the outstanding Western Art book of 1969 by the National Cowboy Hall of Fame; the work was also named winner of the 1969-1970 Western Heritage Award. Reed is president of Frontier Heritage Press and is currently engaged in the biography of Tucson artist Ted De Grazia.

Don Rickey, Jr., lives in Hagerstown, Maryland, and is assistant director, U.S. Army Military History Research Collection, Carlisle Barracks. He obtained his doctorate from the University of Oklahoma and is the author of *Forty Miles a Day on Beans and Hay* published by the University of Oklahoma Press in 1963. He served aboard the USS Enterprise during WWII, in the Pacific, and on the USS Bache during part of the Korean conflict. He is a member of the Western History Association and the Company of Military Historians.

Harry Aaron Shiley, compiler of the bibliography for this volume, and producer of the maps, holds a BA degree from San Diego State College in geography and history. He graduated Summa cum Laude, is a member of Phi Kappa Phi and Phi Alpha Theta. He is a Master's candidate in history at the University of San Diego.

D. Harper Simms was born in Almagordo, New Mexico. His father was the trading post operator, and his grandfather the missionary on the Mescalero Apache Indian reservation at Dulce, northern New Mexico. Close contact with Apaches in his youth led to a lifelong interest in their history and customs. He graduated from the University of Missouri, worked for the Soil Conservation Service in the Southwest and in Washington, D.C., for thirty-three years. An editor of *Corral Dust* published by the Westerners of Washington, D.C., for seven years, he has, since his retirement in 1968, written a book about the history of soil conservation movement in the United States.

Dan L. Thrapp, graduated from the University of Missouri School of Journalism, joined the United Press, and lived in Argentina. He spent four years in the Army, emerging as Captain, Infantry, having served in Burma and China. After his service, he worked with the UP in London, Greece, and Italy and then freelanced in Africa. Since 1951 he has been with the staff of the *Los Angeles Times*. As a young man he traveled the American West working on cattle ranches; he once took part in a dinosaur-collecting expedition in the Big Horn Basin, and has packed in and out of the great rivers of the West. His two outstanding nonfiction books are *Al Sieber, Chief of Scouts*, and *The Conquest of Apacheria*, both by the University of Oklahoma Press.

Robert A. Weinstein, research associate in Western History for the Los Angeles County Museum of Natural History, is a specialist in several fields. His authority lies in Pacific Coast maritime history, and the history of early photographers in the western United States. He is honorary consultant to the Special Collections department of the UCLA library on photo archives, and Southern California representative for the San Francisco Maritime Museum. He is also Graphics Editor for the *American West* magazine. His most recent work is *Will Soule: Indian Photographer at Fort Sill, Oklahoma, 1869-1874*.

Photo by Frank Ferreira, Tucson, Arizona

De Grazia

by William Reed

THE SETTING WAS THE COLONIAL ROOM of a luxury hotel in Tucson, Arizona. Guests in formal attire wandered in boredom from busy group to busy group, sipping champagne while waiting for the guest of honor. The occasion was a press conference and cocktail party honoring the release that evening in New York of a De Grazia television special. A film of the special was standing ready on a projector in the center of the room, and the master of ceremonies had a worried look on his face. "What if De Grazia didn't show up? One never knew...he was a bit eccentric, you know."

Suddenly the front door swung open, and all eyes shifted to focus on the reason for their being there. He was a man of medium stature, with an unruly beard and a mischievous twinkle in his eye. He was wearing Levi denims and a Levi jacket with a large tear in one elbow. In stark contrast, his shirt was a pleated "after six" variety, open at the neck and topped with a red and white polka dot cowboy neckerchief. An Indian medicine bag hung from his neck on a strip of rawhide leather. As the television cameras swung in his direction he grinned, held up one hand signalling a pause, and pulled from the bag a pint of whiskey. He took a quick drink from the bottle, wiped the back of one hand across his beard, smiled at the group and walked forward to his seat of honor. The party was officially commenced. "Who in the hell is that?" asked one uninitiated guest. "You mean you don't know?" his friend replied. "That's De Grazia, the artist."

2   De Grazia the artist indeed, but no ordinary artist. He is an institution. The platform of his institution is the Southwest, which he knows and loves. Not just the land; not just the precise history of its peoples — although these are primary ingredients of his artistry — but also the color and life and movement which are unique elements essential to understanding this harsh but beautiful country. His major subjects are the Mexican and the Indian, and his success lies in the fact that he not only understands their language, but their philosophy. He understands also that quiet and unspoken something which enables them to hang on when seemingly all is lost. His understanding is not as a dilettante; it is the result of a learning process based on hard experience and keen observation. One must know the route well before he can draw a map for others to follow. It is apparent that the Southwest is a trail which De Grazia knows as few other men.

For Ettore "Ted" De Grazia the trail started in 1909 in the small mining town of Morenci, Arizona. As a boy, he grew up as lean and hard as the desert environment in which he worked and played. From the beginning he was an enigma, a "loner," a stark individualist. While other children played collective games, Ted often sat alone carving figures from the hard desert clay which, to his mother's dismay, he then insisted upon baking in her oven. His artistic ability was apparent at an early age, but this was not a golden key to societal acceptance and praise. This was not Vienna; this was Morenci. Here, life was tough and hard — there was no room for artistic nonsense and daydreaming. Survival depended upon pitting one's wits against the environment, not embracing it as a friend. Ted De Grazia never learned to accept this philosophy. For him, the desert is a thing of inestimable beauty; a flowing form of color, silent sounds, and delicate movement. This is the magic he has succeeded in capturing in his art. Add to this the spirit and drama of its Indian inhabitants, who love the desert in like manner, and his canvasses come alive. He puts it this way:

> Some people object to my art on the grounds that it is not photographic. They think I'm too abstract. They say, "That horse's neck is too long," or "That saddle doesn't even have a cinch!" It's funny, but that's the same objection I have to most of the art of the "realistic" school. You know, life is not a precise "slice of pie." It is not a "frozen movement," no matter how beautifully captured. We observe life around us as movement and color and sound; ever-changing and evasive of precise interpretation. It comes in chunks too big to digest at one setting; too immense to comprehend at a glance. Most of what we see around us is on the periphery of our vision — we feel it more than we see it. This is the essence I try to capture in my paintings.

There is little doubt he has succeeded. De Grazia's acceptance by the public in the last decade has been phenomenal. Rarely will he sell an original, but cards and prints of his works have been circulated throughout the world. Well over a thousand of his paintings have been reproduced. To this, Ted has the following comment:

> Artists sometimes approach me and ask what I think of their work. Sometimes it is good, and I tell them so. "Well," they say, "if it's good, why doesn't it sell like yours does?" Of course there is no way to answer this, but I usually tell them, "Go home and paint one thousand paintings, and you'll be good!" I seldom hear again from those who take me seriously. If they get through a thousand paintings, they will be good. They won't need me any more.

Success has come to De Grazia, but it was not an easy road, and it was no accident. It came as the product of great determination. His early education was one of experience and observation. He entered the first grade when he was sixteen years old, and graduated from high school at the age of twenty-three. In 1932, with fifteen dollars in his pocket, he enrolled at the University of Arizona in Tucson. Thirteen years later he graduated with three degrees, bachelor's of art and music, and a master's degree in music. His thesis was titled, "Art, and Its Relation to Music in Music Education." He then abandoned a proposed teaching career and, against the objections of his family, returned to his first love. De Grazia set a hard course; he would make it on his own as an artist. He almost starved. Even while in school he traveled constantly. In Mexico City in 1942, he met and studied art under both José Clemente Orozco and Diego Rivera. Both men were impressed with his talent and predicted in writing that he would "find his place in the sun." Orozco wrote in November, 1942:

> De Grazia's painting has all the freshness, simplicity and power of youth. He is able to go from the simple and graceful movement of the "Cocks Fighting" to the understanding of human misery as in the "Boy Playing the Violin." He will be one of the best American painters some day.

Their encouragement gave De Grazia new impetus, and in 1944 he built his first studio complex in Tucson. There were many lean years, and on one occasion he found himself painting decorations on mailboxes for fifty cents each, but he determined to stick it out. Slowly his work began to catch on. Eventually he saved enough money to build a new studio northeast of Tucson. Its setting was on the side of a desert hill, and its construction was accomplished in the most part by De Grazia and Yaqui Indian friends. The adobe of its walls and the dried cactus spines of its fences and ancillary structures come from, and blend harmoniously into, the rocky desert surrounding. It is not a static monument, it is rather a flowing form. De Grazia named it the *Gallery in the Sun.* De Grazia has found his place in the sun, and the world of

4 art has discovered De Grazia.

What kind of a man is he? This is an almost impossible question. De Grazia is ever-changing. Faced with challenge he is a tough opponent. When confronted by the demands of a society which insists upon a mediocre "normality" of behaviorism, he rebels. This has earned him the reputation among some as being an impossible eccentric — a classification which he shrugs off with a tolerant smile. Relieved of the necessity of defense, and secure in the intimacy of his own life-style, he is a warm and generous personality who gives unstintingly of his time and talent. More important than the viewpoint of others, is the way in which he views himself:

> A man has to believe in himself. I don't compare myself with another painter. When I paint, there is no other painter. That's why I never join art groups. Anyone can compare, copy and criticize, but when you face that empty canvas you are ultimately alone with your talent, creative ability, and determination to succeed. I was on a television show recently, and the interviewer asked me, "Why do you consistently sell so well when other good painters are having such a hard time?" "It's simple," I replied. "It's because I am the best!" Of course, the reaction to that attitude is explosive. "Did you hear what he said?" people will ask. They don't seem to understand that I *have* to believe that I am the best. In actuality, I don't waste my time comparing myself with other painters. I only know that each painting I do is in competition with myself, and it is hopefully the best that I can do. People ask me, "What is your best painting?" I tell them, "The next one. I haven't painted it yet."

My Frisky Horse

Apache Guide

Taos Rabbit Hunt

Stampede

Mud House and Indians

Apache Hunter

From the Collection of
Mr. and Mrs. Robert L. Walker
Tucson, Arizona

One Little World

DeGrazia
ARIZONA USA
SUMMER of 1970

Mangas Coloradas: King Philip of the Apache Nation

by Ray Brandes

FORTY YEARS AGO Will Levington Comfort wrote a fictionalized biography of Mangas Coloradas, or Red Sleeves, the "King Philip of the Apache Nation."[1] Despite the fact that there have been nine printings of the novel, few men have had much to say about *Apache*;[2] yet J. Frank Dobie called it, "...the most moving and incisive piece of writing on Indians of the Southwest that I have found."[3]

Comfort read numerous newspaper accounts and interviewed old-timers to create the breathtaking story.[4] As he developed the life of Red Sleeves, a majestic tale unfolded. Comfort not only pierced the warrior's character, but he reflected a deep sensitivity to the nature and character of the Apache Indians.

Comfort wrote other books but not one compares with the spell-binder—*Apache*—as it struck me those forty years ago—a myopic lad whose adventures had no limits while he held *Apache* in hand. So, too, had Comfort, as a young man, vicariously lived the essence of the way of life that was the frontier and of every Indian whose survival depended on the demands of a single day at a time. After Comfort introduced Mangas to the public, Elliott Arnold wrote his fictionalized biography of another Apache—Cochise, or *Neh-des-ee-chin*[5]—which rivals the Comfort work in style and character. Cochise, because of *Blood Brother*,[6] and with help from motion pictures and a television series has become legendary. These portrayed the Chiricahua chieftain, his friendship with gallant Tom Jeffords, and took note of two sons of the chief, Tahzay and Nachise.[7]

Mangas, a Warm Spring (*Chienne* or Red people) Apache has remained an elusive figure in narratives.[8] What little has been written has been highly fictionalized. Comfort and Arnold, though primarily *raconteurs*, could not have put their words down on paper in the effective manner which was theirs without having immersed their minds in the culture of the Apache. These men knew their subject, its time and its place. The dialogue in *Apache* and *Blood Brother* is not proved, yet it conveys the real sense of Apache life.

As nearly as can be determined Mangas was born about 1790, somewhere in the four-corner area where Arizona, Sonora, New Mex-

Captain John C. Cremony, with the California Column who took part in the Battle of Apache Pass, and who recorded many conversations with Mangas Coloradas. Arizona Pioneers' Historical Society photo.

ico, and Chihuahua meet. It may have been that life came to him in the Burro Mountains, or in the Gila Valley; his birth may have taken place at the Presidio of Janos in Chihuahua, or at Ojo de Mancus Colorado (so misnamed on military maps of the 1850's). One can only imagine those early years as he came to manhood, devoting his growing years to the hunt and the chase, and in the years of his marriage to Carmen (a Mexican captive) fathering a large family.[9] Red Sleeves grew in stature among his people. Physical prowess, and an inborn gift of diplomacy led him to become war chief of nearly all the Apache nation.[10] As a leader he suffered with the decline of this nation. And, after Mangas Coloradas had been murdered[11]—a disaster in the mind's eye of all Apache—his people did not cry *tats-an*, he is dead; they softly said *yah-ik-tee*, he is not present—he is wanting.

Had Mangas been educated by Father Font at the Santa Rita del Cobre presidio as is suggested but not authenticated by a number of secondary authors? Is it possible that Mangas was half *Mejicano* and half Apache as is implied in some primary documents? Physical characteristics of record—pictorial and written—and other evidence point strongly to such a conclusion. Yet Apache vehemently deny that a man could have become a chieftain were he other than an *Indio puro*.

His mastery of the Spanish language suggests there is no questioning the fact that his contact with the Mexicans had been more than that of casual meetings. He and his warriors rode along the main streets of Chihuahua City and Guaymas, circled at full gallop the walled cities of Tubac and Tucson and held the residents of these presidios at bay, and no doubt exists that they visited Santa Fé with regularity.[12] This man was no ordinary hombre.[13]

Mangas Coloradas appeared, at least to his contemporaries, as a giant of a man. Captain John C. Cremony, who had stood alongside the chief, described him as:

> ...something over six feet in height.[14] His frame was powerfully built, corded with steel-like sinews, and capable of any amount of endurance. His head was enormously large, with a very ample forehead; strong, aquiline nose; capacious mouth; broad, firm chin; and thick, pendulous ears. His deep, wide chest, long arms, and thin flanks announced the possession of more than ordinary strength. There was not the slightest evidence of obesity, but he could not have weighed less than two hundred pounds. His complexion was rather fairer than usual among the Apache warriors; and the expression of his sharp, brilliant, black eyes was not displeasing....[15]

Cremony could not be charged with exaggeration. He despised Mangas for the raids and crimes committed against the Americans and Mexicans, but had great respect for the ability of this Apache to maneuver the tribes when the occasion demanded.[16]

Some United States military officers compared Mangas to European leaders, but when Cremony wrote of Mangas he extolled his qualities in these words:

> Neither King Philip nor Logan, Uncas, nor Keokus, Black Hawk nor White Cloud, ever possessed the genius and ability of Mangas Colorado. None had his broad mental grasp; his wonderful craftiness; his unbounded ambition; his subtle and comprehensive knowledge of the elements he collected and managed; and none ever equaled him in blood-thirsty ferocity.[17]

Mangas won the respect of the foremost of the Apache, whose very names belied their hatred of the Mejicano.[18] The Apache bands were semi-nomadic, acting and living free and unfettered—the nature of the land on which they roamed making it nearly impossible for any large number of people to survive as a group. The desperate need for food resulted in tribal warfare. Yet, when an exterior force threatened the entire nation, the Apache warriors joined and selected leaders. At times Apache and Navajo fought side by side. Such contradictions demanded the adroitness of a strategist among these peoples—a diplomat. In the midst of tribal disunity the need of a joining together of groups in time of danger demanded a person greatly feared yet highly respected. Mangas shrewdly united his tribe to three most powerful Indian groups when he gave his daughters in marriage to the chiefs of the Navajo, Coyotero Apache, and Mescalero Apache bands.

As the Spaniards and other Europeans entered their domain, the question of self-preservation became paramount to the Apache. They found that they were being pressured by the Spaniards who were entering their lands from the south and that they had natural Indian enemies to the north and to the east. All of these sought the land and the game and some of the Europeans sought gold and silver and other minerals. As tides of Mexican settlers moved into the southern areas of New Mexico conflicts occurred with the Apache, and a feeling of hatred smoldered until it erupted into open warfare, and brought about retaliation in the forms of slave trade and scalp hunting. These pursuits came to be an accepted way of life—in fact, they developed into a form of "commissioned" warfare.[19]

Treaties, and peace establishments arranged by the state government of Chihuahua for the Apache failed to bring about a state of friendship or peaceful coexistence for any length of time. When Anglo-Europeans entered the southwest there is ample evidence that, despite the fact that Mangas and other Apache leaders sought alliances that would establish a sense of trust and a state of peace, the newcomers brought with them a hunger for land and a greed for minerals.

Red Sleeves recognized the signals of the might of the American government: its finest leaders were being ordered to the areas the Apache felt to be his own domain. Mangas parleyed with General Stephen Watts Kearny and the Army of the West; the Patties, father and son trappers—knew the chief; Major John Russell Bartlett of the Boundary Survey Commission ransomed captives from Mangas; Benjamin Wilson, the first Anglo mayor of Los Angeles, credited the chief with saving his life; and a virtual parade of travelers, Mexican and Anglo, mounted or afoot, wrote of this leader of men.[20]

Although Albert W. Aiken in *Kit Carson, King of Guides . . .*, credits the famous scout with having fought Mangas in "single combat" no such incident took place.[21] The two did meet during that time Carson worked at the Santa Rita Copper Mines.[22]

Mangas met with American authorities at Santa Fé in 1852, and figured prominently in the negotiations concerned with the Apache hope for peace and with faith in a nation much stronger than they. Mangas knew how to negotiate, and he trusted those with whom he was negotiating. His sensitiveness to the thoughts and needs of other men shows well in the agreements. While the Apache and the Indian agents waited for the United States Senate to ratify the Treaty of 1852, the agents had instructions to try to get their groups of Indians to turn to farming. Could these agents convince these nomadic raiders—these warriors who had stormed the adobe citadels of Sonora and Chihuahua over a period spanning several centuries—that they should take up the hoe and shovel, and do the type of work the Apache had always considered to be the work of women?

One man—Michael Steck—the agent of the southern New Mexican Apache, did just that.[23] In a fanciful account of early day Arizona, James Henry Tevis, one time Arizona Confederate, in his reminiscences titled *Arizona in the 50's*,[24] described Steck as a coward who had run from the Apache. Tevis had wrongfully tagged the man. On most occasions Steck went alone to the rancherías though at times he is known to have been accompanied by an interpreter. He became a beloved and trusted friend of the Apache from the Rio Grande to the Santa Cruz rivers. Steck put the Gila, Mimbreño and Warm Springs Apache to work. Mangas heeded Steck's counsel and they became trusting friends and allies. The Mimbreño Apache constructed and shaped irrigation ditches, plowed fields, and dug rows in which they planted melon, corn, wheat, and vegetables. Steck hauled in his wagons the seeds, tools, supplies and goods they needed. This Indian agent reported in 1858, that Mangas had settled many of the younger braves down and had prevented them from making their sporadic raids on the Mexican settlements in the south.

Congress, dealing with the Indians as a foreign power, delayed too long the ratification of the Treaty of 1852, and Bureau rations for the Apache failed to reach Steck's charges. The Apache found no recourse but to live on the gifts of nature and the better fortunes of others, bringing in its turn a resurgence of the hunt and the raid.

From that time forward Steck's influence proved to be no match for those of the civilians and the military who considered the land their own and who, little-by-little, drove the Apache from their reserves and to the south—in the only direction in which they could go. The Mimbreño and Gila warriors disappeared with their families into Chihuahua to take refuge at such presidios as Janos, where they had lived and traded from time to time in the historic past. But even there, as had happened earlier, soldiers from Sonora crossed the state boundaries in violation of peace treaties the Apache had made with the government of Chihuahua and entered the compounds to attack and kill the Indians.

Survivors fled back into New Mexico, to the sites of their old encampments in the Mimbres or Gila Cañon where some of their people had remained. Around Piños Altos and Santa Rita miners had moved in without regard for the rights of the Indian to the land. Citizens of Doña Ana formed vigilante groups to rid the Mesilla Valley of the Indians. The Apache committed their share of thievery, but they also had to take the brunt of charges which on many occasions should have been leveled at others. Steck's papers are filled with accounts of investi-

Apache Pass, Arizona. Cannon on wall of Old Fort Bowie overlooked the vital waterhole *Puerto del Dado*. Taken from illustration in the book by William A. Bell, *New Tracks in North America* (1869).

gations which revealed how cattle had been rustled by vaqueros who had come out of Mexico and how, on at least two occasions citizens of southern New Mexico communities, disguised as Indians, had made night raids into other towns to create confusion and raise a hue and cry against the Apache. Indians who came into Mesilla met hostility and were taken captive. Mangas, beaten and flogged—a humiliating experience for an Apache—hid from his family until he had recovered.

Mangas still wanted to work with Steck and still trusted his American allies, but by 1858 the chief had become a man possessed of the thought that trust and hope alone could never bring about a state of peace. Within the five following years, the forces he brought to bear played a vital role in creating a far larger and more forceful story.

The newspapers of Chihuahua and Sonora carry the quintessential accounts of these forays. The stories of the raids do not make pleasant reading but they are reality. Led by Mangas and Cochise the Apache stormed Bacuachi presidio. The walls of this presidio were twenty feet high but these warriors successfully broke them down. One can envision Mangas' entrance into the plaza at Guaymas; his storming of the walls of the Tucson presidio; his raids on Tubac and on Mesilla where his tormenters cringed in fear and then fled. *La Voz de Sonora*, the official newspaper of that State, regularly carried a headline titled "Incursiones de los Barbaros," which accurately noted that "Coyoteros, Chiricahuas, and other Apache have joined with Mangas Coloradas in the attacks on our communities."

The whole of the Gadsden Purchase flared and flamed as the Apache attacked wagon and supply trains. Mangas and the united Apache Nation, whose lands had been overrun by miners and settlers, made a desperate attempt to force the Anglos to leave. The braves raided and looted ranches and settlements almost without opposition. Those settlers who stayed behind sooner or later met the Apache in combat. Small parties of "over-landers" and miners, aware of the dangers, left Mesilla for Tucson and points west. After September 1860, few men who chose to court death in this way succeeded in completing their journey over that southern route.

In September 1860, Apache led by Mangas and Cochise boldly attacked the mining camp of Piños Altos. The pitched battle in the streets brought death to men of both forces. In February 1861, the two chiefs brought their forces into Apache Pass, and the encounter there with Lieutenant George Nicholas Bascom and the troops from Fort Buchanan lit another fuse, and through the spring and summer of 1861, a number of parties met horrible fates at the hands of the Apache.

The American Civil War—spreading out, finally to involve such Confederate and Union forces as were stationed in the west—only served to further kindle the anger of the Apache, who knew only too well that any disruption would furnish an opportunity to step up the tempo of their attacks. At Dragoon Springs the Confederate forces found the Apache to be a formidable foe and left several men buried near that stage station. A report in the *Los Angeles Star* of June 15, 1861 confirmed what most southwesterners already knew, that "...the Apache Indians seem to have control of the [New Mexico] Territory...."

Numerous blood-chilling encounters took place in the summer of 1861. One of these, the Battle of Cook's Springs, illustrates the problems which the historian faces in his efforts to separate fact from historical myth and legend. The life of Mangas Coloradas is filled with such fragmentary stories; most of these stories require careful sifting of evidence which has been assumed to be correct but frequently has been found to have been distorted. Mangas won the Battle of Cook's Springs but lost the war. This forceful tale must be put in context as to its importance, by reason of the fact that this conflict became the first of three tragedies which brought his life to a conclusion.[25]

Two eyewitnesses gave versions of the battle. Mangas gave his account to Jack Swilling at Piños Altos, New Mexico; Swilling gave "Uncle" Billy Fourr the account which he recorded. Cochise told of the fight while in Corralitos, Mexico. No Anglos survived the battle, nor did any Anglo see the battle in progress, so there can be no other versions than those related by the Apache. Expressmen and freighters who passed through the canyon two weeks later had a firsthand view of the tragedy.[26]

On the morning of July 20, 1861, seven men stood in front of the stage station in Mesilla. Each man was an experienced frontiersman and all had volunteered for the dangerous duty of transporting mail across the desert country, while on their way to California. The men were well known by residents in the Rio Grande Valley and none doubted they would safely cross the worst stretch of the road from Mesilla to Apache Pass nearly 200 miles away. As each man climbed aboard Conductor Freeman Thomas checked out weapons. Joseph Roacher, Matthew Champion, John Pontell, Bob Avlin, Emmit Mills and John Wilson[27] rode away with little, if any, notice.

The group covered the route in good time that day and night and the day of the twenty-first of July.[28] On the evening of the 21st, the coach started the climb up a difficult mountain pass.[29] About a mile from the summit a combined force of warriors,[30] led by Mangas Coloradas and Cochise, arose from behind rocks and other places of concealment in ravines to pour a murderous fire into the group.

Thomas ordered the driver to pull to the brink of the hill—to a place where the Indians could not move forward without exposing themselves to gunfire. In the race to the summit, Pontell, riding on the box of the coach, took a wound. The animals pulled the coach to the spot where the men took their arms, ammunition, and canteens of water and abandoned the vehicle. Thomas sent the stage careening along the road down the hill in an attempt to draw off the savages. The Apache stampeded the animals as the animals plunged down the grade and the coach overturned. The Indians then rushed forward to plunder the baggage and mail.[31] Thomas rallied his men to build a breastwork of slate slabs for protection. Each time the Indians stopped firing the men gathered more slate, and built up the parapet until it stood two feet high for good protection.[32] At dusk on the twenty-first the Apache suddenly withdrew and Thomas crept out to see if the warriors had left

Mangus, the son of the chieftain Mangas Coloradas. Arizona Pioneers' Historical Society photo.

the area. To his dismay he saw nearby some very well armed Apache watchfully on the alert.

This was not the first time Freeman Thomas had been in a tight spot—he had covered the route before and knew every possible avenue of escape. But Thomas saw the strength and disposition of the Apache force—a complete encirclement of these seven luckless men. As night drew on a sentinel was posted; the others slept. At daybreak the Apache attacked again and made every effort to dislodge the Americans. At midday the Indians put slabs of slate in front of themselves as armor and "belly-crawled" up the hill. Luck was not with them and Apache upon Apache became an easy target for the gunfire of the embattled Americans.

The hillside was strewn with battered bullets. Every rock and stone within many yards of the small fortress which might have concealed an Indian had bullets lying near. A small tree some 150 yards from the wall bore the marks of eleven balls.[33] A diminishing supply of ammunition and water brought a sense of panic to the Americans. Thomas made an attempt to snake his way down the hill to the springs on the evening of July 22. Again, he found the place too well guarded. The twenty-third of July proved to be a repetition of the preceding day. As the heat and the lack of water weakened the Americans, consolation could only be found in the mounting toll of Apache deaths. Each engagement brought down more of the Indians around the knoll. Each death increased the exasperation of the warriors and each new attack became more daring and persistent.

As night fell on the twenty-third of July Thomas, Avlin, and Wilson agreed they could not hold out another day without water and decided to try for the springs. For a few moments the men saw no movement; their hope that they could get to the water was roused and they agreed that two of them would cover the third man while he filled the canteens. Unknown to them a trap had been set. Mangas and Cochise let the men get near the waterhole and then closed the trap from all sides. Thomas took gunfire in both legs and fell. Avlin died without a word.[34] Wilson moved farther up on the ridge; the warriors went around, took a stand on top of the ridge and poured a dozen arrows into him. Thomas, wounded again, blood flowing from wounds above and below the knees, crawled and moved about on the stumps, firing with each move. When out of ammunition he threw, first, his pistol, and then, rocks, at the braves. Aroused by their success the Apache rushed the parapet and killed the four remaining men.[35]

The freighters Daguerre and Thabult, on their way through the pass a few days later, found and buried the bodies. They reported that everywhere the evidence of the terrible struggle appeared. All the bodies had been stripped of clothing and three had been scalped. The arms of nearly all had been broken; all had been shot through the head. Four of the bodies were found within the walled area; one in front of it; and two some fifty yards to the rear.[36] Under a stone on top of a wall Daguerre found a penciled note dated July 23, 1861, stating the men had fought for two days; that they had killed many Indians; that all the Americans had been killed or wounded but two; that they had run out of water and would make an attempt to escape that night.[37] Some time later Cochise related that out of 310 Apache he and Mangas had taken into the fight, only 125 came out alive. The victory had been an expensive one. Mangas is reported to have said later that the battle had uselessly weakened the combined warrior strength of the tribes. Whatever the correct figure for their losses might have been, Mangas and Cochise could not afford such a loss.[38]

One year later the California Column left Tucson and headed east to engage the Confederates in New Mexico. The Apache harassed every patrol sent out ahead, and sniped at the main body of troops as it lagged behind. In Apache Pass the combined forces of the Chiricahuas under Cochise, and the Mimbreños and Gilas under Mangas met the California Column head-on. In this engagement the California troopers clashed with, and dislodged with artillery fire, the warriors from the spring known as *Puerto del Dado*[39] and from the surrounding crags. This first use of artillery completely dismayed the Apache. Later, in a needless

The cemetery at Fort Bowie, Arizona, 1886. Whitewashed headboards and rough hand lettering marked the burial sites of soldiers and civilians of the period 1861-1891. Photo from Arizona Pioneers' Historical Society.

exchange of rifle fire with Trooper John Teal, Mangas was so seriously wounded that the Apache found it necessary to transport him to Janos on a horse, where he could be cared for by a presidio doctor. Within a few months Mangas had returned to his ranchería near Piños Altos, but this second of a series of three successive disasters had brought Mangas to his knees.[40]

In the spring of 1863, death came to Mangas at Fort Thorn, in southern New Mexico where the seventy-year-old chief had been imprisoned after having been taken prisoner at his ranchería. The story of deceit that culminated in his death by bayonet thrusts and minnie musket balls was an incongruous ending for this outstanding character and personage who had, in all good faith, placed his trust in the very pillars of the U.S. army in New Mexico.

Within a few months the army had routed the Gila and Mimbreño Apache and Mangas' wife had been severely wounded in an ambush. The strength of the warriors now having been sapped, by the year 1867 most of them had given up and submitted themselves to the way of life of the reservations. An era had been concluded and a way of life ended: a time not to be matched in ferocity until the last gasp of the Apache wars in 1886-1887. Of his entire family only Mangus, the younger, remained to act as a bridge between his people and the Anglos, and it fell to his lot to be able to act on numerous occasions to ease tensions. It is interesting to note that Mangus the son, never spoke of Mangas the father, that having been the custom of the Apache.

Could Mangas Coloradas have been the magnificent man—so dominant, proud, and honorable—as the Anglo leaders portrayed him to have been? Could he have been so treacherous and cruel as Mexican governors, Mexican soldiers, and the Anglo scalp hunters claimed him to have been? The truth is that Mangas exemplified all these traits. As a man who loved his wife and his sons and daughters he had been at the same time a man embittered by the breaking of treaties. He had placed full trust in special Anglo allies and their agents but had been at the same time filled with hatred for the miners who had trampled down his people's cornfields. He despised the cavalrymen who rode unmercifully and stupidly through the rancherías and killed his Mimbreño people.[41]

Mangas Coloradas, still a warrior at seventy, was so feared by U.S. military officers that, to make certain that he would not return—in life as a threat or in death as a martyr—field Army officers ordered him decapitated, drawn and quartered. In whatever perspective one may view this leader of men, Mangas Coloradas from 1842 until 1863, held in his hands the balance of military and diplomatic power in the American Southwest.

NOTES

1. In the biography of Mangas Coloradas, near completion by this author, there is still an uncertainty as to the origin and spelling of the name. John C. Cremony in "Some Savages," *Overland Monthly*, vol. 3, no. 3, March 1872, pp. 201-210, called Mangas Colorado the "King Philip of the Apache Nation," and stated he received his name from the practice of smearing his hands and arms with human blood. A number of authors give the spelling as Mangus Colorados, Mangas Colorado, and other varieties on the basis of the long, red-sleeved shirts the chief supposedly wore.

Evelyn Lillian Mangus Gaines, daughter of Carl Mangus, son of Mangus (and her daughter Martine Mangus) say that Mangas Coloradas does not mean Red Sleeves but Pink Shirt. (Letter from Mrs. Eve Ball to author, May 22, 1970.) Yet the name may stem from other associations. Francisco Velasco's work translated by William F. Nye, *Sonora*, San Francisco, H. H. Bancroft and Company, 1861, notes that "the region between Arispe and Gila ... is a place where there were medicinal herbs of marvelous efficacy, one of which called 'Colorada' is used by the Apaches for the treatment of wounds." There are other works cited in this present work which reflect a number of Apache who utilized the name "Coloradas," and William B. Griffen's very fine work, *Culture Change and Shifting Populations in Central Northern Mexico*, University of Arizona Press, 1969, suggests the use of "Colorados" as a band or group name in the Coahuila and Parras region from perhaps the year 1629.

2. *Apache* was first published by E. P. Dutton & Co., in 1931; an English edition by Stein appeared in that year; subsequent editions include the Bantam paperback of 1968. Reviews of *Apache* appeared in *Booklist*, May 1931; *Bookman*, April 1931; *Boston Transcript*, Feb. 28, 1931; *New York Times*, Feb. 8, 1931; *Outlook*, Feb. 11, 1931; and *London Times* Literary Supplement, Dec. 3, 1931.

3. J. Frank Dobie, *Life and Literature of the Southwest*. Dallas: Southern Methodist University Press, 1965 printing, p. 180.

4. James V. Mink, "The Making of a Southwestern Novel," in *Manuscripts*, vol. IX, no. 3 (Summer 1957), pp. 163-170.

5. Gordon C. Baldwin, *The Warrior Apaches*, Tucson, Dale S. King, 1965, pp. 29-30, who cites a conversation with Eugene Chihuahua of Mescalero, New Mexico, in 1961.

6. Elliott Arnold, *Blood Brother*, New York: Duell, Sloan & Pearce, 1947, 1954: in paperback as *Broken Arrow*, New American Library, Signet Book, 1966. No reviews of either edition of this work have been located. One should also see Arnold's article, "Cochise—Greatest of the Apaches," *Arizona Quarterly*, vol. 7, no. 1, 1951, pp. 5-12.

7. A few years back, while on the Apache reserve at San Carlos, this author sat in a small theatre and watched the youthful descendants of Cochise and Mangas cheer the horse-soldiers as they chased the Apache across the screen.

8. According to Mrs. Eve Ball, the "Red People" so took their name *Chienne* because of a red band from ear to ear across the nose. The Mimbreños and Warm Springs Apache are considered as one Apache band.

9. Mangas had at least two brothers, one named Felis (Phalis) Palacio, and another whose name is not known. Arnold, in *Blood Brother*, provides the name of a sister of Mangas who had married Cochise. Arnold called her Tesalbestinay. Mangas and Carmen had three sons—Mangas Chie, Salvador, and a third whose name is not known. All that is known of this third son is that he had been killed in an interband dispute in 1858. Arnold gives the names of three of Mangas' daughters but does not document the names. Cremony in "Some Savages," states there had been

three daughters, but does not provide their names. "Amelia and Christian Naichi say their grandmother, wife of Cochise, was the daughter of Mangas Coloradas," states Mrs. Ball. See also Col. H. B. Wharfield in *Cooley: Army Scout, Arizona Pioneer...*, the author, 1966, p. 7, note 7, notes "There is a surmise extant that Mangas Coloradas was the grandfather of Molly Cooley. If true, perhaps a daughter of the chief was married to Pedro of the White Mountain [Mescalero] Apache...."

10. Some of the Apache groups included the Jicarilla, Mescalero, Lipan, Pinal, Coyotero, Chiricahua, Warm Springs, Mimbreño, and Gila. Two factors make the determination and location of groups complicated: the various names and spellings given throughout the historic past for the same groups; the amalgamation of groups when the number of men in the bands dwindled.

11. The evidence for this assertion is conclusive. A few definitive sources include *The War of the Rebellion: a Compilation of the Official Records of the Union and Confederate Armys*, published under the direction of the Hon. Elihu Root, Secretary of War, Washington, G.P.O., 1901, Series I, vol. L, part 2, pp. 296-297; Daniel Ellis Conner, *Joseph Reddeford Walker and the Arizona Adventure*, Norman: Univ. of Oklahoma Press, 1956; Correspondence from Judge Knapp of Mesilla to the Superintendent of Indian Affairs, in the papers of Michael Steck, Zimmerman Library, University of New Mexico (reel 4 on microfilm); the *Santa Fé New Mexican*, April 14, 1865; diary of George Hand, on file at the Arizona Pioneers' Historical Society, Tucson, entry for January 12, 1863; and the various documents from General James Henry Carleton to officers in the field, January 1863, in English and in Spanish, ordering the death of Mangas. See Adjutant General's Office records.

12. (Chihuahua) *La Coalicion* (1859-1860); (Ures) *La Estrella de Occidente* (1858-1863); (Ures) *La Voz de Sonora* (1855-1859); (Ures) *El Nacional* (1853-1855); (Ures) *El Voto de Sonora* (1845-1848); (Santa Fé) *Republican* (1847); *Santa Fé Weekly Gazette* (1853-1865); *Rio Abajo Weekly Press* (1863-1864), and the *Mesilla Times* (1860-1862).

13. Major Horace Bell, *Reminiscences of a Ranger; or Early Times in Southern California*. Los Angeles, Yarnell, Caystile & Mathes, Printers, 1881, pp. 276-277.

14. The several accounts which describe Mangas' height vary from "over six feet" to "six and one-half foot," to "six feet six inches."

15. Cremony, "Some Savages," p. 201.

16. Cremony, "Some Savages," pp. 201-210.

17. Cremony, "Some Savages," pp. 201-202.

18. Among them: Delgadito (Dudeevia), Cuchillo Negro (Baishan), Costales, Veinte Reales, Han, Serjeanto, Josecito, Pino Blanco, Pionsey, and Geronimo (Goyakla) who proudly declared he had made his first foray, while yet a youth, into Mexico, under the generalship of Mangas.

19. For one account of this type of activity see "The Scalp Business on the Border, 1837-1850, Accounts of the 'Hair Raising' Exploits of two of History's Bloodiest Barbers, Kirker and Glanton," by Ray Brandes and Ralph A. Smith, in *The Smoke Signal*, Tucson Corral of the Westerners, Fall 1962, no. 6, 16 pp.

20. For a few primary contacts with Mangas see John R. Bartlett, *Personal Narrative of Explorations...*, New York: D. Appleton & Co., 1856, 2 volumes; William Elsey Connelly, *Doniphan's Expedition and the Conquest of New Mexico and California*, Topeka: the author, 1907; Samuel Cozzens, *The Marvellous Country, or Three Years in Arizona and New Mexico*, Boston, 1874; and John C. Cremony,

Life Among the Apaches, San Francisco, 1877, reprinted Tucson: Arizona Silhouettes, 1951.

37

21. Albert W. Aiken, *Kit Carson, King of Guides; or Mountain Paths and Prairies*, March 22, 1882, published in the Beadle's Boy Library. Too often stories in this dime-and-nickel novel have been stated as fact.

22. M. Morgan Estergreen, *Kit Carson: A Portrait in Courage*, Norman: University of Oklahoma Press, 1962, pp. 152-155. The Journal of Captain Abraham R. Johnston, 1st Dragoons, also notes a meeting of these two men. The Journal is included with Lt. Col. William H. Emory, "Notes of a Military Reconnoissance from Fort Leavenworth in Missouri to San Diego in California...," 30th Congress, 1st Session, *House Ex. Doc. No. 41*, 1848, pp. 579-589.

23. The Michael Steck papers are at the Zimmerman Library, University of New Mexico.

24. James Henry Tevis, *Arizona in the 1850's*. Albuquerque, University of New Mexico, 1954.

25. Several of the accounts of the Battle of Cook's Springs are noted here, but this is by no means a complete bibliography. See Cornelius C. Smith, Jr., *William Sanders Oury: History Maker of the Southwest*, University of Arizona Press, Tucson, 1969, which cites Oury's account in the (Tucson) *Arizona Daily Star*, July 27, 1879; Dan L. Thrapp, *Conquest of Apacheria*, Norman: University of Oklahoma Press, 1967. Thrapp cites Thomas Farish, *History of Arizona*, vol. II, Phoenix, Filmer Brothers Electrotype Co., 1915—but Farish provides no authorities for his data; Tevis, *Arizona in the '50's*, p. 229; Paul I. Wellman, *Indian Wars of the West*, New York, 1956.

  Other accounts are a creditable novel by Brian Garfield, *Seven Brave Men*, New York, David McKay and Co., 1966; the primary account of W. W. Mills, whose brother Emmit died in the battle, as recorded in George Griggs, *History of Mesilla Valley; or the Gadsden Purchase*, Las Cruces, Bronson Printing Co., 1930, and Mills own work, *Forty Years at El Paso: 1858-1898*, El Paso, 1901. (W. W. Mills, Emmit, were brothers of the army officer Anson E. Mills. The abbreviated article by my good friend, the late Douglas Martin, in *True West*, titled "Battle at Cooke's Canyon," in the Sept.-Oct. 1962 issue, pp. 16-17 should be consulted, and as well the article in the *San Francisco Evening Bulletin*, Sept. 6, and 7, 1861. Uncle Billy Fourr's manuscript, in the files of the Arizona Pioneers' Historical Society, Tucson, undated, pp. 119-120, contains one Apache account of the fight.

26. The *San Francisco Evening Bulletin*, September 6, and 7, 1861, carried accounts as reported by an expressman (unnamed) and the freighters Daguerre and Thabault —who buried the bodies.

27. The *San Francisco Evening Bulletin*, September 6, 1861, provides the accurate spelling of names of the men. Oury in the Tucson newspaper account of July 20, 1879, says six men left by stage from Mesilla; and Farish, vol. II, pp. 59-60, states that this was the Free Thompson party which left by stage. Tevis says eight or nine men left Mesilla, while Comfort called it the Free Thompson party which left by pack train. Farish says only that it happened in the spring of 1861. Historians believe that Farish took most of the information for his 8 volume *History of Arizona* from newspaper accounts. A study by this author suggests that Farish sprinkled his works with reminiscences and documents. Unfortunately his *Works* have a very slim bibliography, and a search for his notes has not turned up a leaf. The account as by W. W. Mills states that eight men were killed (in Griggs, p. 51).

28. The *Mesilla Times* for January 15, 1862 (copy by courtesy New York Historical

Society) indicated the distances along the mail route as:

Mesilla to

Rough and Ready	12
Goodnight	52
Cooke Spring [Cook's Springs]	14
Mowry City	18
Dinsmore Spring	16
Soldier's Farewell	14
Barney's Station	19
Steen's Peak	21
San Cimona [San Simon]	13
Apache Pass	18

29. Except for Farish who said it occurred at Stein's Pass, all accounts agree that the place was Cook's Canyon.

30. The precise number of warriors is difficult to ascertain. Farish said "400 or 500 men"; three accounts say, "300 Indians"; others do not hazard a guess. Four probably came closest with "a war party of 60"; the *San Francisco Evening Bulletin* of September 7, 1861, stated, "It is supposed that the Indians numbered at least 100."

31. Tevis testified not too long afterward, he had seen the overturned stage. One assumption is that Tevis may have been the expressman, unidentified in the San Francisco newspaper. Oury notes that some years later that the charred remains of the wagon destroyed by the Apache in 1861 had been seen.

32. Fourr says the men had a few rocks to hide behind, p. 119. Mills said in Griggs, *History of Mesilla...*, p. 65, the men built stone breastworks two feet high and enclosed a space twelve feet square.

33. All accounts agree the fight lasted 3 days. The account by Daguerre and Thabault in the *San Francisco Evening Bulletin*, Sept. 7, 1861, described the battle site. W. W. Mills in *El Paso...*, gives precisely the same information; he visited the site where his brother had been killed.

34. The various accounts disagree on minor points but Tevis reported nearly this same information and Farish, pp. 59-60, said that the "Tucson party" which buried the men found that one man, wounded and bleeding badly, had dragged himself from one vantage point to another around the hill—[the man was Thomas].

35. *San Francisco Evening Bulletin*, Sept. 7, 1861.

36. *San Francisco Evening Bulletin*, Sept. 7, 1861.

37. W. W. Mills, a brother of the Emmit Mills killed in the fight, had been imprisoned in Mesilla, during the first months of the American Civil War. While in jail, someone handed him a copy of a newspaper which related the account of the battle and the death of his brother.

38. Fourr, pp. 119-120, said that Mangas had bragged to Swilling about the fight at Piños Altos, stating that the white men at Cook's Canyon had killed 25 Indians and crippled many more. Mangas, much impressed by the bravery and fighting ability of the Anglos said, if his Indians had been as fearless as those few men he could have whipped the world. According to Oury's account in the *Arizona Daily Star* (Tucson), July 27, 1879, Cochise went to Corralitos to dispose of the loot and said that with 25 such men he could undertake to whip the whole United States. Douglas Martin in "Battle of Cooke's Canyon," said "a more conservative estimate based on other studies indicates that less than forty Apaches were slain and another twenty wounded...," p. 17. Briggs citing Mills says the Indians sold the arms and

watches taken from the Anglos after the battle in Mexico and said they lost 40 warriors in the fight, p. 16.

39. This waterhole, now so diminished as to be hardly worthy of note, a very significant point along the trail east and west was known from Spanish times as an assured source of water. A procession of travelers passed that way; miners, '49ers and Union and Confederate soldiers moved back and forth through the pass which was ringed with the rancherías of Cochise's Chiricahuas.

40. For the official accounts of the Battle of Apache Pass see *War of the Rebellion...*, Series I, vol. 50, various documents; Cremony, *Life Among the Apaches*, and articles which appeared in *Arizona Highways* in issues of Dec. 1935, January and February 1936, and May 1938.

41. The Steck papers and various letters in the records of the Adjutant General's Office substantiate these statements. As one example, on April 6, 1856, Steck wrote to George Manypenny, Commissioner of Indian Affairs, about an expedition out of Fort Thorn led by Colonel Chandler in pursuit of renegade Apache in the Mimbres Mountains. The troops espied a ranchería, rode into the camp, and fired for some twenty minutes before the discovering that these Apache had been members of a peaceful group who had been assisting the army. Chandler admitted to the mistake at the time, and offered to pay for the killed and wounded. Steck, called to the scene by the Apache to ease tensions, said, "not all the children who fled the scene were found." Steck Papers, roll 2, pp. 63-163.

Warrior-Soldiers:
The All-Indian 'L' Troop,
6th U.S., Cavalry,
in the Early 1890's

by Don Rickey, Jr.

THE ENLISTMENT of Brule Sioux men in L Troop, 6th Cavalry, in the early spring of 1891 on the Rosebud Reservation in South Dakota, came at the end of what was probably the worst winter of hunger, want, and black despair the western Sioux had ever known. Thousands of United States soldiers had campaigned over and occupied the Rosebud and Pine Ridge Reservations during the Ghost Dance disturbances. Terrified Sioux families had fled their homes in fear of the troops, becoming war refugees in their own homeland; leaving their cabins and camps to be looted and ransacked while they themselves sought shelter at the agencies or hid shivering in the badlands.[1]

War, famine, disease, and despair had stalked the land. Women, children, and old people had suffered—but perhaps the active Brule men in the twenty to forty age group had suffered most of all. Not only had they been living under the same physical hardships as the others, but in addition opportunities to fulfill their traditional roles as self-respecting Brule men and warriors had not existed since the end of the buffalo hunting life, confinement to reservations, and enforcement of intertribal peace and white concepts of law and order imposed on the northern plains Indians almost ten years before. For the active men, the reservation world of early 1891 seemed to offer no hope for a people whose traditions of manhood were rooted in the achievement and display of warrior-hunter virtues of bravery, courage, and physical strength.

By March, 1891, troops had been withdrawn from the reservations, and the Brule people were picking up life threads disrupted by the troubles of the previous winter. When Army officers began to speak of an opportunity for eighteen to thirty-five-year-old men to enlist as soldiers in the Army, with all the privileges, duties, and status of regular soldiers, the idea was very appealing to many Brule men.

The concept of enlisting Indians in all-Indian units, as part of the United States Regular Army rather than as scouts, had been under consideration for over a year before the order to do so was issued as General Orders No. 28, 1891, from the office of the Adjutant General of the Army.[2] Inspector Frank C. Armstrong, Indian Department, had formally proposed the enlistment of Indians in a letter sent to the Secretary of the Interior in January, 1890.[3] Armstrong was a man of wide, varied, and long experience in the Indian service. He understood the restlessness and frustrations affecting active Indian men restricted to life on reservations, where there was nothing for them to do to be men as their traditional way of life had taught them how men should be. This had been an important factor in troubles on several reservations, such as the November, 1887 outbreak among some of the restless young men on the Crow Reservation.

Enlistment in the Army was proposed as a way of offering active Indian men an opportunity to achieve status as soldiers, learn the ways and values of white civilization, and at the same time keep the more restless among them under the close supervision and control of the Army. The experiment had worked very well during a time of threatened outbreak among the southern Cheyennes in western Oklahoma in 1885, when General Philip H. Sheridan had asked Armstrong to recruit and organize a unit of soldier-scouts. Armstrong, drawing on his experience as a Brigadier General in the Confederate Army and his personal contacts with western Indians as an Inspector, enlisted 120 members of the Cheyenne Dog Soldiers, the most restless men on the Cheyenne-Arapaho Reservation, and peace and order were consequently maintained by the very Indians whom it was feared would have been the most turbulent.

The Indian soldiers suggestion was forwarded to the Secretary of War by the Secretary of the Interior. War Department consideration followed; including the requested opinions of several of the Army's highest ranking and most experienced officers. General O. O. Howard favored enlisting Indians, as an experiment, provided their number would not be subtracted from the already inadequate number of enlisted men allowed in the Army by existing legislation. General George

Crook was against the concept of trying to make precision, drill-ground, spit-and-polish soldiers out of Indians, because he believed that Indians were too individualistic and unused to acceptance of guidance and controlling authority over every aspect of their daily lives as would be demanded of them as regular soldiers. Instead, Crook advocated enlisting Indians in scout units, to be stationed on their own reservations and not moved away to strange surroundings unlike their reservation homes. General Nelson A. Miles agreed in general with Crook's recommendations. Generals John R. Brooke, Wesley Merritt, John Gibbon, and Colonel B. H. Grierson all recommended against the idea. Only General Howard and General T. R. Ruger, who had been associated with Armstrong in settling the Crow troubles in the fall of 1887, and General David S. Stanley replied that they favored the experiment.

Six of the nine high ranking officers whose opinions were asked came out opposed to the idea of enlisting Indians as soldiers. And of the six, at least one, Colonel Grierson, expressed an attitude that was openly prejudiced against Indians; replying that in his opinion Indians would not make good soldiers because they were sullen, indifferent, superstitious, and untrustworthy.[4] Grierson's attitude seems a little surprising and ironic, considering that he himself had led non-white troops, the black soldiers of the 9th Cavalry, for over twenty years, was very biased in their favor, and had good reasons to know that racial prejudice had often been unfairly directed against his own troops.

Although the majority of high ranking Army opinion opposed enlisting Indians, the Secretary of War, Redfield Proctor, was very much in favor of doing so; and, accordingly, the order to enlist Indians for L Troop, 6th Cavalry was issued early in 1891.

Brule reaction to the idea was interested but wary and questioning. Leading men among the Brule were, at first, of different viewpoints on having their young men join the Army as soldiers. Two Strikes, however, was one who took the lead in promoting enlistment. He believed this would be a fine way to show the loyalty and good faith of the Brule people toward the Government and the Army, and he wanted his position of peaceful cooperation made clear. Two Strikes' son and nephew were among the first to enlist, early in April, 1891. His attitude toward the idea was written down, at his request, by Lieutenant E. E. Dravo in a letter that Two Strikes asked him to send to Captain R. H. Pratt, head of the Indian School at Carlisle, Pennsylvania. Pratt had written asking Two Strikes about rumors of more trouble brewing among the restless young men on the reservation. Two Strikes replied that such rumors were false, and that he had encouraged the younger men to enlist to show good faith in keeping the peace, explaining, "we see that this is a very good chance for our young men to do something for themselves, and make men of themselves, and we let them enlist.[4]

Recruiting for L Troop, 6th Cavalry, began when 1st Lieutenant Edward E. Dravo arrived at Rosebud Agency from Ft. Niobrara, Nebraska, with a detail of three non-commissioned officers and six privates of the 6th Cavalry the evening of March 28, 1891. He discussed the project with Captain Jesse M. Lee, who had long standing contacts with and the confidence of the Brule people, and who was then on special detail at the agency. Captain Lee had already spoken of the enlistment idea to several leading men among the Brules. After talking with Captain Lee and Agent Wright, Lieutenant Dravo announced that he would explain the enlistment offer to all interested men in a meeting at the agency on Friday, April 3.

The day of the meeting saw a very large turnout of Brule men. The Lieutenant explained that the enlistments would be for five years, as they were for white soldiers, that Indians who joined would be treated the same as white soldiers in every way, and that ten out of the desired fifty-five recruits would be allowed to have their wives and families with them at Ft. Niobrara. This last was a special consideration, as Army policy in the early 1890's was very much against allowing private soldiers to be married and have their families living at Army posts. Monday, April 5, was set as the day when enlistments would begin, when all the men who wanted to join the Army, and could pass the physical examination, would be signed up as regular soldiers in L Troop, 6th Cavalry.[5]

Following his speech explaining about enlistment, Lieutenant Dravo was asked many questions, and some older Brules spoke against the idea of enlisting in the Army. Objections were raised about having the young men taken away from their people and reservation—that they might be sent to some far-off place as a form of exile, as had happened to some Apache and Cheyenne scouts who had been exiled to Florida and the Indian Territory along with their hostile kinsmen. Captain Lee and Lieutenant Dravo assured the Brules this was not going to happen, but, that those who served in the Army might indeed have opportunities to travel around in far places of the Great Father's land and learn much in their travels. Several of the older men, who had been on trips to Washington and other places in the east, echoed the officers' viewpoints. "The old men grasped this idea with wonderful quickness, and...told the young men it would be a good thing for them to go all over the Great Father's country."[6]

Another point raised by the Brules was that of rank and promotion, as they said that they wanted corporals and sergeants appointed right away among those who enlisted and that some of the enlistees should be made officers as soon as possible.[7] Dravo reported that this demand was overcome by "...some of the young men who had been to Carlisle [explaining]...in their own way, how impossible such a condition was."[8] Lieutenant Dravo ended the meeting by emphasizing that the Brules would be "showing their friendship for the Great White Father by entering his service."[9]

The recruiting meeting was very successful. Two Strikes, Sky Bull, High Bear, Turning Bear, Big Turkey, and Fast Thunder were all in favor of having their men enlist. By the end of the meeting sixty-seven men had offered to enlist.

By Wednesday, April 8, thirty-two men had passed the physical examination and were enlisted. Applications dwindled for the next few days, due to opposition on the part of people who did not want any of the Brules to leave the reservation. But, reported Dravo, "...assisted by the young men who had already enlisted, we were able to overcome this opposition."[10] A total of fifty-four Brule men had been enlisted by April 23.[11]

The recruiting trip had been entirely successful, and much good will had been built. Twenty-three men had come from what the Indian

Fast Thunder, Dakota Sioux, the chief who led the move to get warriors to enlist in "L" Troop, 6th U.S. Cavalry. Studio portrait by Heyn and Matzen; copyright c1900. Smithsonian Institution photo.

Bureau termed the "non-progressive" camps of Sky Bull and Big Turkey. Turning Bear, a leader among the warriors who had been out in the badlands during the Ghost Dance troubles, wanted his sixteen-year-old son to be enlisted. When the age limits were explained to him, both he and High Bear asked that they be notified if ever L Troop should be called out to fight, so that they could go along as volunteers with their soldier kinsmen.

Once the enlisting was completed, all those who had joined were told to assemble at the agency on April 24. Then, Lieutenant Dravo explained that the new troop would be sent out on a tour of the reservation just as soon as they were uniformed, armed, mounted, and had learned the basic military drills. This announcement greatly pleased the enlistees and their relatives, and the new soldiers were eager to go to Ft. Niobrara and get their uniforms. When the Army wagons came to get them that evening, the new troopers were very happy and sang far into the night; looking forward to the morning when they would journey to the Army post near Valentine and become blue-uniformed soldiers in the Great Father's Army, as befitted warriors and the sons of warriors.*

*A listing of Brules who enlisted for L Troop, 6th Cavalry, in April, 1891, appears as an Appendix at the end of the article.

Two Strikes, Brulé Dakota, the chief who took a lead in idea that warriors should enlist in "L" Troop, 6th U.S. Cavalry. It was one of his sons, Yellow Hand, who became the close friend of Private Hartford G. Clark. Photo taken by Gardner in 1872. Smithsonian Institution photo.

Above: High Bear, Dakota Sioux, too old to enlist in
the 6th U.S. Cavalry, told troopers if he was ever needed
he would volunteer to fight. Studio portrait by Heyn
and Matzen, copyright 1900. Left: Big Turkey, Dakota
Sioux, wearing hair-fringed shirt and feather bonnet.
He agreed to let his braves enlist in "L" Troop,
6th U.S. Cavalry. Photographer of this studio portrait
unknown, 1904. Smithsonian Institution photos.

48 At Ft. Niobrara the Brule cavalrymen would enter a new life entirely strange to most of them; for the fort was a gateway opening into the military aspects of the white culture and civilization whose coming had doomed their old free life as hunters and warriors. In the Army post these Brule men would live and serve like white soldiers, and through their training and close contact with white men learn much about the white people and their customs. Daily contacts with white soldiers and officers enabled the Brule soldiers to learn the ways of white men, and at the same time white soldiers, who had only a few months before campaigned against the Sioux on the Rosebud and Pine Ridge Reservations, had continuing opportunities to understand the Brules as men and soldiers like themselves.

One of the white 6th Cavalrymen stationed at Ft. Niobrara was Private Hartford G. Clark, and it is through his diary entries for the year 1891 that much of the history of L Troop, 6th Cavalry is reflected.[12] Harry Clark was an active, adventurous young man from Exeter, New Hampshire, who had joined the Army for adventure in the West. Before the winter campaign of 1890-1891, he had no personal contacts with Sioux people; but from several of his early diary statements written in January, 1891, he had heard and absorbed many prejudiced stories about the Sioux, and generally believed them to be murderous "red fiends" and much inferior in every way to white people. He had taken part in at least one small action with Indians, had participated in looting Indian homes—noting in his diary that he thus acquired many Indian objects and "relics," including a pair of leggings he stripped from a warrior's corpse on Wounded Knee Battlefield—and he wrote that when he heard the warriors yell in action it made him "feel like killing them all or seeing them killed."[13] Clark even went so far as to obtain a Sioux scalp from one of Lieutenant Casey's Cheyenne Scouts, so he could hang it over his bed "... to kindle a strong temper against the Indians."[14] Beyond a doubt, Private Harry Clark was a thorough-going Indian-hater as of January, 1891.

Like most hatreds, Clark's was rooted in prejudice directed against

a people he had no real personal knowledge of, except as enemies.
Changes in Private Clark's viewpoints towards Indians, after he became acquainted with some of the Brule men of L Troop, indicate, however, that he was not a man who continued to be prejudiced against all Indians as a group, because he became a good friend to at least one of the Brule cavalrymen and treated other men as individuals rather than as members of a despised alien race far different from his own.

"L Troop of 6th Cavalry composed of Indians came in tonight from Rosebud agency," wrote Private Clark in his diary for April 25, 1891. "They have got on their buckskin suits, as they have not been issued the blues yet." The Brule recruits rode into the post in wagons. "They were feeling very jolly and kept singing while going through the post." Two days later, after the L troopers had been settled into their barracks, Two Strikes and a party of Brule people from Rosebud visited the fort to see how their young men were being treated—and to talk with the post commander in hopes that he could help get their beef ration increased at the agency, because it was far from enough for the number of people to be fed.

On April 28, the Brule soldiers received their uniforms, and felt "...very proud when dressed in Uncle Sam's clothes." Meanwhile the Brule recruits were getting acquainted with Ft. Niobrara and its white soldiers. Harry Clark mentions that he "got acquainted with...a son of Chief Two Strikes" a few days after the L troopers arrived.[15]

The commanding officer of L Troop, the same Lieutenant Dravo who had recruited the troop, was very pleased with the way things were going, and was convinced the Brules would make good soldiers. "I have them now in uniform," reported Dravo on May 2, "and have commenced their drill and instruction in the care of barracks, kitchens, etc. They are very proud of their position, and I never saw a lot of men try so hard to [learn]...They will, I believe, make a magnificent troop of cavalry."[16] Within a week or so of their arrival, the men of L Troop were beginning to be integrated into the life of the post—hair trimmed in Army fashion, dressed in brass-buttoned blue uniforms, and learning their military drills as soldiers. One major factor kept them from becoming more rapidly assimilated into the Army and the life of the post, and that was the fact that very few could speak or understand English. All being from the same background, they naturally tended to keep to themselves and somewhat apart from the white soldiers, especially for having dances and singing sessions at night in and near their own barracks; which occasioned considerable interest and attracted white soldiers, first as spectators and later, in some cases, as participants. On their part, the Brule soldiers were interested in watching white soldiers participate in such activities as baseball, and at least one of them, who

told Private Clark that his name was Yellow Hand, became a player on the post baseball team.[17]

Some sports, common to both white and Brule soldiers served as a meeting ground for these men of different cultures. Writing in his diary on a warm Sunday evening in late May, Harry Clark noted, "... some fellows came running in the [troop] library shouting 'Clarkie, come and see the race." So off I went for the scene of excitement, and there found several Indians having a race, ... and they could run too. Tappan of A Troop ran against one of them (Cheyenne) and got beat — quite a little excitement prevailed."[18]

By the end of May, Private Clark thought the L troopers were getting along very well, that they would escort General John R. Brooke when he came to Ft. Niobrara on his way to the Rosebud Reservation, and that L Troop would also be chosen to go on a trip to Chicago.[19] On May 26th, two wagon loads of Brule women and children, the ten families authorized for the married L Troop members, arrived at the post. "Some very pretty squaws and Indian girls were among them," noted Harry Clark.[20] Wooden-floored tents had been prepared as quarters for them behind the post hospital. Their L trooper husbands were very glad to have them in the post, as they had been left behind until quarters could be made ready. Since nearly all the Brule soldiers were married, and only ten families were authorized for the fifty-five men in the troop, many L troopers' families remained back home on the reservation, spending only part of the time camped in or near the post in their own tipis. This factor grew to cause much dissatisfaction as time passed, and was probably the main reason that some L troopers chose to purchase discharges after one or two years of service. The presence of their families was very important to the Brule soldiers, and more than the ten authorized wives and families were present at the post from time to time. In January, 1892, several families of Indian soldiers were living among the laundress-wives of the white soldiers; a situation that made for inter-action between the wives and children of the Indian and white married enlisted men, giving each group opportunities to learn the ways of the other.[21]

As the end of May, 1891, drew near, Private Harry Clark's diary made increasing mentions of his Indian friend Yellow Hand. The two went hunting together, exchanged gifts, and got to know one another quite well. Apparently, the two young men shared several interests, as both liked hunting, riding, and baseball. Clark pitched for the all-post team, and Yellow Hand was at least a part-time player. On May 30, Decoration Day of 1891, the Ft. Niobrara baseball team went into Valentine to play the local team as part of the day's celebration; the events of which were to further cement the friendship between these two young soldiers from different cultures.

Arriving at the baseball field in Valentine, the Ft. Niobrara team found that they had to loan some players to the local team in order to make up two teams. After the first half of the fourth inning, the Valentine team gave up, as the score was thirty to one in favor of the soldiers, and the Valentines' only run was scored by Yellow Hand. Shortly after the game, wrote Clark, "Yellow Hand, my Indian friend, came near getting cut pretty bad with a dirk in the hands of a drunken cowboy. The cowboy came up to Yellow Hand and told him he was no good, nor any of his race, and that he could lick him—I told this fellow to go about his business, as he would surely suffer by fooling with Y[ellow] H[and]; and at the same time he pulled a dirk...and said he would cut the heart out of him anyway. But Y[ellow] H[and] was too shrewed [sic.] for him; he grabbed him by the arm and I pulled the knife out his hand, and then Y[ellow] H[and] gave him a good thrashing."[22] Valentine could be a very tough place in 1891, and Private Harry Clark proved his friendship there for his fellow soldier, a Brule Sioux trooper of L Troop, 6th Cavalry, in a way that Yellow Hand did not forget and that he understood very well.

The following night, the Indian soldier invited Clark to meet his family, living in a tipi about a mile from the barracks. "I went in to the teepee [sic.]," said Clark, "and had a chance to see the finest little Indian baby (8 months old) I ever saw. He has also," noted Clark, "got a pretty wife."[23] After the visit Clark took Yellow Hand to meet his friend Fred Bloom, an 8th Infantryman in charge of the post pump house and a practising photographer. On the way back to the post, Clark and Yellow Hand ducked into the L Troop barracks when a heavy rain began—and Yellow Hand insisted that Clark take a rubber coat to keep dry in the down-pour. The Indian soldier and the white trooper had become fast friends—and personal contact had overcome the prejudice and hatred that Private Clark had reflected in his diary only five months before.

As the weeks passed, L Troop was trained and drilled as soldiers, and learned a great deal about the Army—including participation in the old Army habit of payday drinking sprees. As enlisted soldiers, the men of L Troop were permitted to purchase beer and wine at the post canteen, the same as any other soldiers. Naturally, some got into trouble as a result—one L Trooper being hospitalized June 6, 1891, after being injured in a payday free-for-all. However, reports on Army alcoholic problems reveal that there was less, or at least no more problem drinking among the Indian soldiers than among their white comrades.

As of June 6, L Troop still had not its horses and full equipment. Private Clark noted that the Brule soldiers didn't seem to have much to do, and that this caused some resentment among white troopers, who were compelled to prepare for inspections and drills that L Troop was not yet a part of.[24] A few days later, Clark said that some of the Brule soldiers had gone Absent Without Leave from the post—but he was sympathetic, writing, "they miss their old ways of freedom—and who can blame them."[25] Plenty of white soldiers did the same; deserting into the bargain. None of the Indian soldiers meant to desert though, and like many white absentees, soon voluntarily returned to their duty station.

As the summer of 1891 progressed, so did the military indoctrination and training of L Troop at Ft. Niobrara. Shooting and riding were skills the Brule men took great joy in, but the language problem continued to hamper their training in military matters, and not all aspects of life as Army soldiers were well understood and adapted to by the Brule soldiers. Some of the medical treatments seemed strange to them, and several suffered from sore legs as the result of vaccination for small-pox.

"Five Indians of L Troop—Spotted Eagle, White Horse, Black Horse, Omaha, and Cheyenne came to the hospital...with sore legs, the effects of being vaccinated a few days ago," wrote Harry Clark. The L troopers didn't like being confined to the hospital, and "the steward had hard work to keep them in, they are continually getting up and going out, and that is against the rules of the hospital."[26] Unable to keep the Brule soldiers inside the hospital, the steward tried another tactic the next day, July 31, when he "...took away the Indian's clothes ...to keep them from going out so much, but it did not work. "Soon as night came," said Clark, "they went to see their squaws in their under-clothes and did not get back until 9:30 pm."[27]

Toward the end of August, 1891, the men of L Troop finally were given an opportunity to pay a visit to the Rosebud Reservation, in connection with a large gathering of Sioux people for meetings at the agency. L Troop left the fort August 27, marched to the reservation, and camped for about ten days near St. Mary's Mission; where they were visited by many relatives and had ample opportunity to impress the home folks with their new status as United States cavalry soldiers. Since L Troop was now considered adequately trained, mounted, and equipped, their service as soldiers took on much more variety.

Immediately after returning from the Rosebud Reservation, L Troop joined the rest of the Ft. Niobrara garrison, five other troops of the 6th Cavalry and two companies of the 8th Infantry, for a week or so of maneuvers at Camp Carr, five miles from the post. The L troopers enjoyed this thoroughly, as there was a great deal of skirmishing practice, fast riding, and shooting. Private Harry Clark liked all this activity too, especially the sham battle on September 8, 1891; writing,

> As soon as we discovered our supposed enemy, we threw out
> our skirmish line consisting of the whole [G] troop, and then
> began firing blank ammunition, and finally made a mad charge
> with our sabres. L Troop had no sabres, so used their pistols...
> the Indians dashing into the other side war whooping and firing
> off their weapons, and the lieutenant could not stop them. They
> began firing without the command 'commence firing.'[28]

This was the sort of training practice the Brule soldiers thought was really worthwhile. Some were old enough to have participated in fights with soldiers and Indian enemies in the late 1870's, and the sham battle was a taste of the old time warriors' experiences for them.

Towards the end of September, 1891, Secretary of War Redfield Proctor visited Ft. Niobrara and reviewed all the troops in the garrison, including L Troop, which, however, was the only unit not yet fitted

The 1888 delegation to Washington from the Rosebud Agency. (l. to r.): (front row) Black Wolf, He Dog, Quick (Fast) Bear, Good Voice, Yellow Hair, Swift Bear, and Thomas Flood (interpreter); (middle row) Grey Eagle Tail, Sky Bull, whose warriors were first to enlist in the U.S. Cavalry (the Indian Bureau had labeled his camp "non-progressive") Eagle Horse, Pretty (Good) Eagle, and Ring Thunder; (back row) Ugly (Bad) Wild Horse, Red Fish, Two Strikes, Col. L. F. Spencer (Agent). Smithsonian Institution photo.

out with dress uniforms.[29] Early in October, the post began to settle into its winter garrison routines. For the men of L Troop, this was supposed to mean increased concentration on schooling in English and other basic education to help the Brule soldiers advance and improve as United States cavalrymen. However, there was no competent teacher who could speak and understand both Sioux and English, so that the language barrier continued to be a major problem.[30] That this schooling opportunity was and continued to be a matter of serious interest to a number of the Brule troopers was reported in August, 1892, when, in explaining the status of schooling for enlisted men at Ft. Niobrara, the point was made that although the white enlisted soldiers cared little about schooling several men in the Indian troop were very interested in education and regularly attended classes.[31]

At the end of October, 1891, L Troop made another trip to Rosebud Agency, which no doubt pleased them and their relatives at home. Four L troopers were promoted to the rank of sergeant during the fall of 1891: Lewis Dorian, Samuel High Bear, Charles Steed, and Arthur Two Strikes. All the Brule soldiers were attending school classes in their barracks at this time for one and a half hours each day. Six of the L Troop men made another official trip to Rosebud Agency, probably in November, to help Captain W. H. Clapp recruit for an all-Indian I Company, 16th Infantry, to be stationed at Ft. Douglas, Utah.[32]

While becoming increasingly integrated into the military life at Ft. Niobrara, the Brule soldiers likewise enjoyed sports and past-times of their own, some of which drew the participation of white soldiers. Private Harry Clark saw a group of Brules playing a sort of polo on the parade ground one late November day, and, being a good rider and athlete himself, rode into the game. All the players were very excited, now urging their mounts in one direction and turning sharply in another, heel-drumming their horses' flanks, and curbing them in abrupt stops. Private Clark wrote that he "... got one whack at the block, when an Indian knocked it back and it struck me on the shin and I got a little huffy and struck an Indian—and then excitement prevailed, because I struck an Indian with a club; but it came off all right, as I apologized to the Indian. Yellow Hand, a big Indian friend of mine, kept yelling, 'My friend Clark, look out.' Well, it passed off all right though, between the Indian and white soldiers."[33] Clark may not have known that the blow he struck could mean a deadly insult, but he did have the good sense to realize he was in the wrong and make an apology. Again, this event showed the strong personal friendship between Private Yellow Hand and Private Clark.

L Troop remained in post at Ft. Niobrara with the other five troops of the 6th Cavalry during the winter of 1891-1892, but their area of experience was soon to be broadened, when all the 6th Cavalry troops at Niobrara were ordered out in June, 1892, to maintain law and order in eastern Wyoming between the so-called "rustlers" and the big ranch owners in the after-math of the Johnson County War. Participation in this summer campaign provided many new experiences for the Brule L troopers; not the least of which was their status as representatives of the authority of the United States Army, policing white citizens in Wyoming, many of whom had been eager for the Army to severely punish the Sioux only eighteen months before during the winter of 1890-1891. This reversal of roles must have caused many a chuckle among the Brule soldiers, and it would be extremely interesting to have heard what they thought about the matter.

The 6th Cavalry's summer camp was set up near old Ft. Fetterman, about eight miles from Douglas, Wyoming, late in June, 1892; from which L Troop and the other five troops, marched, had annual target practise, and patrolled the countryside for most of the summer. "On Suncers," wrote Harry Clark, "a majority of the dwellers hereabouts visit camp to hear the music given by the band of the Sixth Cavalry. The Indian soldiers of L Troop are a great attraction to the visitors, who cannot understand how the red warriors can be utilized, but... they are as well disciplined as any of the white troops, glory in field service, and are always ready for the march."[34]

Shortly after returning to Ft. Niobrara from summer camp in Wyoming, L Troop learned that it and all the other troops at the post would travel to Chicago to take part in ceremonies and celebrations in connection with the World's Columbian Exposition scheduled for October, 1892. A few of the L troopers had been east, as students at the Carlisle school, but most had never been as far east as the Missouri River, so the trip to Chicago was a new and vastly different experience for most of the Brule soldiers. Arriving by rail in mid-October, L Troop went into camp with the rest of the 6th Cavalry troops, at the fair grounds adjoining the fashionable Hyde Park section of Chicago's lake shore south side. Thousands of Chicagoans visited the Army camp, where the Brule troopers quickly found themselves the center of visitor interest.[35] Several Brule soldiers were interviewed by a newspaper reporter from the Chicago *Tribune*, whose story, "Red Men in Blue," was featured on page one of the next day's paper. "They are all good Indians now," wrote the reporter, "and those of them that speak the English language say they like the Army service."[36] One of the L troopers told the reporter about the railroad trip east, and complimented the troop cook, Jim Claymont, for having prepared such good meals on the trip. The reporter was particularly impressed with a Brule corporal named Little, who struck the newsman as being a very modest, unassuming soldier, though he had served as the model for a sculptor's mounted statue of a Sioux warrior.

The high point of the Chicago ceremonies came on October 20, 1892, when L Troop, 6th Cavalry was chosen to lead the dress parade through Washington Park, mounted and turned out in dress uniforms with plumed helmets.[37] All the troops left Chicago October 22; L Troop and the other five troops of the 6th Cavalry returning to Ft. Niobrara for the winter.

By the spring of 1893, L Troop had completed its first two years of service in the Regular Army. The Brule soldiers had developed into a good troop of U.S. cavalry, although the language barrier was still a problem, with a performance record as good as the average troop of white cavalry. Unlike some units, L Troop recorded no desertions.[38] However, the year 1893 proved to be a crucial one in the Army's experiment to train and maintain all-Indian units, as regular soldiers rather than as scouts. This was especially true in the case of L Troop of the 6th Cavalry. The office of Secretary of War was now occupied by a man not particularly interested in the idea of all-Indian units, and the 6th Cavalry had received a new colonel as regimental commander. The new colonel arrived in March, 1893, and from the outset opposed the continuance of the all-Indian troop. By the fall of 1894, all the Indian soldiers had been mustered out of L Troop, 6th Cavalry. Although originally enlisted for a term of five years, and it seems apparent that the Brule troopers were being pushed to do so, as all were discharged about three years after enlistment and the troop was disbanded.

About two-thirds of the L troopers received their discharges after three years of service; seven or eight of them purchased earlier discharges at the end of one or two years, most likely due to the pull exerted by their families' needs for them back on the reservation. Five received discharges for physical disability in the line of service, two died in service, and only one Brule received a dishonorable discharge.

Between 1894 and 1897, all of the Army's all-Indian L troops of Cavalry were mustered out of service. Captain Hugh L. Scott, who had

Captain Nicholson's 7th U.S. Cavalry troopers. U.S. Signal Corps photo, U.S. National Archives.

commanded the Indian troop of the 7th Cavalry at Ft. Sill, Oklahoma, later wrote that he was certain that the change in office of the Secretary of War and the prejudice of several high ranking officers served to effectively scuttle the experiment. "The truth was," wrote Scott, "that the Army was angry at General Schofield for mustering out the white men in two troops in each regiment L and M in the spring of 1890, and did not want the experiment to succeed."[38] Scott also added that he believed the experiment was very worthwhile; noting that the experience had proven very valuable to many of the Kiowa and Comanche men who had served in L Troop, 7th Cavalry, as several of these men were noted as important and leading men among their peoples for many years after discharge. Tabbytite, a young Comanche 7th Cavalry L Troop soldier, learned a great deal about the white culture, becoming something of a living cultural bridge himself between his own people and the white culture. His granddaughter, Mrs. Fred Harris, is the wife of a United States senator.

Although the all-Indian Army unit experiment was terminated by 1897, it had by no means been proven to be a complete failure. That the lack of English on the part of many of the Indian soldiers proved to be a major handicap is no doubt quite correct; however, no great effort was made by the Army to remedy this situation, as no heavy emphasis was placed on providing teachers and instructors for the Indian soldiers other than what was casually available in the way of a teaching staff at the posts where Indian units were stationed. Likewise, the Army's traditional insistence that all its enlisted soldiers be trained first and primarily as parade ground automatons, in the European manner, did not suit the psychological background and individualistic personalities of the but recently reservation-bound Indian men. Official Army policies on this matter have modified considerably over the years, and it is doubtful that this would have been nearly as important a consideration in more recent times. As it was, it is not surprising that the routine drills and irksome restrictions of enlisted Army life in the 1890's grew boring and tiresome to many of the Brule soldiers after two or three years of service. White soldiers of the 1890's often grew tired of routine Army life too, as a large percentage of them likewise chose to take their discharges at the end of three years rather than to complete the original five-year term of enlistment. Added to these negative factors for the Brule troopers was some degree of prejudice against them as Indians on the part of some white officers and soldiers, and the fact that only ten of the L troopers could have their families with them at the fort.

The experience of serving as regular soldiers in the United States Army had been a significant one for the Brule men who lived it. It had

58 provided many opportunities for not only learning about the Army, but for observing and participating in many aspects of the white civilization. At the same time, service in L Troop, 6th Cavalry, had provided an opportunity for Brule men to at least in part perpetuate the values of the warrior culture they had been born into.

After leaving the Army the men who had served in L Troop, 6th Cavalry, and I Company, 16th Infantry, returned to the reservation with a very real and deserved sense of pride in having been part of something important. Many of them became leading men on the reservation, and several served for years as reservation policemen. The Army experience had been a high point in the lives of many of the Brule men, and the spirit and tradition of military service remained high among the Rosebud people. Research has not indicated whether or not any of the men who served in L Troop at Ft. Niobrara volunteered as individuals for service during the Spanish-American War in 1898, but this writer believes that the prospect is very likely that some of them did. Chauncey Eagle Horn, the first Brule to die in action in France during World War I, is believed to have served in I Company, 16th Infantry, at Ft. Douglas, Utah, in the early 1890's. He was among the many Brule men who volunteered early in 1917. Mr. Charles Kills in Water, the son of a Brule L trooper, recalled that his father had been very proud to have been a member of L Troop, and that when he heard that the United States had entered the War in 1917, he immediately advised his son to go down to Ft. Niobrara and volunteer to join the Army. Pride in their willingness to perform military service has remained high among the Brule people of the Rosebud Reservation to the present time. Some have considered the application of draft laws to the Brules as a form of insult, casting aspersions on their bravery by implication.

There are no surviving members of L Troop now living. But they are well remembered by their children and grandchildren, and in the history of the Brule people, the story of the Brule L troopers of 1891 to 1894 will not be forgotten.

NOTES

1. Troops campaigning on the Sioux Reservations in the winter of 1890-1891 eagerly scrounged through abandoned Indian homes for Indian relics and artifacts, and frequently made use of fence posts, sheds, etc., as firewood in their camps. Many Sioux refugees were convinced that the soldiers had been sent there to kill them.

2. General Orders of the Army, 1891. General Orders No. 28, Office of the Adjutant General of the Army, March 9, 1891, Washington, D.C.

3. Frank C. Armstrong, U.S. Indian Inspector, to Secretary of the Interior (copy), January 22, 1890, AGO, 1839-PRD-1890, Record Group 94, National Archives.

4. "Replies of Division and Department Commanders on the Subject of Organizing a Regiment of Indians for the Regular Army...," Adjutant General's Office, March 22, 1890.

5. 1st Lieutenant Edward E. Dravo, 6th Cavalry, to Assistant Adjutant General, Department of the Platte, ms, Ft. Niobrara, Nebraska, May 2, 1891, AGO 7922, Record Group 94.

6. Dravo, ms.

7. Dravo, ms.

8. Dravo, ms.

9. Dravo, ms.

10. Dravo, ms.

11. Of 54 men enlisted at Rosebud Agency five were one-half white, two were one-quarter white, and 47 were noted as being full-blood Brule. Two came from Two Strike's band, four from the Northern Band, twenty-three from the bands of Big Turkey and Sky Bull, three from the Hollow Horn Band, thirteen from the Loafer Band, 7 from the Wassage Band, and 2 from the Big Thunder Band. The youngest was 19 and the oldest 35, with the average being a little over 27.

12. Private Hartford G. Clark's Diary for the year 1891 was loaned for research use to the author by Mrs. Pearl Clark, widow of the diarist. A transcript of the diary is on file in the research records of Jefferson National Expansion Memorial, St. Louis, Missouri.

13. Clark Diary, Jan. 1, 1891.

14. Clark Diary, April 28, 1891.

15. Clark Diary, May 1, 1891.

16. 1st Lieutenant E. E. Dravo to Assistant Adjutant General, Dept. of the Platte, ms, May 2, 1891....

17. The name Yellow Hand does not appear on any of the L Troop muster rolls or in the enlistment records. Several L Troop men are listed with white names, however, and it is most likely that the Brule soldier in question told Private Clark what his personal, Indian name was rather than a white, "agency name." Preliminary inquiries on the Rosebud Reservation have so far failed in the author's attempts to further identify Yellow Hand. From mentions in the Clark Diary Yellow Hand did have some command of English, knew how to play baseball, and was married and the father of an eight-month-old child as of May-June 1891. Since Private Clark relates his being taken by Yellow Hand to see his wife and child in a tipi about one mile from Clark's barracks, it also appears that Yellow Hand was not among the ten Brule soldiers whose families were provided wooden-floored tent quarters at Ft. Niobrara.

18. Clark Diary, May 24, 1891.

19. Clark Diary, May 25, 1891.

20. Clark Diary, May 26, 1891; "Letters Sent," Ft. Niobrara, Jan. 18, 1892, Record Group 98, National Archives.

21. Opportunities for cultural exchange between the families of the white and Brule enlisted men would have extended to matters of dress, use of native berries and

fruits, food preparation methods, play practises of children, and inter-personal family relationships observed by members of each culture group.

22. Clark Diary, May 30, 1891.

23. Clark Diary, May 31, 1891.

24. Clark Diary, June 6, 1891.

25. Clark Diary, June 10, 1891.

26. Clark Diary, July 30, 1891.

27. Clark Diary, July 31, 1891.

28. Letter from Private Clark printed in the *Exeter* [New Hampshire] *News-Letter* Sept. 21, 1891.

29. Clark Diary, Sept. 21, 1891.

30. "Letters Sent," Ft. Niobrara, Oct. 10, 1891.

31. "Letters Sent," Ft. Niobrara, Aug. 24, 1892.

32. Muster Roll, Troop L, 6th Cavalry, October 31-December 31, 1891, Record Group 94, National Archives.

33. Clark Diary, Nov. 29, 1891.

34. Letter from Private Clark printed in the *Exeter News-Letter*, July 28, 1892.

35. *Chicago Tribune*, Oct. 18, 1892.

36. *Chicago Tribune*, Oct. 18, 1892.

37. *Chicago Tribune*, Oct. 18, 1892.

38. Hugh L. Scott, *Some Memories of a Soldier*, New York, 1928, p. 170.

APPENDIX

Roster of Indian L Troopers, 6th Cavalry, April, 1891

From Register of Enlistments, Regular Army, 1891, National Archives Micro-Film, and Muster Roll, L Troop, 6th Cavalry, April, 1891.

Frank Brings Them, *Awieagli*, 19, farmer
Bear Man, *Matowicaxa*, 23, laborer
Bear That Fights, *Mato Wickiza*, 21, farmer
George Bull, *Tatanka*, 27, baker
Beads, *Pxite*, 30, farmer
Jack Bear Heel, *Jiyete*, 21, laborer
John Black Horse, *Nimgrapa*, 29, farmer
Walter Bull Man, *Tatanka Wncasa*, 31, blacksmith
Catch Alive, *Niyakegta*, 23, laborer
Cheyene, *Salinjela*, 32, farmer
*James Claymount, 29, farmer
*Louis Dorion, 35, blacksmith
Ralph Eagle Feather, *Wapobleca*, 29, carpenter
*David Eastman, 22, farmer

*Louis Greenwood, 21, farmer
Hollow Horn Bull, *Tatankaturlgeca,* 30, farmer
Samuel Highbear, *Pupahumaza,* 29, baker
Holy Man, *Wakinn,* 26, farmer
Horned Horse, *Tashumkeheton,* 35, farmer
His War, *Okicizeitama,* 29, laborer
Holy Cane, *Togye Wakan,* 25 farmer
Head, *Nata,* 20, farmer
Cecil Ironwing, *Matontankatoya,* 26, farmer
Ironhand, *Chetonmaza,* 22, laborer
*Edward Iron Boy, 30, farmer
Kills The Enemy, *Togtewicakiya,* 21, laborer
Kills In The Water, *Minijawicagte,* 21, farmer
Makes First Trouble, *Tokeniyawasieca,* 26, farmer
Noisy Owl, *Hihanzso Huhononga,* 34, farmer
Omaha Boy, *Hogrita,* 35, teamster
Ring Eagle, *Wanblicangleska,* 27, farmer
Charles Running Horse, *Toximkinizauke,* 24, shoemaker
Red Bull, *Tatnka Luta,* 35, farmer
*Conrad Roubideaux, 25, painter
Shoots The Enemy, *Tokute_____,* 26, farmer
*Charles Steed, 34, farmer
*William Simpson, 30, farmer
Spotted Eagle, *Waubli Gleska,* 35, farmer
Two Charger, *Nonpa Wicahia,* 23, farmer
Arthur Two Strikes, *Nomhaipa,* 25, tailor
Turns Twice, *Nompa Kawinge,* 25, farmer
Under The Water, *Minne Matrel,* 29, farmer
*Morris Walker [Janis], 25, blacksmith
Wing Shot, *Wankalivichalda,* 28, laborer
White Horse, *Xungrka,* 28, farmer
White Bank, *Mayaska,* 35, farmer
White Boy, *Hogxilaaka,* 19, farmer
Charles P. Loader, *Opagain*
Fast Dog, *Nimkaluzahan*
Frosted Bear, *Aweyimka*
Four Feathers, *Wiyakatopa*
Good Killer, *Tehia Wichakta*
Ghost Bird, *Joutkala Waingi*
*Iron Hawk,_____
*Little Bull,_____
Little, *Ciqa*
*Asterisked names indicate no Sioux name listed

Pawns of Conquest:
The Jicarilla Apaches
of New Mexico

by D. Harper Simms

IN 1541, FRANCISCO VASQUEZ DE CORONADO, after exploring part of the upper Rio Grande valley, set out to find the fabled land of Quivira somewhere eastward across the Great Plains. As his party entered the buffalo country they saw, at one point, strange marks in the ground, such as would be made by dragging lances.

Following the tracks, he came upon an Indian village and learned that the scratches in the earth had been made by the dragging of poles —poles with which these native people built "tall and beautiful tents."

So it was that the first white men encountered the people who followed the buffalo and depended upon those animals for a living. These were Apaches, one of many bands of an Apache nation the Spanish would come to call "Vaqueros" because they followed the "cattle." One of those Vaquero bands, although it may not have been the group Coronado encountered, came to be called the "Jicarilla Apaches" or, as the Spaniards usually recorded it, "Apaches de la Jicarilla."

"Apaches de la Jicarilla" is a phrase that occurs repeatedly in the official papers that document the Spanish conquest and settlement of New Mexico. Reports of the early American Indian agents in the Territory of New Mexico—John S. Calhoun, Michael Steck, Christopher (Kit) Carson, Lorenzo Labadie and others—likewise had frequent occasion to refer to the Jicarilla Apaches.

But, while every television viewer knows about Geronimo and Cochise, few have heard names like Chacon or Lobo—chiefs of these

New Mexico Apaches who, with their tribesmen, played a significant if less spectacular part in the history of the Southwest.

The Jicarilla Apaches today are a progressive and prospering tribe with some 1800 members who live on a 750,000-acre reservation in north-central New Mexico. But before they went on the reservation in 1887, the Jicarillas, and their kinsmen in bands with other names, ranged over and called their own a vast region—upwards of 61,000 square miles in northeastern New Mexico, southeastern Colorado, and the Panhandle of Oklahoma.

This was a good region. It's extensive grasslands once were dotted with buffalo and antelope. To the west were rugged mountains with great forests of pine, fir, spruce and aspen. Its foothill valleys were watered by clear streams and the alluvial soils were well suited to the growing of corn, squash, beans and melons.

It was a good region, but no better or worse than many other regions of its size in the Southwest. Two circumstances, however, have singled it and its inhabitants out for special recognition in Southwestern history.

First, it was the place of crossing between the mountains and the plains. Through it Navajos, Pueblos, Utes and Spaniards traveled eastward to make war or to hunt buffalo. And here, too, crossed the westward-bound people—the plains Indians and later the Americans. The former went to raid and trade; the latter went to trade and, finally, to invade!

Secondly, this Jicarilla homeland proved to be the fateful point where the territorial ambitions of three non-Indian nations—the Spanish, the French, and the Americans, would collide.

The Jicarillas were, however unwittingly, heavily involved in the circumstance of their location. They not only played a role in the unfolding of history that took place here but were, inescapably, effected by the interplay of cultures and international politics that enveloped them. The wonder is not that the Jicarillas retained any of their own culture but that they even survived. That they did both is a tribute to the native tenacity and adaptability of these people.

"When the world was new there were only the Jicarilla Apache living; there were many of them then." So begins one of the tales in Jicarilla mythology. And so it must have seemed, for at the beginning of recorded history in the Southwest there were a number of these closely related Apache bands of the great northern Athapascan linguistic family living in a large area of the Great Plains, from Nebraska to Texas, as well as in the mountains and plains of northeastern New Mexico. These small tribes or bands bore names, usually given them by the Spanish explorers, that stemmed from their location, their leader, or some characteristic trait or custom of the tribe.

There were, for example, the Carlanas, Cuartelejos, Trementinas, Chipaynes, Calchufines, Conejeros, Limitas, Palomas, and several others. The Jicarillas, presumably, got their name because women of the tribe wove small, tight baskets that reminded the Spanish newcomers of the chocolate cup—*jicara*—used commonly throughout Latin America.

Of all these tribal names once applied to Apaches of the region, only one—Jicarilla—survived beyond the middle of the 18th century. It is a safe assumption, therefore, that in today's Jicarillas flows the blood of these many other decimated and displaced Apache bands whose survivors joined with the Jicarillas a century or more ago.

After Coronado returned to Mexico in 1542, the Apaches were not to see much of the Spaniards for the next half-century. It was not until 1598 that Don Juan de Oñate came with colonists as well as soldiers and established a capital at San Gabriel, near present-day Española. Santa Fé, the second capital, was not founded until 1610.

Oñate was recalled in 1607. New Mexico had a long succession of governors, some good, some bad. More settlements were established and some fifty churches built in the first quarter of the 17th century. Priests worked diligently to convert the Indians. A long severe drought in mid-century caused the hostile tribes to step up their raids on the settlements. The Pueblo Indians began to resent their Spanish masters and rumblings of revolt began to be heard.

In 1680 that revolt came and all Spaniards were driven out of New Mexico, not to return until Don Diego de Vargas made his triumphal reconquest in 1692.

After the reconquest there was no further hostility of consequence from the Pueblo tribes. Close ties were formed between the Spanish settlers and the Pueblo people, partly because they were neighbors in the Rio Grande valley and partly because they needed to join forces to protect themselves against relentless depredations by the plains tribes and the Navajos—depredations now more formidable because the hostile tribes had obtained horses and were now mounted warriors.

Besides the continuing threat from Indian enemies, there was the ever-present fear of encroachment on Spanish territory by the French, in particular. This kept the Spanish government nervous and they hastened to extend and strengthen their frontiers. The border settlements of northern New Mexico, therefore, and any native peoples there who could be counted upon as allies, were expected to serve as buffers, not only against hostile Indians but also against the possible invasion and seizure of land (and rich Mexican mines) by any other power.

This role, as a buffer nation for the Spanish kingdom, began to emerge for the Jicarilla Apaches. With minor exceptions, these Apaches had always been at peace with the Spaniards, a first requirement. Furthermore, most of them lived, strategically, between the northernmost Spanish settlements and the Arkansas River beyond which, until 1763, lay French territory.

They lived, too, between the Spanish, and Pueblo, towns and the mountain hideouts of the Comanches and Utes. Equipped with firearms provided by the French, and with horses, these two tribes swept down upon the Jicarillas and their allies with intensified fury in the early years of the 18th century. The Apaches, by now, were not strong enough to withstand these assaults alone and turned to the Spanish government for protection. A mutual benefit was thus obtained and Spanish leaders sought to take full advantage of the arrangement.

The first step was development of a plan to establish a Spanish fort at one of the Apache settlements in northeastern New Mexico or southern Colorado. The first proposal was for a presidio at El Cuartelejo, in what is now southeastern Colorado. But that site was abandoned, on second thought, because it was too far removed from any Spanish settlements or reinforcements and might, therefore, be too vulnerable.

A second proposal, long debated, was to set up an outpost at La Jicarilla, an Apache ranchería near present-day Cimarron where a substantial number of Jicarillas lived. In spite of much support for this

Santiago Largo, Jicarilla Apache chief, and one of five Jicarilla leaders who went to Washington in 1880, to negotiate for a reservation for the tribe. Photo by C. M. Bell, April 2, 1880. Smithsonian Institution photo.

location, somehow the ponderous bureaucracy of the Spanish government never got around to building and equipping the fort. But Viceroy Baltasar de Zuñiga, the Marquís de Valero, ordered the New Mexican governor to "hold" the Apaches, whatever that meant, because of word of new activities and new settlements by the French beyond the Arkansas.

Specific evidence of how the Spaniards expected to use the Jicarillas came from Governor Tomás Velez Cachupin. In 1752 he reported to his superior that he regarded the Apache bands of that region as trustworthy and that, during the past winter, "three hundred men of these tribes have been in the environs of the pueblo of Pecos....*I keep them in this limited area with whatever guile I can in expectation of an action on the part of the Comanches and to enlarge my troops with their support in case of necessity*" (underscoring supplied).

As this would indicate, the Apaches were expected to be more than spies for the Spaniards. They were frequently invited, or conscripted, to join Spanish military expeditions that probed out into the Plains, or northward into French territory. The Indians were usually happy to go along for it gave them a chance to strike back at their old enemies with less danger to themselves.

The Jicarillas paid a price, then and later, for this relationship. The Comanches and Utes hit them repeatedly, sometimes in raids aimed

James Garfield Velarde, Jicarilla Apache leader, and his wife, taken about 1896. Velarde lived to be more than 100 years of age, dying in 1958.
Photo courtesy Denver Public Library Collection.

at the Apaches alone and sometimes, just in passing, as the hostiles rode farther south to strike Spanish towns and the pueblos. Early in 1724, for example, the Comanches virtually wiped out the Indians living at La Jicarilla, killing many of the men and carrying off the women and children. The Jicarillas were so demoralized by this attack that they considered moving far west, into the Navajo country, to get out of reach of the Comanches. But that would have ended their usefulness to the Spanish government which made great effort to dissuade the Apaches from moving. With Spanish help and encouragement, the Jicarillas moved, instead, closer to Spanish protection.

Some came, at this time, to live near Pecos Pueblo. Others were settled on the Rio Trampas, not far from Taos. They made a formal request to be baptised even though they, unlike the Pueblos, had not heretofore been receptive to the religious efforts of the Spanish priests, some of whom were skeptical of the true motives behind this new interest.

Even at Pecos, and especially at Taos, the Jicarillas were still in strategic position to serve as eyes and ears for the Spanish government. Both pueblos were traditional gathering places for people of many tribes and nations. Traders, trappers, and Indians from tribes ordinarily hostile to the New Mexicans mingled freely at the periodic fairs in Taos. Here the Apaches were frequently able to pick up word of impending hostilities. Don Pedro Tamarón, Bishop of Durango, visited the northern settlements in 1760 and commented on this.

Speaking of a visit to a settlement near Santo Domingo, he wrote: "Here the captain of the peaceful Apaches came to call on me. This man is esteemed in the kingdom because of his old loyalty. He warns of the coming of the Comanches and in war he and his men are a safe ally."

A little later, on returning to Santa Fé after visiting another outlying church, the bishop wrote again: "I also experienced another alarm about the Comanches, the news of which was given by the peaceful heathen Apaches." And he saw that the relationship worked both ways for, concerning his visit to Taos, he reported: "In this valley we kept finding encampments of peaceful infidel Apache Indians, who have sought the protection of the Spaniards...."

In the middle of the 18th century the Utes and Comanches came to a parting of the ways. This, then, led to a close Jicarilla-Ute alliance pleasing to the Spaniards, and the Utes came into the Spanish fold. And, before the end of the century, the Spanish government made peace with the Comanches who then shifted their focus of attention farther east and south in the Great Plains.

In 1763 all of the old Louisiana territory west of the Mississippi was ceded by France to Spain. It was returned to France, briefly, in 1800 but went to the United States in the Louisiana Purchase of 1803. This ended the threat of French encroachment. But now that the United States had a common border with Texas, Americans began moving into that region and another threat loomed before the eyes of the Spaniards.

The intentions of the Americans became more clear when Zebulon M. Pike and his party of exploration were caught inside Spanish (actually Jicarilla) territory in 1807. After Pike's release from custody he made reports which further whetted American interest in New Mexico. American traders foresaw new and lucrative markets and the New Mexicans were eager to get American goods. The Spanish government resisted the tide in vain. Jicarilla Indians began seeing American trappers along their mountain streams and undoubtedly served as guides for some of the mountain men of the era.

Mexico declared its independence from Spain in 1821. In 1836 an American-dominated Texas declared its independence from Mexico and obtained United States statehood in 1845. This touched off the war between the United States and Mexico and on August 18, 1846, in Santa Fé, General Stephen W. Kearney, without opposition, took possession of the territory of New Mexico in the name of the United States.

Kearney promised the citizens of New Mexico that their rights and religion would be honored, and that they would be protected from attack by hostile Indians, naming specifically the Utes and Navajos but not mentioning the Jicarillas. For many days thereafter, representatives of various New Mexico towns, the Indian pueblos, and Navajo, Ute and Apache bands came to Santa Fé to talk with the general and to offer their allegiance.

One of these was a group of Jicarillas. Their chief, not named in the record, spoke at length in the classic fashion of Indian orators. He said, in part: "The Apaches are poor; they have no clothes to protect

them from the cold, and the game is fast disappearing from their hunting grounds. You must, therefore, if you wish us to be peaceable, speak a good word to the Comanches, the Yutas, the Navajos and the Arapahoes, our enemies, that they will allow us to kill buffalo on the great plains. . . .''

This plaintive plea happened to be an accurate description of the plight of the Apaches—their legacy as "pawns of conquest" over three hundred years. The general gave them blankets, butcher knives, beads, mirrors and other presents and they left with a promise that they would be good and faithful citizens of the United States.

But the Jicarillas, for a time at least, were not to receive much better treatment at the hands of the Americans than they had from their Spanish and Mexican governmens. Charles Bent, whom Kearney had named as provisional governor of New Mexico, was not sympathetic. In his first report to the Commissioner of Indian Affairs he reported that the "Jicarillas have no permanent residence but roam through the northern settlements of New Mexico." They numbered "about 100 lodges or 500 souls," he said, but were "indolent" people "living principally by thefts committed on the Mexicans."

John S. Calhoun, the first Indian agent, later the first territorial governor of New Mexico, appeared to be little more sympathetic with the condition of the Jicarillas. He referred to them as a "mixed band

Jicarilla Apaches in ceremonial garb at Dulce, New Mexico, about 1900. Photo from Simms Collection, photographer unknown.

termed 'Jacarillaras'... who for years past, have infested the vicinity of San Fernandez de Taos, the country between it and Bent's Fort, and that part of the Santa Fe road (Trail) which crosses the Rio Colorado."

It was true that the Jicarillas had no permanent residence at this time for they had been dispossessed and displaced from every place they called their own. In the next 40 years agency headquarters, of sorts, were established first at once place, then another. Efforts were made to move the Jicarillas into the Bosque Redondo encampment at the time of the Navajo roundup, but the Apaches successfully resisted this incarceration. Twice they were moved to Fort Stanton to share reservation lands with the Mescaleros—a related band but one for whom the Jicarillas had little love.

At one point, possibly with an eye on the still hostile Navajos in eastern Arizona and western New Mexico, and knowing that the Jicarillas and Navajos were traditional enemies, Governor William Carr Lane moved one band of Jicarillas under Chacon, their chief, to a site on the Rio Puerco, west of the Rio Grande. But the Jicarillas mostly wanted to be allowed to stay in their more familiar homeland—the Taos, Mora, Cimarron region, the heart of which was the huge Maxwell Land Grant.

During this period the Jicarillas, hungry and demoralized, began to resort to raiding and thievery on a stepped-up scale. They attacked a number of parties on the Santa Fé Trail, making off with livestock and supplies and killing a few travelers.

The most publicized of these incidents was the so-called "White massacre" at Point of Rocks in northeastern New Mexico. It took place in 1849 when a party of Jicarillas attacked J. M. White, of Santa Fé, and his family who were traveling westward. The Indians killed White and several other men. They took as captives Mrs. White, their small daughter, and a Negro maidservant. Mrs. White was later killed by the Indians just before soldiers caught up with the marauding group. But the little girl was never rescued and the occurrence of a few blue-eyed Jicarillas in subsequent generations has led some observers to believe that she was kept in the tribe the rest of her life.

In March of 1854 Lieutenant David Bell of the Second Dragoons, operating out of Fort Union, caught up with a band of Jicarillas accused of having robbed a rancher on the Canadian River. During this encounter Lobo, a principal chief, although pierced by seven bullets, drew his bow and killed a young soldier named Arnold. They both fell and died grappling in each other's arms.

On Christmas Day of 1854 Utes and Jicarillas raided the town of Pueblo, Colorado, killing fourteen men, carrying away a woman and two children, and making off with 200 head of livestock. Before the army could get organized to do anything about it, they struck the same town again, killed four more people and stole 100 more animals!

These, and a number of other hostile acts finally brought down upon the Jicarillas the heavy hand of military force and soon after the 1854 incidents, they came to Santa Fé and sued for peace.

They were not through with the warpath, however. In 1864 seventy-two Utes and Jicarillas were invited to join Col. Kit Carson in an expedition against the Comanches and Kiowas ordered by Brigadier General James H. Carleton, U.S. Volunteers, then commanding the Department of New Mexico.

The New Mexico Indians accepted the invitation with alacrity, for it promised some food and equipment and also because they were told they could bring home all the plunder they could manage. In the engagement, which took place at the Adobe Walls on November 25, Carson's force succeeded in destroying a winter-quarters village of the Kiowas and a large amount of their supplies. Carson withdrew, however, in the face of a much larger enemy force of Comanches and Kiowas and headed back to New Mexico. The Jicarillas managed to take a number of enemy horses and one enemy scalp—which they bought from a young Mexican soldier who had risked his life to "lift the hair" of a Comanche warrior he had killed.

Because the Jicarillas insisted on living there anyway the government, in 1862, established an agency on the Maxwell Ranch at Cimarron. One band of Jicarillas, together with a band of Utes, lived there and drew rations for a number of years. But in 1870 Lucien Maxwell, the owner, sold the ranch and moved away. In 1876 the Cimarron agency was discontinued.

For the next fifteen years the Jicarillas were continually on the move. A reservation in Rio Arriba County, on the Navajo River, was established, abolished, then established again. Finally, in 1887 the Jicarillas were permanently assigned a piece of country, on the western edge of their pre-reservation territory, that they could now call their own. It was not their beloved Cimarron region but it was familiar land and they gradually settled down into reservation life.

During the War Between the States, although they took part in no engagements of record, the Jicarillas and Utes were credited with being, along with the Pueblos, "Union" Indians. This didn't mean much but, as Hubert Howe Bancroft aptly put it, this fact, in view of their holding (as foes of the Navajos and plains tribes) a sort of balance of power, made them in later years the recipients of many complimentary allusions.

So, the Jicarillas came to their reservation with not much to show for their three-hundred-year alliance with the Spanish and 150 years of contact with the Americans. Most of them had adopted Spanish names—for the rolls, at least—like Largo, Baltazar, Veneno, Vicenti, and Tafoya. They had picked up the Spanish language as a second tongue. They had learned about liquor from the Spaniards and their proximity to the settlements had helped many of them develop too strong a liking for whiskey.

It should be acknowledged that, without Spanish help in the worst days of Comanche aggression the tribe might have been wiped out. But the net effect of their role as a buffer group for the Spanish kingdom, and other developments of that era, was to render the Jicarillas poor, homeless, degraded, and demoralized.

Their culture, heavily oriented toward that of the plains tribes, became markedly influenced by their close contact with the Pueblo Indians throughout the Spanish era. An example is their annual ceremonial relay race, rather directly adopted from similar Pueblo rituals. Their clothing and dwellings, in pre-reservation days, resembled those of the plains Indians but they cultivated (when they could stay in one place long enough to do so) the same food crops as the Pueblos.

Jicarilla mythology, according to anthropologists, is very similar to that of the Navajos. A small percentage of today's Jicarillas are members of a Christian church of one denomination or another but most still cling to their own religion. A mission of the Reformed Church of America has operated on the reservation since 1913 and, for many

These five Jicarilla Apache leaders went to Washington, D.C., in 1880, to plead in person for the establishment of a suitable reservation for their people. (l. to r.) Santiago Largo, Guerito, Augustin Vigil, San Pablo and Juan Julian. Photo taken at Corcoran Gallery, April 2, 1880. Smithsonian Institution photo.

74 years, conducted the only school available to the Jicarilla children. This circumstance, plus the influence and help of a wise and benevolent trader to whom the Jicarillas looked for leadership for many years, has contributed much to the progressive character of today's Jicarilla tribe.

Notwithstanding the poor treatment the Apaches suffered in the earlier decades of the American era, they perhaps have more to show for their years of exposure to the Anglo-American culture than some would acknowledge. They were dispossessed of their original homeland but, however tardily, are about to be reimbursed for it. They were given land, finally, although it is no credit to the U.S. government that the land selected for the reservation turned out to be rich in gas and oil resources. But before that bonanza was discovered, the government had helped the Jicarillas get a start in livestock and they were on their way to being self-supporting. Today, from these various sources, the Jicarillas reap a harvest that causes them to have one of the highest—if not the highest—per capita income of any Indian tribe in the nation. They have good schools, and a tribal fund that provides scholarships for Jicarilla youths who wish to leave the reservation for advanced education. Industry and tourism are providing jobs and training for these Apache citizens and helping them take their place in the society of the 1970's.

The United States Indian Claims Commission, after long study and litigation, has ruled that the Jicarillas should be compensated, at a rate per acre not yet determined, for 9.2 million acres of land in northeastern New Mexico which was taken from them without treaty or compensation in 1883. Depending upon whose evaluation is finally accepted, the Indians could be paid anywhere from $3.5 million to $12.6 million.

We can only hope that the Jicarilla ancestors who were driven from La Jicarilla in 1724 and those who were evicted from the Maxwell Ranch 150 years later are looking down from whatever happy hunting ground they now enjoy when that payment is made.

BIBLIOGRAPHY

Annie Heloise Abel (ed.), *The Official Correspondence of James S. Calhoun while Indian Agent at Santa Fe and Superintendent of Indian Affairs in New Mexico, 1849-1852*, Washington, D.C., 1915.

Eleanor B. Adams, *Bishop Tamaron's Visitation of New Mexico, 1760*, Albuquerque: Historical Society of New Mexico Publications in History, vol. xv, 1954.

Albuquerque Journal, May 17, 1969. "A Report on the Jicarilla land claim."

Hubert Howe Bancroft, *History of Arizona and New Mexico, 1530-1888*, San Francisco: A. L. Bancroft and Co., 1884, and reprint, 1962.

Herbert Eugene Bolton, *Coronado on the Turquoise Trail*, Albuquerque: University of New Mexico, 1944.

Chris Emmett, *Fort Union and the Winning of the Southwest*, Norman: Univ. of Oklahoma Press, 1965.

George P. Hammond and Agapito Rey, *Narratives of the Coronado Expedition, 1540-1542*, Albuquerque: Coronado Cuarto Centennial Publications, 1940.

John T. Hughes, *Doniphan's Expedition*, Cincinnati, 1847.

George E. Hyde, *Indians of the High Plains*, Norman: Univ. of Oklahoma Press, 1959.

David Meriwether, *My Life on the Mountains and on the Plains*, Norman: Univ. of Oklahoma Press, 1965.

Morris Edward Opler, "Myths and Tales of the Jicarilla Apache Indians," *American Folk-Lore Society* Memoirs, No. 13, New York, G. E. Stechert and Co., 1938.

George H. Pettis, *Kit Carson's Fight with the Comanche and Kiowa Indians*, Santa Fe: Historical Society of New Mexico, 1908.

Albert H. Schroeder, "A Study of the Apache Indians," in 2 mimeo. vols., Santa Fe: U.S. Department of the Interior, 1959-1960.

Alfred Barnaby Thomas, *After Coronado, Spanish Exploration Northeast of New Mexico, 1696-1727*, Norman: Univ. of Oklahoma Press, 1935.

_____*The Plains Indians and New Mexico, 1751-1778*, Albuquerque: Univ. of New Mexico, Coronado Historical Series, vol. 11, 1940.

Ralph Emerson Twitchell, *The Leading Facts of New Mexican History*, Cedar Rapids: The Torch Press, 1911-1912; reprinted Albuquerque, 1963.

Robert M. Utley, "Fort Union and the Santa Fe Trail," in manuscript. Washington, D.C.; U.S. Department of the Interior, 1959.

Clyde Wilson, *Jicarilla Apache Political and Economic Structures*, Berkeley: Univ. of California, 1964.

Lost River Raid

by Richard Dillon

LONG AGO, Europeans used to argue as to the number of angels capable of dancing on the head of a pin. For some years, Americans have indulged in a similar pursuit—toting up the causes of individual Indian wars of the Western frontier. An obvious example is the Modoc War of 1872-1873 on the border of California and Oregon where, as usual, *the* cause of it is obliterated in a long train of events (no one of which was worth a war) but which brought on the sad conflict as surely as if it were, somehow, fated to occur despite the efforts of those who sought to prevent it.

If it is difficult or impossible to assign a single cause to the Modoc affair, it is easy enough to determine what ignited the bloody warfare. It was Captain James Jackson's raid on the twin villages of Subchief Captain Jack on November 29, 1872. Jack's band had split off from the main body of Modocs led by Chief Sconchin. The latter were making the best of a bad situation on the Klamath Reservation north of Upper Klamath Lake, accepting the taunts and harrassment of the more numerous Klamaths. But Jack and his followers refused to swallow the Klamath bullying and left the reservation set up by the October 14, 1864 treaty signed at Council Grove. They returned to their homeland on lower Lost River, near the ford called Natural Bridge and the mouth of the river on the north shore of Tule Lake, barely across the California Line into Oregon.

Captain Jack's band of so-called renegades was tolerated on Lost

River until 1872 when the annoyance of their mere presence in the path of settlement, plus a little petty thieving and insolence on their part, led the growing number of ranchers in the area to express their exasperation to the Superintendent of Indian Affairs for Oregon and the military officers at Fort Klamath. This post was established adjacent to the Klamath Reservation (1863) to keep an eye on Modocs and Klamaths, particularly. Petitions were signed and a flurry of paper-work in both Oregon and Washington, D.C., resulted in a communication of July 6, 1872, from Commissioner of Indian Affairs F. A. Walker. In it he gave Oregon's Superintendent of Indian Affairs, T. B. Odeneal, a peremptory order—"You are directed to remove the Modoc Indians to Camp Yainax on the Klamath Reservation, peaceably if you possibly can, but forcibly if you must."

Odeneal sent his Sub-Agent, Ivan Applegate, to Fort Klamath to ask its commander, Major John Green, for a force of soldiers to compel Jack and his Indians to go back on the reservation. Like Walker, the Superintendent urged that bloodshed be avoided if at all possible. Perhaps because the Fort, as usual, was understrength or perhaps because Odeneal ended his letter, "I think they might be induced to surrender and come upon the reservation without further trouble," Green did not wait for the reinforcements promised him by General E. R. S. Canby from California and Oregon posts (should real trouble develop with the mildly annoying Modocs) but decided to send only James Jackson's "B" Troop, First Cavalry, to round up the Modocs and escort them under

Camp Warner, Oregon—1873. U.S. National Archives photo.

arms to the Klamath Reservation. "B" Troop's Lieutenant Frazier A. Boutelle later claimed to have been dumfounded by the order to march and to have screwed up his courage enough to question Green's order. The Major, sensitive to criticism of the Army for a do-nothing policy in regard to the Modocs, answered by saying "If I don't send the troops, they will think we are afraid."

Green was not really going off half-cocked. White opinion of Captain Jack's men was that they were a beggarly band, no match for men of a cavalry regiment fresh from the Apache campaigns and with a tradition stretching back to the Seminole War. Green had personally scouted out the Modoc country in September. He was an experienced officer with two brevets won in the Civil War and he would pick up a Congressional Medal of Honor during the Modoc War. Since he knew that Jack had only fifty-odd warriors, he thought that Jackson could handle them. Still, he took the precaution of asking—*after* he had sent "B" Troop—for the reinforcements at his disposition at Camp Warner, in the Oregon desert to the east of Fort Klamath.

Captain Jackson and Lieutenant Boutelle led thirty-five enlisted men out of Fort Klamath, accompanied by Assistant Surgeon Henry McElderry. Four more soldiers brought up the rear with a pack train. It was a light one, for so confident of success was Major Green that he had ordered only three days' rations to be issued the yellowlegs. Boredom and peace had been the hallmarks of Fort Klamath history since its founding in the Civil War, so the troopers moving through the rain on November 28, 1872, were enthusiastic for a scrap—to break the dulling monotony of garrison life in the pines of Oregon. A little of this enthusiasm was washed away by fatigue and cold as the rain turned into a numbing sleetstorm before they reached Linkville, now Klamath Falls, still two dozen miles short of their destination.

At Linkville, Jackson rested his men and consulted with Superintendent Odeneal, who met him there. The latter assigned Ivan Applegate to Jackson as his guide and interpreter and then made suggestions which were virtually orders since the commanding general of the whole Department, E. R. S. Canby, had required his officers to implement the Indian Bureau's plans. One wonders if Jackson felt some of his confidence ebbing as he foresaw the effect on his surprise raid of Odeneal's requirement that he "request an interview with the head men" upon his arrival at the Lost River camps of the Modocs. Surely he was troubled by the impossibility of mixing military surprise and diplomatic palaver as he heard out Odeneal—"Talk kindly but firmly to them and, whatever else you may do, I desire to urge that if there is any fighting, let the Indians be the aggressors. Fire no gun except in self-defense after they have first fired upon you."

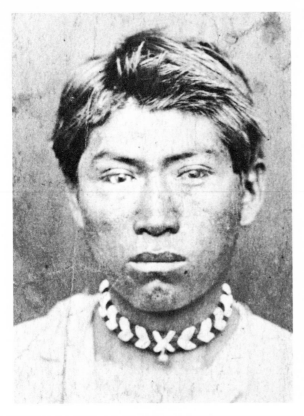

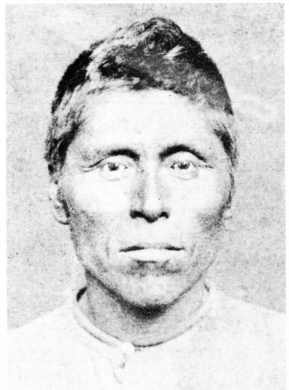

Upper left: Hooker Jim, major sub-chief of the
Modocs. Photo taken by L. Heller, 1873.
Smithsonian Institution photo. Above: Scarface
Charley, Modoc, and Captain Jack's right hand
man. Almost six feet tall, his Indian name
was Chikchikam Lupatkuelatko. Photo taken prior
to 1877. Smithsonian Institution photo.
Left: Curley Headed Doctor, the Modoc medicine
man who, following the Lost River Raid, led his
warriors on a trail of blood around Tule Lake.
Photo from U.S. National Archives.

Ivan Applegate ran into his brother Oliver at Linkville and when the latter learned of Jackson's upcoming uninvited visit to Jack's camp on the right bank of Lost River, he decided to form up a unit of citizen-soldiers to support the Captain in the village across the river from Jack's Lodge. By the time Jackson reached his destination, Oliver Applegate had at least eight armed settlers with him although strategy—or even tactics—he had none. Captain Jackson later claimed that his civilian auxiliaries were to protect the family at Crawley's ranch (near the Modoc camps) and to prevent any attack on his Troop's rear. But his recollection came twenty years after the event and just might have been askew from the facts. In any event, Oliver Applegate's absurd little Army ignited the Modoc War even before Jackson could light the fuse.

Jackson's Lost River raid was bungled but since every other Army engagement, except perhaps the last, was also mishandled by the military, few people are aware of the circumstances of this first battle of the Modoc War. It was an important battle, too, for its repercussions had much to do with later Modoc refusals to surrender, with their spurning of the Peace Commission and their murder of General Canby, and with the trial and execution at Fort Klamath of Captain Jack and his lieutenants. The Lost River raid set a pattern. Hailed as a victory (even before it was fought) it was, instead, a defeat for the Army by a ragged band of renegades. The involvement of civilians in it led to the murder of innocent white settlers upon its conclusion, just as a later battle would bring about the murder of a peaceful young teamster. The murder of civilians brought about the intervention of Oregon (civil) courts and the indictment of Indian men-at-arms for the crime of murder, an unusual circumstance in the Far West's Indian warfare. Most curiously, perhaps, the battle of Lost River taught the Army nothing. Whipped there, the military rushed to drub the miserable Modocs and was again rebuffed, twice, in the Lava Beds before being shockingly chopped up at Sand Butte (now Hardin Butte) by Scarfaced Charley and his men. Ironically, the only clear-cut victory for the Army over the Modocs before the latter split into groups, to be hunted down, was the Battle of Sorass Lake. In this skirmish, it was the Modocs who were the attackers—by surprise—and, for once, the legendary Captain Jack actually led his men into battle. The result was unexpected, to put it mildly, the Modocs were defeated, for once.

But neither cavalrymen or troopers had any real idea of Modoc mettle at dawn of November 29, 1872. Both sides were largely untested in genuine warfare, as contrasted with drills and reconnaissances on the one hand and cattle raiding or bullying of travelers or settlers on the other.

Jackson's command followed the ridge of hills paralleling Lost River on the south until he came within half a mile of Captain Jack's camp at daybreak. He gave his men the order to dismount and rest while he looked over the terrain. His troopers were saddle-weary and soaked to the skin—"a tired lot of men" in his own words, but his surprise appeared to be complete, to be perfect. No one was stirring in the camp which lay before his command. As he broke his company into two platoons, with Boutelle in charge of one and himself in command of the other, the Lieutenant doffed his overcoat despite the icy temperature, saying, "If I am going into a fight, I want my deck cleared for action." Most of the enlisted men followed suit. They remounted and closed at a trot with the sleeping village. At about 7 a.m., they halted near the lodges of the Modocs, dismounted and turned their mounts over to the horse holders and formed a skirmish line, awaiting Captain Jackson's orders.

Meanwhile, across Lost River, Oliver Applegate's misguided minutemen, hiding in a gully 400 yards from the village presided over by Hooker Jim, were undecided as what to do next. Their only plan of action seemed to be the denial of access by the Indians to their canoes, in case they wished to reinforce Captain Jack across the river or attack Jackson. As usual, Fate played a hand. One of Applegate's men returned from the river bank to tell him, erroneously, of course, that Jack's men were surrendering to the Fort Klamath troopers. This news so emboldened Applegate's men that they decided they might as well capture a village, too. They pushed into the camp and shook hands with a surprised Curley Headed Doctor but Hooker Jim, the other major subchief resident there, made for the river. O. C. Brown stopped him and forced him to surrender his gun. But another Modoc, Miller's Charley, snatched it away. As the confusion deepened, a Klamath scout with Applegate, Dave Hill, took it away from Miller's Charley. Still there was no shooting. There was yet no Modoc War. Only one shot had been fired, a warning signal by Scarfaced Charley.

But the settlers now realized that they had bitten off more than they could chew and they began to back off. Suddenly, there was a blaze of fire in their faces, almost coinciding with a rattle of small arms fire from across Lost River. Applegate's Cincinnati retreated pell mell for Crawley's cabin, where they forted up. George Fiocke cut loose with his double-barreled shotgun but unfortunately shot down, by accident, a squaw and papoose rather than a brave. This, naturally, enraged the Modocs who were not expecting hostilities of any kind on that late November dawn. Thus, when three civilians (either not in the fight at all or not *yet* in the fight) came in view, they were fiercely attacked. John (Jack of Clubs) Thurber and the pioneer settler of Linkville,

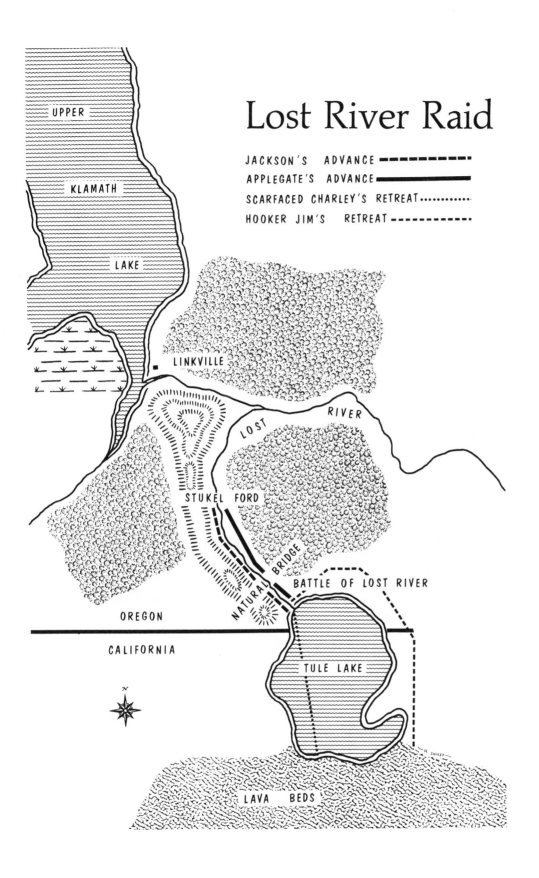

Lost River Raid

JACKSON'S ADVANCE ----------
APPLEGATE'S ADVANCE ━━━━━━━━
SCARFACED CHARLEY'S RETREAT ············
HOOKER JIM'S RETREAT -·-·-·-·-

UPPER

KLAMATH

LAKE

LINKVILLE

LOST   RIVER

STUKEL FORD

NATURAL BRIDGE

BATTLE OF LOST RIVER

OREGON

CALIFORNIA

TULE LAKE

LAVA   BEDS

Wendolin Nüs, were shot dead and Joe Pennig was wounded and maimed for life. He escaped on his fleet horse and did not fall from the saddle until he reached a safe zone. According to Applegate's men, Thurber was shot in cold blood as he was shaking hands with an Indian. Already the Modoc War was taking a bitter and brutal turn; not only was Thurber a civilian and quite possibly uninvolved in Applegate's militia, he was stone deaf and could not even hear rifle shots! Amongst Applegate's unit itself, no one was wounded although Jed Small's horse went *loco* with fright and pitched and sunfished around the Modoc village. Small hung on for dear life, regained control of the animal and galloped to Crawley's and safety. Besides the child and squaw shot by Fiocke, Miller's Charley, Duffy and Black Jim were wounded among the Modoc men. Since there were probably only fifteen warriors in all, and they had no idea of the disposition of troops and civilian auxiliaries, they withdrew to the eastward. Had they attacked Crawley's they would have probably wiped out Applegate's force. Lieutenant Boutelle was particularly critical of the blundering of Applegate: "The citizens who attacked the Indian camp on the left bank of Lost River were there without order or authority and had no more right for their attack than if it had been made on Broadway."

Jackson's raid on Captain Jack's camp was almost, but not quite, a complete surprise. One Indian was up, fishing, and he ran from the water's edge to the cluster of lodges, shouting "Soldiers! Soldiers!" A much more dangerous Modoc was already up, also. Scarfaced Charley, Captain Jack's righthand man — the Crazy Horse of the Modoc War, to Jack's Sitting Bull — was not only up and around but had canoed over to visit Hooker Jim's camp. When he saw the approach of the cavalrymen he fired his rifle into the air as a signal (later telling Boutelle that the weapon had "accidentally" discharged) and paddled back across the river.

As Scarfaced Charley came up the bank to a helpless village, Captain Jackson drew his revolver from his holster and ordered him to halt. Charley ignored him, continuing on and exhorting his comrades to fight to the death. Jackson, hamstrung by Odeneal's orders not to fire the first shot and commanded to secure the Modocs "peaceably if you can," did nothing. He recalled, bitterly, in later years, "Had they been undoubtedly hostile, there would have been no Modoc War." No; there might have been another Washita or Sand Creek near the shores of Tule Lake.

Ivan Applegate understood Modoc and he heard Scarfaced Charley tell the other warriors that they could kill every soldier without losing a man, if they acted quickly. But Captain Jack was nowhere to be seen and the Modocs were only slightly less muddled than Jackson's command. According to tradition, Jack was there, all right, but asleep in bed. The story goes that he sent out Bogus Charley to dicker while he yelled to the troopers not to shoot as he pulled on some clothes. But there was no parley and Captain Jack never appeared. Not one soldier saw him. Ivan Applegate wrote, "I was not able to find Captain Jack." Boutelle wrote that he could "neither get a talk with, or a sight of, Captain Jack." Jackson wrote that Jack "did not put in an appearance and, so far as is known, took no part in the subsequent fight." This was in character. Captain Jack has been transformed by legend and fiction into a dashing field commander of the Modocs although Scarfaced Charley eminently fitted that role.

Whether Jack was absent, pulling on his Levi's in his winter lodge, or lighting out through the sagebrush, Scarfaced Charley assumed command of the Modoc force. After disappearing into a lodge, he emerged through the smoke hole stripped for battle and accompanied by Bogus Charley. Scarfaced Charley, almost six feet tall (a

Captain James Jackson with a group of cavalrymen in the captured Modoc stronghold. He thought he had won a victory at Lost River, but the Modocs escaped and went on the rampage. U.S. National Archives photo.

giant among the bowlegged Modocs), was waving his rifle in one hand and haranguing his comrades. Jackson's "surprise" was now paperthin but Ivan Applegate actually thought that the Captain's gamble had paid off. He walked to the riverbank to call across to One Armed Brown to tell him everything was settled. This led to Oliver Applegate's bad miscalculation at Hooker Jim's camp.

Jackson, through Ivan Applegate, tried to get Scarfaced Charley's attention as Captain Jacks proxy, *wa-waing* about peace, protection from Klamaths on the reservation, and ample provisions for the Modocs if they would come in. They were largely ignored although there is considerable doubt that Charley really did as H. C. Rambeau said, that is, raised his gun and cried "I'm going to kill an officer." More likely, it was a Mexican standoff as Jackson demanded the surrender of the Modocs' weapons and, when it was not obeyed, asked his subordinate, "Mr. Boutelle, what do you think of the situation?" Boutelle's answer was, "There is going to be a fight and the sooner you open it the better, before there are any more complete preparations."

The next act of the tense drama was clear enough. Jackson ordered

The Modoc Winema (Toby Riddle) (center, back row) with Frank Riddle to her left in picture and O. C. Applegate to her right. Other Modoc women not identified. Oliver, brother of Indian sub-agent Ivan Applegate, formed armed citizens' group to support Captain Jackson in the action which ignited Modoc War before the U.S. Army had become involved. Photographer unknown, but c1873. Smithsonian Institution photo.

Boutelle to take four men from the line of skirmishers to arrest Scarfaced Charley and "the boldest spirits" among his followers. In an apologium written many years later, Boutelle insisted that he said not one word to the Indians as he advanced on them but it is much more likely that other witnesses had more reliable memories. With the aching tenseness of the situation there is no need to be surprised that Boutelle would curse and threaten his enemy as he faced them, gunsight to gunsight. In any case, when Captain Jackson again ordered Scarfaced Charley to take off his pistol after he had dropped his rifle, Charley retorted, "You got my gun. The pistol all right. Me no shoot you." Boutelle then took over. "Here, Injun," he said, "Give me that pistol here, damn you, quick! Charley laughed at him. "Me no dog," he answered. "Me man. Me no 'fraid you. You talk to me just like dog. Me no dog."

At this point, the Modoc War *might* have been averted, at least for a time. But it is unlikely, both because of the explosive situation in Captain Jack's camp and the even more deteriorated conditions across the river. But Charley did offer what amounted to an olive branch to Boutelle—"Talk me good, I listen you," he said. Boutelle spurned the peace offer. He pointed his Colt at the warrior and said, "You son of a bitch, I will show you not to talk back to me." Scarfaced Charley looked him in the eye without flinching and repeated cooly, "Me no dog. You no shoot me. Me keep pistol. You no get him, my pistol." As Boutelle squeezed the trigger, the scarred Indian brought up his own pistol to fire.

All hell broke loose. Ivan Applegate rushed up to Captain Jackson and using his brevet rank, shouted, "Major! They are going to fire!" Boutelle called to his men "Shoot over [sic] those Indians," whatever that meant. He then fired at Charley at the same instant that the Modoc shot at him. The two reports sounded as one. The Lieutenant's pistol ball tore the red bandanna which Charley wore around his black hair. Scarfaced Charley's slug cut through Boutelle's uniform blouse and cardigan jacket but did not tear either his shirt or undershirt sleeve. In later years, Boutelle was able to joke about the simultaneous exchange of fire—"Great minds appear to have thought alike."

The two hurried shots signalled general firing in the camp. According to Boutelle, there were only twenty-three men on the skirmish line. According to Jackson, only seventeen! In any case, the skirmishers began to fall back as Modoc rifle balls took effect. Private Harris was shot to death. Corporal Fitzgerald and Privates Gallagher and Kasshafer were severely wounded and Corporal Challinor and Privates Totten and Doyle less badly hit. A snapped shot by Boutelle caused Scarfaced Charley to drop to the ground and crawl off into cover. Boutelle's attention shifted when a warrior knelt in the opening of a lodge to take aim at him with a bow and arrow. "This I dodged," recalled the Lieutenant, "and the subsequent proceedings interested him no more."

With eight of their effectives knocked out of action, it was hard to hold the skirmish line but a little charge led by Boutelle drove the Indians out of the village. As they fell back, firing steadily, Boutelle halted his men in a picket line and secured the village. Ivan Applegate always said that Boutelle's coolness saved all of them. The Army, belatedly, concurred; in 1890 it awarded him the brevet of first lieutennt for his gallantry at the Lost River fight.

Somehow, Captain Jackson persuaded himself that the village had held 120 warriors, that he had whipped the Modocs, killed eight or nine warriors, including Captain Jack and Scarfaced Charley, and had won a fine victory. Actually, Charley had been playing possum. As Ivan Applegate observed, "The Troops were certain that Charley had been killed and one man was willing to take an oath that he was dead; but Charley, in reality, never received a scratch." Captain Jack was not even involved in the fight. The eight dead warriors shrank to actually one brave killed, Watchman, and six wounded. So elated was Jackson with his "victory" at Lost River, however, that he believed there

Lt. Frazier A. Boutelle with other officers at Fort Keogh, Montana, in the winter of 1870-71. He and Scarface Charley engaged in face-to-face pistol duel. Photo from U.S. National Archives.

would be no further Modoc resistance. Therefore, he had no objection to the squaws and children leaving the village (which he set afire) to join their scattered menfolk. A sick squaw was burned when the lodges were fired. It was probably an accident rather than an atrocity. She was apparently overlooked.

Oregonians like B. F. Dowell praised the "victor," Jackson, for his "prompt and effective march and attack and signal success." But the Captain began to have his doubts and even though he began his report of the Lost River raid thus, "I have the honor to report that I jumped the camp of Captain Jack's Modoc Indians yesterday morning, soon after daylight, completely surprising them...," he had to admit tht he had not tried to pursue the Modocs. His excuse was his wounded men, the weakness of his force, and his desire to protect the citizens gathered at Crawley's cabin.

So it was that Klamath scout Dave Hill ferried the wounded over the river in canoes as Jackson led his men seven miles upstream to Stukel Ford (the Natural Bridge ford being under too much water for safety at that season) while the ubiquitous Boutelle commanded the rearguard which repulsed a half-hearted attack by a small party of braves. Boutelle remarked later, "They had had enough and did not want any more."

Unfortunately, this was not the case with the band of Modocs on the left bank of Lost River. While Scarfaced Charley's men made their way in boats across Tule Lake to the safety of the labyrinthine Lava Beds of its southern shore, the band led by Hooker Jim and seconded by Jack's medicine man, Curly Headed Doctor, left a trail of blood as they rode all around the north and east side of Tule Lake to join the others in the Lava Beds. They spared all women they met but killed (and, it is said, mutilated) all men and boys on the ranches and farms in their path. At least fourteen, and probably more, noncombatants were murdered in Hooker Jim's bloody withdrawal after Jackson's raid.

Where Major John Green had erred in sending too few men to round up Jack's band, Captain Jackson really bungled his operation by immobilizing himself at Crawley's ranch after his "victory." He left the warning of settlers to Odeneal's men and, as a result, the blood of the unsuspecting ranchers was partially on his hands. When he finally sent a patrol to the Boddy ranch, only three and a half miles from his headquarters, the troopers did not reconnoitre thoroughly enough to even discover the massacres committed by the Modocs.

Not until December 1st did the full horror of his "victory" dawn on Captain Jackson, when travelers arrived at Crawley's with word of the butchery at Boddy's place. Not until December 2d, four days after the fight, did Jackson send a detachment out to pick up the Modocs' trail. He finally sent a patrol to Clear Lake, too, but stayed put, himself, at Crawley's ranch, awaiting supplies and reinforcements promised him by his C. O. at Fort Klamath, Major Green; by the Commander of the District of the Lakes, Colonel Frank Wheaton; and by the Commander of the Whole Department of the Columbia, General E. R. S. Canby.

But when the Army again tried to corral Captain Jack and his band—this time in far more difficult terrain (the Lava Beds) than in the Lost River Valley, they did not trust Jackson or even Green with the command. The great offensive of January 17, 1873, against Captain Jack's Stronghold was led by Colonel Wheaton, himself. It was a horrible fiasco but Wheaton's defeat at least improved both the military and civilian estimate of Captain James Jackson's ability. It was not that he and his troopers were so bad, after all; the facts of the case were that the embattled Modocs were ready to fight the toughest little war the yellowlegs of the First Cavalry had ever run into, since they were dragoons in the Everglades. To the Army's credit, Jackson and Boutelle were not made scapegoats, although everyone explained away

Loa Kum or Nub Scouting, a Modoc. His U.S. Army issue equipment including the Spencer rifle and Hardy hat ranges the time period from 1851 to about 1870. U.S. National Archives photo.

the thumping of the Army, the militiamen and the peaceful settlers of
Lost River and Tule Lake. Both men served throughout the war with
Boutelle participating in the turnabout victory at Sorass Lake and Jackson and his troops were in on the final capture of Jack and his last
loyal lieutenants.

NOTES

The chief sources of information about Captain Jackson's Lost River raid are, for
the most part, the best books about the Modoc War in general. But while there is
no dearth of books about the war and, especially of volumes which include the
war in a general roundup of American Indian campaigns, only a handful of them
are really dependable. Two are outstanding—Keith A. Murray's *The Modocs and
Their War* (Norman, University of Oklahoma, 1959) and Erwin N. Thompson's
Modoc War (Washington, D.C. [?], U.S. Department of the Interior, 1967). The
latter was largely an "intramural" report of the National Park Service and is virtually unobtainable. However, a California antiquarian book dealer is planning
(1970) to issue a reprint edition for a wider readership. With these two works
should be used the government document "Correspondence and Papers Relative
to the Modoc War," *House Executive Document No. 122*, 1st Session, 43d Congress, 1874. (Serial set No. 1607.) This document, for example, contains the ver-
batim reports by Captain Jackson and his superiors on the Lost River fight.

Three older books are useful but are so flawed (carelessness, inaccuracy, in-
vented conversation, &c&c&c) that they cannot be considered to be primary sources
although their authors were participants or witnesses to events of the Modoc War.
These are Jeff C. Riddle's *The Indian History of the Modoc War*...(n.p., D. L.
Moses, 1914) and Alfred B. Meacham's *Wigwam and Warpath*...(Boston, John
P. Dale, 1875) and *Wi-ne-ma* (Hartford, American Publishing Company, 1876).
None of this bibliographical trio is common but a West Coast publisher is (1970)
considering the reprinting of Riddle's underdog version of the sad conflict.

My own volume, William Henry Boyle's *Personal Observations on the Conduct
of the Modoc War* (Los Angeles, Dawson's Book Shop, 1959) is useful but picks
up the story of the campaign after Jackson's Lost River strike. And the same ap-
plies to the Modoc War portion of Oliver Knight's *Following the Indian Wars*
(Norman, University of Oklahoma Press, 1960). For additional background on the
events both preceding and succeeding the first battle of the Modoc War, a perusal
of the government documents of the 1860's and 1870's is recommended, particularly the annual reports of the Secretary of War and of the Commissioner of Indian
Affairs. And, hopefully, my study, *Fort Klamath and the Modoc War*, scheduled
for 1972 publication by Prentice-Hall in its American Forts Series, will throw light
on the broader campaign in the Lava Beds and around Lost River and Tule Lake.

Of particular value for this chapter were the personal accounts of participants
in the Lost River raid. Captain James Jackson's "The Modoc War—Its Origin,
Incidents and Peculiarities" appeared in *The United Service* for July 1892 (pp. 1-12)
while the activities of Jackson, Ivan Applegate and especially Lt. Frazier Boutelle
are detailed in their own words in Cyrus T. Brady's *Northwestern Fights and Fighters* (New York, Doubleday, Page, 1916), pp. 257-279.

Ho-wear: A Yapparika Comanche chief, frequently at Fort Sill in the 1870's.

The Man Who Photographed Indians

by Robert A. Weinstein

WHEN WILLIAM S. SOULE left his Boston, Massachusetts, home in 1867 to photograph the Plains Indians of the Far West, his self-confidence was reassuring, although his evident unfamiliarity with the problems he would certainly encounter should have been frightening. New to the Far West and even newer still to the Plains Indians, he was largely unaware of how a people bound to a sorcery culture might regard the taking of photographs of themselves. He was ignorant, unhappily, of the rather strict prohibitions surrounding the fashioning of a realistic image of a human being in an image-based culture.

In the due course of time Will Soule discovered his Indian subjects and they puzzled him; the Indians—Kiowas, Comanches, Arapahoes, and Apaches found Mr. Soule, his camera and his photographic aspirations equally puzzling. To them the picture-taking process was most bewildering. The engaging young Soule explained that with the help of the sun, the glass eye in his black boxed camera only borrowed the subject's face and then quickly returned it to its rightful owner, plus of course the paper copy of it. Plausible as it sounded, the Indians queried, "How many times might an Indian lend the black box his face before he discovered that he had lost it altogether one tragic morning?" This bit of trenchant reasoning was, apparently, never successfully answered. While many Indian men ultimately accepted the implied risk in being photographed they remained most reluctant to allow their women and children to do likewise.

Presently we have too few daguerreotypes or other photographic images of Southwest Plains Indians before the work of Will Soule. He was much the pioneer in his work in the Southwest Plains and the limited evidence available suggests that his work was undertaken not solely as a commercial project, but in the main for his personal satisfaction.

A scant four years after the close of the Civil War the United States was groping towards the expansion of its western frontier. Raw land was the key, and the new American settlers wanted to settle on it, farm it, mine it and if possible, own it. The trouble about that otherwise excellent notion was that various Indian nations already owned it, hunted on it, lived on it and additionally had every legal, reasonable right to do so.

By 1869 the white bearers of American Manifest Destiny had descended upon these Indians in quantity. Perhaps more important than the land itself, or the wanton slaughter of the sacred buffalo, certain fundamental intentions of the invaders soon became painfully clear. Deliberate disregard of solemn treaty obligations, trickery in negotiations, outright and repeated lies, sudden and savage physical violence were all evidences of the white man's determination to destroy a belief pattern, a cultural heritage, and in the end a way of life and a set of ethical standards both useful and honorable.

The Indians were not slow to resist, and incident and counter-incident followed tragically and swiftly. Fort Sill, newly-located in the heart-center of the ancient Kiowa tribal land, seemed to the Indians another expression of the willingness of the United States government to provide military protection for all those carrying out a brutal program of Indian destruction. The fort was to tragically prove a sore spot, ready tinder for the flame of forthcoming battle.

This was the setting for Will Soule's artistic endeavors. It was to this incipient maelstrom, in the hot dusty summer of 1869, deep in Oklahoma Territory, that W. S. Soule, the younger brother of John P. Soule, successful Boston portrait photographer, made his way with a military party of United States Cavalry.

Arriving at Fort Sill for the dedication ceremonies Soule was quickly torn between the military's demands for his few precious glass plates and his own fascination with photographing the many Indians gathered at the fort for the founding festivities. Clearly his aesthetic impulses won out, for he photographed Kiowas, Comanches, Arapahoes, and even Apaches — many men, a few women and even fewer children in a metier and in costumes closer to their own natural choices than required of them by later Indian photographers. Soule's subjects are not the Indians of twenty or even ten years later, dressed and posed to demonstrate the Indian as the white man wished to see him—conquered, servile, and compliant—the well-known feather "carnival" Indian.

Although there is no evidence that Soule and his camera were accepted enthusiastically by the Plains Indians at Fort Sill, their co-operation, hesitant and wondering as it was, has enabled us to see them once more. A proud, skillful, defiant people, soon to be faced with the bitter choices given them by the march of human events; their like-nesses are available now in memory for the understanding and honor denied them in their lifetime—thanks to the sensitivity and determina-tion of a young Boston photographer.

Look carefully at the faces of these Indians photographed by Will Soule at Fort Sill in 1869. Do we see here the result of the usual pho-tographer's request to "smile and watch the birdie"? No, there is no visible humor here. Resignation perhaps, or hostility, pride, contempt —nearly any emotion—but enjoyment is not visible here. Soule's plates for the most part seem to reflect a kind of mutual respect and mutual cooperation between a white photographer and his Indian subjects re-markably uncommon among Indian frontier photographers.

Look again at the print of White Bear. He has been described as warlike and arrogant. Soule's portrait, however, would describe him

White Bear (Satanta). Known as the "Orator of the Plains," he was the Kiowa's greatest chief and warrior. He is photographed wearing a Major General's uniform presented to him by General W. S. Hancock. Arrested more than once for leading raiding parties, he committed suicide in 1874 by leaping from an upper story of the prison hospital.

differently; here he is at peace. And, who might have imagined that Kicking Bird could be persuaded by Soule to sit quietly for his portrait in 1869 in full regalia, when at the Medicine Lodge Creek Council in 1867 he appeared in only his breech clout and a high silk hat.

So far as we know neither the Comanche, Kiowa or Apache asked for or accepted favors in return for their posing. Further, there is no evidence of their interest in owning photographic prints. Nor can we record, for instance, any example of Lone Wolf offering his portrait, enshrined on a *carte-de-visite* to George Armstrong Custer when they met at Sheridan's camp.

All Indian photographers were not so privileged or so lucky. Attempting to photograph the Utes in 1874, William Henry Jackson encountered very strong opposition and was able to take only a very few pictures. Where Jackson failed, Soule's remarkable collection of glass plates show that he succeeded. Unlike Jackson who managed to travel through Indian areas of relative peace, Soule probably could not have taken these pictures if he had arrived at Fort Sill two years earlier or four years later. Almost as if he knew that he was in the eye of a tornado, Soule had to photograph swiftly, and surely to record this brief moment of tense calm. In a very real way his Indian subjects reflect their own sense that the end was near for themselves as Lords of the Southern Plains.

Their faces reflect many currents and cross-currents as well. What history required of them was the ability to accept cultural change. The kind of cultural change demanded of them was too rapid for most. For certain of them there was no problem. They simply refused to consider a change of any kind—and that is what can be seen in their proud faces. That is what William Stinson Soule—the man who photographed Indians—saw at Fort Sill, Indian Territory, in 1869 through 1874 when his epic work was finished.

Russell E. Belous, Los Angeles County Museum of Natural History, was of great help and extended material assistance in the preparation of this article.

Mow-way (Shaking Hand). Mow-way was a Cochateka Comanche chief of great reputation as a fierce warrior. He surrendered to the U.S. Army at Fort Bascom in 1869. With a group of Comanches he was imprisoned at Fort Leavenworth for a brief time, released and then taken to Fort Sill, Oklahoma Territory. He died there and is buried in the Post Cemetery.

Left: Tosh-a-wah (Toshaway, Tosawi, Silver
Brooch). First chief of the Penateka
Comanches, he was well known for his
peaceful attitude towards the white man and
the U.S. Army. Right: Cry of the Wild
Goose (Sa-lo-so, Tsa'l-au-te). At the United
States Army's attempt to move various tribes
to Fort Cobb in 1868, Sa-lo-so was present
and saw the United States troops under
Colonel Custer and General Sheridan seize his
father, Satanta, and Lone Wolf as hostages.
Later on Sa-lo-so became a valued member of
the Indian Police. Bottom: Walk-u-betta, an
Arapahoe chief, and four members of his
band were photographed by Will Soule at
what is believed to be Camp Supply, in the
Fall of 1868.

Top: Lone Bear (Tarlo). Evidencing uncommon trust between Will Soule and his Indian subjects, this unusual photograph of young Lone Bear dressed in ceremonial garb verifies Soule's amazing relationship with the Plains Indians. Taken out-of-doors, Soule used his "props," a buffalo robe and one or two painted backdrops that can be seen in others of his photographs. Below: These two Wichita women are further evidence of Will Soule's ability in developing a trusting confidence in his Indian subjects. Taking such revealing portraits of Indian women in 1869 in Indian Territory was both difficult and unique . . . more often, as not, impossible.

Above: Horse Back (Tuh-huh-yet,
Nau-qua-hip, Champion Rider).
Born in Texas about 1810, Horse
Back became one of the principal
civil chiefs of the Nocomee
Comanches. Although stern and
just, he was generally friendly to
the whites and he was one of the
ten leading chiefs for whom houses
were built at Fort Sill in 1876.
Right: Big Bow (Zepko-eete). A
Kiowa chief who probably "killed
and scalped more white people
than any of his comrades." He was
so described by Thomas Battey,
minister and teacher, who lived
among the Kiowas. Although he
participated in most of the major
raids he escaped punishment by
surrendering the entire Kiowa tribe
at Fort Sill in 1875.

Left: Sitting Bear (Satank, Set-angya). A Kiowa chief and medicine man, he negotiated the 1840 peace treaty with five Indian tribes. He headed the list of signers of the Medicine Lodge treaty of 1867 as well. Disillusioned by his son's death in battle, he led several raids on wagon trains. In 1871 Sitting Bear was arrested at Fort Sill and deliberately invited his death in an escape attempt. Singing his death song, he was cut down by the guard's bullets. Above: Kicking Bird (Striking Eagle, T'ene-angpote). A friendly Kiowa chief, a signer of the Medicine Lodge treaty. He helped persuade Big Bow to surrender at Fort Sill in 1875, incurring deep hostility from the war chiefs. He died in 1875, it is believed, of poison.

Above: Big Tree (A'do-eete). Kiowa chief who, with White Bear and Sitting Bear, led many raids into Texas. Converted to Christianity, he served for thirty years as a deacon in the Rocky Mountain Indian Mission Church, dying in 1930. Bottom: Woman Heart (Manyi-ten). A Kiowa chief included in an Indian delegation to Washington, D.C., in 1872.

Above: Pacer (Peso, Essa-queta). Chief of the Kiowa-Apaches, this man, singularly intelligent and endowed with considerable ability, advocated peace with the whites consistently. His lifelong ambition to see an Indian school constructed for his people was completed by a Quaker, Mr. A. J. Standing, in 1875, the year of his death. Pacer is buried in the Post Cemetery at Fort Sill.

Where was the Battle of Turret Peak Fought?

by Dan L. Thrapp

At the tag end of winter the wet snows still lay heavy on the Mogollon Rim country, the San Francisco Peaks to the north, on the high Four Peaks to the south and Pine Mountain to the west. Squaw Tit, a landmark for fifty miles up and down the river, had its bonnet of rotten snow too, with a fringe of greenery fed by melted ice waters splotching its precipitous sides a short distance below the white. Big George Randall, Captain of the 23rd Infantry, a brevet Major from the Civil War and one day to become a Major-General, chewed on a live-oak splinter and listened to his scouts. Same old story. They hadn't much to report, although they had been working very hard, climbing like weasels over the points, scrambling through the dry washes and ravines and around the brittle hillsides, slipping through chaparral that would rip a white man's clothing to shreds, all the time seeking hostile sign, day after weary day. Nothing. Or almost nothing. They had managed to capture one woman, but she insisted she had no information about where the enemy camped and wouldn't tell even if she knew, which she probably did. Exasperating. Not since the battle of the Salt River Cave three months ago had the enemy been struck squarely, although there had been a few skirmishes here and there. Now Randall and his command, Company "A" of the 5th Cavalry and "I" of the 23rd Infantry, plus a few Indian scouts, had reached the mouth of the East Verde River after scouting north from Camp McDowell all the way up the main Verde. The hostiles *must* be in this God-forsaken wilderness somewhere. They had to be, for they were nowhere else.

To top it off, now he had lost some mules, and in this country mules were as important as soldiers — almost as valuable as scouts. Without mules a column soon would become immobilized. He would have to put into Camp Verde soon to draw some more. Probably they were stolen by the damned Indians since, shortly after the animals disappeared, signal smokes went up briefly well beyond reach. Eaten by now, the mules no doubt were, damn it all.

Randall surveyed the brown stony hillsides that seemed to push up the skyline all around, as though he were sitting in the bottom of an oversized bowl, as, in fact, he was. An enormous, Indian-ridden, little-known, inaccessible valley that was the bottomless heart of hostile country. It had to be cleaned out, because orders said so. He sat on his flat rock and chewed the twig and reflected. If he could find this main body of Indians, and get a good crack at them, perhaps he could wind up the main offensive, and General Crook would like that.

Full-bearded, active George Crook, brevet Major-General, assigned to the Department of Arizona in 1871 to succeed General George Stoneman, had known that his major mission was not housekeeping the Territory, but settling its thousands of warring, depredating Indians, Yavapais, Apaches and others, on reservations where they could be managed and fed and kept off of the warpath for the benefit of the whites and even, perhaps, for the good of the Indians themselves. He had reached Arizona in late June. Twice he had readied an "offensive" to accomplish this end. Twice he had been forced to call it off while peace emissaries from Washington turned their hands and hearts to bringing tranquility to the blood-soaked region. Twice they had failed. Now it was Crook's turn to prove that he had another answer, and one he believed the only practicable one. The only solution, he was convinced, that the Indians would respect and obey.

His "offensive" was not laid out by the book; it was not orthodox in any military sense. No huge units would go marching out like Braddock's column, seeking a cataclysmic battle with a massed foe. Nothing of that sort would ever succeed in Apachería, Crook well knew, for here the Indians gathered in bands too small, too fragmented to ever be combined for a mighty contest — or for any battle at all which they could avoid. They lived in tiny rancherías, in secluded gorges or on remote mountain tops somewhere, on buttes or in brushy valleys, wherever you least suspected they could survive. It was a case of hunting down each of these bands, one by one, giving each a good clearing out, flushing them from their hidden retreats and stinging them to the point where they would scurry for safety to some waiting reserve. This was a hard, bitter, cruel war, but Crook hoped at least to make it short, and so he sent his columns out from the scattered military posts: Apache, Mc-Dowell, Grant and others, small commands, a company or two at most, under junior officers for the most part, because they, being young and hard and ambitious, were more active and enduring, he believed.[1]

They scoured the back country, some of it little explored, following the streams through the hidden canyons, sometimes splashing up the watercourses themselves for a mile or more, clambering up and down the bluffs, avoiding cactus when they could, occasionally slipping through natural tunnels or narrow defiles to attack unwary Indians on the other side. Crook wrote:

> The officers and men worked day and night, and with our Indian allies would crawl upon their hands and knees for long distances over terrible canyons and precipices where the slightest mishap would have resulted in instant death, in order that when daylight came they might attack their enemy and secure the advantage of a surprise....There is hardly a space of 10 miles square in the country operated over that has not some terrible lava bed or precipitous canyon with fortified caves, which the Indians could have held against all odds and with terrible loss of life, had the enemy been approached in daylight and assailed when they were on the alert....The examples of personal exertions and daring among the officers and men if all told would fill a volume.[2]

Innumerable small fights had taken place, but aside from the major engagement at the cave overlooking Salt River, where about seventy-five trapped Indians had died rather than surrender, it had proven impossible to bring about an action in any way decisive until, perhaps, now. Randall called his chief of scouts, Mason McCoy, to him. McCoy,

Turret Peak, from southwest looking northeast. A lion hunter said he rode a mule to the top of it. Photo by author.

who had scouted for Crook in the Oregon country before the General was assigned to Arizona, knew Indians, knew the Army, and was a man reliable, intelligent. He also shared Randall's impatience with present frustrations.

"Mace," growled the Captain, "the only way we are going to find these hostiles is if that woman talks." McCoy understood instantly. "Yes, sir," he replied. He headed over to where the captive watchfully rested amid the fifteen White Mountain Apaches.

With the woman as a guide, the command prepared to start off at dusk. Crook wrote the story:

> Our soldiers, before starting out, wrapped their feet and knees with gunny sacks, so as to make as little noise as possible. Soon after dark the command started for the camp of the hostiles under the guidance of the squaw. Their route lay down the banks of the river Verde for a ways, and then took up an incline of broken lava that had become detached from a high palisade of the same material. The angle of this incline was about 45 degrees. That, together with the loose rocks, made the ascent very laborious and difficult as great precaution had to be observed, so as not to make any noise.
>
> After traveling this way for quite a while, they came to the foot of the palisades. Here they met with a circular mountain running up into a column, with but one mode of ingress. This was caused by a piece of this palisades fallen down, leaving a notch by which, with great difficulty, our people could get up. On top of this notch was lying a huge rock, so our people had to crawl on their stomachs.
>
> The summit was reached just before daylight, and they found the general surface comparatively smooth. The lava was thrown up in irregular masses while cooling, leaving large fissures running to all directions, with this grown up more or less with brush. They crawled up close to the Indians.
>
> Just at the dawn of day our people fired a volley into their camp and charged with a yell. So secure did they feel in this almost impregnable position that they lost all presence of mind, even running past their holes in the rocks. Some of them jumped off the precipice and were mashed into a shapeless mass. All of the men were killed; most of the women and children were taken prisoners. This is called Turret Mountain from its shape.[3]

Various figures are given as to how many Indians were slain in this fight. The *Chronological List* shows 23 killed and 10 captured, with 10 more killed and three captured in another fight "near" Turret Mountain.[4] The Prescott *Miner*, which had access to reports reaching Fort Whipple, reported 47 killed and seven captured.[5] One serious writer said that Randall captured "the entire group, including some one hundred and thirty-six souls."[6] Crook himself gives no figures.

In any event, this is the most complete summary that can be compiled on the basis of information presently at hand on the important battle of Turret Peak. It was the second of the two decisive engagements which settled for all time the Indian problem in central Arizona, no matter how much hard campaigning after scattered bands remained. The story is neatly packaged: the command worked south down the Verde from its junction with East Verde, then cut overland to Turret Peak, scaled the mountain, attacked at dawn, killed those Indian warriors who did not leap into eternity, captured the noncombatants, and returned to base.

But upon closer inspection, it proves to be not all that simple. Not quite.

The first question to be resolved is whether the Turret Mountain Crook spoke of is the upthrust called Turret Peak today, twelve miles west southwest of the junction of the Verde and East Verde, and about nine and one-half air miles west of the river at its nearest approach. Turret Peak lies between Rugged Mesa and Pine Mountain, the lot making up a range formerly called the Black Hills. It is isolated from its neighbors by ravines and saddles. Turret Peak is crowned by a knob on its southwestern extremity while the remainder of the summit, from a distance, appears as a plateau, and the consequent profile, as Crook pointed out, being responsible for its name. Since it was shown in its present position upon the Smith Map of 1879,[7] a scant six years after the fight, and from other evidence, too — scout reports and so on — one may be fairly confident that the peak is the same. Wherein then lies the difficulty?

The problem is that the mountain does not conform, in shape or geological structure, to Crook's description, although it should be mentioned that there is no record that he ever saw the peak at close hand. Even if the sides are steep, particularly upon a torrid August day, as when I climbed it, they nowhere present an escarpment over which frightened Indians could leap to their deaths. Claude Wright, a lion hunter who has roamed all over that country for many years, told me in 1959 that he once even had ridden a mule to its summit, and this would indeed be possible for a man who understood those remarkable animals and was well mounted. One could not, however, ride a mule up an escarpment over which a startled individual might leap to his demise. Nor is there, anywhere around its rim, a notch which answers Crook's description, or blocks of stone representing the difficulties he describes unless the reality is dosed with lavish ladlings of imagination and a generous indulgence allowed for the troops having climbed the peak in the dark under extreme stalking circumstances. It is most unlikely, however, that hardened soldiers would so describe a climb up

Turret Peak, if that indeed was the mountain where the described battle took place.

When in doubt, with respect to a problem such as this, the best rule is to go to the primary source which, in this instance, would be Randall's report. That should provide a ready solution. But in this case it does not. Recourse was had to the National Archives repeatedly, probing every file where such a document logically might be stored, and by others as well as myself, including a professional researcher. No such report has surfaced to date. Finally, Mr. Elmer O. Parker, of the Old Military Records Division, thought to check the *Chronological List*, and uncovered the source for its entry, the "Record of Events" on the pertinent Regimental Return for April, 1873, for Camp Apache. This reports a scout led by Captain Randall and Second Lieutenant Alexander O. Brodie, 1st Cavalry, which left Apache January 10, scouted to New Camp Grant, left there in February, rummaging through the Tonto Basin, touched old Fort Reno and reaching Camp McDowell, then working north along the Verde, making foot scouts to either side, hunting sign. It continued:

> On March 25 a detachment of 'A' Troop, 5th Cav. under command of 1st Sergt. [James M.] *Hill* struck an Indian Camp near *Turret Mountain*, killed 10 Indians and captured 3 women, destroying a large amount of mescal. On March 27th Capt. *Randall*, 23rd Infty, with Guide *Mason McCoy* and detachments from 'A' Troop, 5th Cav. and co. 23rd Infty and 15 White Mountain Indian Scouts surprised the Indians in the rocks on *Turret Mountain* at day light and after about two hours engagement killed 23 Indians, captured 10 women, destroyed their camp and a large quantity of supplies, arrived at *Camp Verde* on the 29th....

Having traveled 404 miles from New Camp Grant, it left Verde April

Skeleton Ridge, the long ridge to right; Pine Mountain in background. At the base of this ridge human bones have been found and it is on this butte that one of the two fights described may have taken place. Photo by author.

15 and reached Camp Apache April 29, after a trip of 745 miles, in
addition to all the side scouts that were made.

This is about as close to an official report of the battle one can come to until some Archives researcher, in a more thorough, or luckier, examination, comes across the misplaced item in some bundle of reports not yet studied. Since few reports which reach the Archives are ever actually "lost" forever, this some day may well happen.

Even this brief account includes statements of interest, however. It mentions that the important fight on Turret Peak lasted two hours, which scarcely matches Crook's description of an opening blast of fire so startling the Indians that they jumped to their deaths, the camp apparently overrun in a matter of minutes. It also remarks upon the interesting fight of Sergeant Hill—where did this occur? All that the summary says is that it took place "near" Turret Mountain. Neither incident, as summarized, contains the identifying details Crook wrote about; of course, such a brief summation could not. But these facts, plus the results of a personal inspection of the site, made me dubious about the story as told, although there appeared no further way to get at the underlying truth.

Then one day at Pine, Arizona, I was chatting with a good friend, James Blackburn, 62 years old now, who knows the rough country of central Arizona perhaps more intimately than anyone since Al Sieber a century ago. There is scarcely a trail, not a waterhole, no butte, canyon, mesa, point, headland, mountain, rim or ravine that Blackburn is ignorant of or has not explored. He learned about the ranges west of the Verde starting in 1929 when he was a cowboy there, rousting out wild cattle, and his 30 years with the Forest Service, later as a sheriff's deputy, and particularly with a search and rescue team, have given him a unique body of lore about that last remaining wilderness that some-one should make a matter of record. Jim Blackburn, as one who knows him well puts it, is of a vanishing breed; the Southwest will be the poorer when the last few survivors of his type have finally gone.

At any rate, Jim and I were talking about Indian fights and sites in central Arizona this particular day, and he mentioned Skeleton Ridge.

"Skeleton Ridge?" I echoed. "Where's that? What is it?"

"Oh, it's over just this side of Pine Mountain," Jim replied. "Stands up there like a box, a table." Then, as an afterthought, he added, "I clumb it once, when I was supposed to be chasing cows. Flat on top. Found some bones in the rocks below the fartherest end."

"What kind of bones?"

"Oh, some skulls, or parts of them. Few ribs. Stuff like that."

I wondered what had taken place on this mysterious ridge. Jim passed along the gossip he had picked up forty years earlier. It was shaky on facts, but nonetheless stimulating. He said he had asked the same question of a man named Woodward, then about 75 and an old-timer in the area.

"There wasn't much brush in the country in those days," Jim explained. "The Indians kept it burned off. It wasn't until the Forest Service moved in and stopped the annual fires that all this chaparral sprang up. Woodward told me that a party of white troopers from Fort Dewey had a parley with Indians in what is now Bloody Basin. Both sides were to approach without arms. The troopers did so, but the Indians tied bows and lances to their toes and dragged them through the tall grass until close enough, then massacred all but two of the soldiers. In retaliation, the troops later cornered the Indians on what is now called Skeleton Ridge. They camped in the saddle between it and Pine Mountain, where there is a spring. No Indian could escape. They all perished."

George Crook, who directed the offensive against the Apaches in 1872-4 as a Lieutenant Colonel, was promoted to Brigadier General because of its success. U.S. National Archives photo.

No fort named "Dewey" is known to have existed in Arizona, but there was a Camp Lewis from about 1865 to 1870 on deep-canyoned Fossil Creek above its junction with the Verde,[8] probably about where the present road from the Verde valley crosses Fossil Creek enroute to the Tonto Basin. Perhaps this was the camp meant. No such massacre is known to have occurred in Arizona, either, but many of the early skirmishes, particularly those between the California Volunteers and the Yavapai and other Indians were imperfectly recorded, and a fight something like this is not beyond possibility. It might even have been responsible for the labeling of Bloody Basin, whose name otherwise is a mystery that no authority has ever unraveled. No such incident as the besieging of Indians atop Skeleton Ridge is known to have taken place, and it would be impossible in any event, since the walls of the ridge are scalable in many places, if with difficulty. No Indian would

George Morton Randall, who led the attack on Turret Peak, in the uniform of a Brigadier General. He made Brigadier General of Volunteers in 1898, and of the Regular Army in 1901, later rising to Major General. He died in 1918. U.S. Signal Corps Photo, National Archives.

remain atop to starve if he could readily flee.

There is the added factor of the naming of Skeleton Ridge. Barnes, in his superb compendium, *Arizona Place Names*, quotes an informant: "This ridge derives its name from its shape. When seen from higher country [i.e., Pine Mountain] it is a very narrow sharp ridge from which numerous ribs or ridges branch off, giving it appearance of a huge skeleton,"[9] which is a fanciful explanation, but probably wrong. The fact that, as Blackburn said, "many old-timers for many years have found bits of bone, along with metal uniform buttons and other objects" along the base of the ridge suggests a more plausible explanation. It was named Skeleton Ridge because skeletons lay about it.

With Blackburn's recollections before one, it became essential for anyone intrigued with the problems of southwestern history to visit Skeleton Ridge itself and see whether it met any of Crooks specifications, and to what extent. Jim was certainly willing. He always is ready for an interesting trip. So were Jim Walker and Wendel Towse; they wanted to go just for the hell of it.

The map showed the ridge to be 5,953 feet in altitude, lower than 6,821-foot Pine Mountain behind it. The butte was seven or eight miles northeast of Turret Peak, and rising about a hundred feet higher. Turret Peak was nine and one-half miles from the Verde, remember, and Skeleton Ridge a little over five miles, although in either case the climb upwards was considerable, since the river flows at an elevation of only about 2,300 feet. The climb, however, was steeper than this figure suggests, since the intervening countryside in either case was chopped up with enough precipitous ravines, buttes, points, gorges and other geographical impedimenta to exhaust anyone less enduring than a toughened scout.

It is not easy to approach Skeleton Ridge even today, since no road goes very close to it. The first reconnoitering trip took us to where we could size up the route, but little more. The second attempt was called off because the Verde was too high to ford at Verde Hot Springs. On the third go, however, we got our International Scouts across the river, and ground away up the long ranch "road"—little more than a trail, really—toward Bloody Basin. Once atop Long Mesa we bore to the right up another similar trace that followed power lines a short distance, then curved around a boulder-littered hill toward Pine Mountain, over a road Blackburn himself had scraped out with a bulldozer when working for the Forest Service. Apparently no one had dared use it since, until we came along. It took us but a short distance, and with fearful jouncing, but to Blackburn, as true a cowpuncher as ever straddled a conveyance, each step ridden is a step saved.

Despite his age, Jim is as tireless a rock jumper as anyone could be; he regularly wears out much younger men on expeditions into the boondocks. From where we were forced to leave the vehicles, the climb to Skeleton Ridge was up a rising hogback whose spiny, undulating outcroppings rose steeply higher and higher and higher, leaving one gasping for breath, praying for rest, particularly desk-hardened swivel-chair jockeys like his companions.

But Blackburn is as contemptuous of rest as he is of those who "cain't keep up," and his party struggled after him, guided when he was beyond sight by brown splotches of tobacco juice with which he doused each prominent rock. Just short of utter collapse we gathered at the base of a red-stone cliff that was the eastern nose of Skeleton Ridge. We slapped it unbelievingly, gratefully, and sank back at last to rest, gazing up its fifty-foot sheer rise, wondering if anyone truly had ever leaped down it.

Was this the site of the Turret Peak fight?

The escarpment was sheer, or almost sheer, in most places, but elsewhere it was broken, with junipers and, near the top, live oaks grown up from the cracks. These stubby trees helped us struggle to the top. A wilderness of brush and stunted timber obstructed the view, except from the rim outward, toward distant horizons. The top was flat as a pond, except for the undergrowth, with here and there a bald spot of open rock for a few yards. We enjoyed the view, as any Indians who had lived there also must have appreciated it so long ago. On the far northern horizon the San Franciscos, rising to 12,670 feet and the tallest mountains in Arizona, were white-capped still with late snows. Far below us, in its deep, meandering basin, rolled the Verde, a ribbon of silver, visible in dots and dashes. Beyond Squaw Tit and the river's junction with the East Verde was Polles Mesa, a flatiron of level rock, looking from this distance as smooth as a billiard table but which we knew from other expeditions, presented in truth a wrenching havoc for any wheeled vehicle. Beyond and to the right, was dark and gloomy

North Peak, the long ridge of the Mazatzals, where Blackburn often had fought brush or forest fires when with the Forest Service. They terminated to the south in the classic Four Peaks, which the Indians called, "Three Passes," and there is a lesson in psychology there somewhere.

Just beyond Long Mesa on this side of the Verde we could see the depression of Bloody Basin, named long ago for some forgotten incident. Behind us, screened from immediate view by the tangle of brush, was dingy, wooded Pine Mountain, a long upthrust curving off to the southwest where, beyond Mockingbird Pass, it would meld into Turret Peak, not quite visible to us.

After he had given us, with waving arm and from his impressive fund of knowledge, this Cook's Tour of central Arizona, Jim turned back to the problem at hand. "Never saw so damned much brush up here," he muttered. "Let's whack our way through it. I clumb up the other end."

Skeleton Ridge is a block of a butte, about a quarter mile long, in most places about one hundred yards wide, and one can force a way only with difficulty through its tightly thicketed scrub oak, manzanita and other growth. It is necessary to step carefully, for the rim is sometimes concealed, and there are cracks and holes everywhere. At about the center of this sky island, a notch comes in from the south and almost meets one from the north, but it is possible to pass, with some trouble, across the somewhat broken surface to gain the western portion of the plateau. The western half is more broken than the eastern, with great

Lieutenant Charles B. Gatewood's Scouts camped near the Mexican border in about 1883. Arizona Pioneers' Historical Society photo.

blocks of stone sheered from the sides of the structure as though it were incomplete—or perhaps falling into ruin.

We found no relics on Skeleton Ridge. Nothing but its physical structure and a rattlesnake or two which we avoided but did not harm, nor did they attempt to injure us. If a big fight took place there, some relics of it must still exist, but they would be difficult to find, given the brush cover and the extreme impracticability because of it to use a metal detector or other modern search gear.

Physically the site matches Crook's description far more exactly than does Turret Peak.

Crook wrote that the men muffled their feet and knees before leaving the Verde, but that is unlikely to have been done so far distant, eight or ten miles before the men would approach within ear-range of the enemy by the way they would have to go. He says that they traveled up a 45-degree incline "quite a while," which holds true in either event, but more precisely for the Ridge. They then "came to the foot of the palisades." There are no palisades on Turret Peak, but there are on Skeleton Ridge. "Here they met a circular mountain, running up into a column." This does not fit Turret Peak very accurately, but it can easily become a description of the Ridge. There was, wrote Crook, "but one mode of ingress. This was caused by a piece of this palisades falling down, leaving a notch by which, with great difficulty, our people could get up. On top of this notch was lying a huge rock, so our people had to crawl on their stomachs." There is no such notch on Turret Peak, nor any need for it, since access to the summit may be had by a man on foot, albeit with some trouble, almost anywhere. Nor is there any such block of stone as Crook describes. Yet these things exist on Skeleton Ridge. There is the notch, two of them to be precise, but in the dark one could not surmise that, and great blocks of stone are littered in such a way that it is readily possible by one route or another that the troopers would have to crawl on their bellies beneath one of them to gain the summit. On top, wrote Crook, "they found the general surface comparatively smooth," which is the case on the Ridge, but not on Turret Peak, which presents a humped configuration. "The lava was thrown up in irregular masses while cooling, leaving large fissures running in all directions, with this grown up more or less with brush." Again this is not the picture of Turret Peak, but it assuredly is that of Skeleton Ridge. When fired upon the Indians "lost all presence of mind, even running past their holes in the rocks. Some of them jumped off the precipice and were mashed into a shapeless mass." As previously noted, there is simply no place on Turret Mountain or Peak where this could readily occur, but it is a distinct possibility on Skeleton Ridge, where conditions are more or less exactly as Crook described them. The finding of human bones and other relics around its base suggests that people had died there at some time in the not too distant past, either in a leap from the rim, or from some other cause.

All of this is not to argue that Randall had no fight on Turret Peak, for there is little doubt that he did. But here we have a report of *two* fights on the same scout, and a description of the one, purportedly on Turret Peak, and no description, not even a line, of the other, except that Hill "struck an Indian camp near Turret Mountain." Where was this fight? What were the circumstances?

I believe that here we have a case of transparent confusion, although it will never be finally cleared away until someone finds the detailed report of the actions, if it ever is discovered. But it seems rather apparent that one of these two fights took place on Turret Peak, and the other on Skeleton Ridge. Their being but seven or eight miles apart would make them easily "near" each other in the parlance of scouting commanders of the 1870's, for whom rugged marches of thirty or forty miles a day, over terrain then, as now, almost beyond belief, were so routine as to merit scarcely a mention. Perhaps because the formal report of these actions was terse, brief, the tale of the fights became soldiers' gossip which Crook listened to eagerly, as he did to all accounts of adventure and service in the Arizona wilderness under his command. John Bourke records this interest with amused indulgence in his great books about his admired commander. When Crook wrote them in his autobiography he had but scant written versions to go on, but he recalled the soldiers' tales and wrote them as he remembered them or as they had been told to him, and in doing so, they became confused, the one with the other.

Indians continued to roam and camp near Turret Peak even after this offensive and the great battle there,[10] because there usually was water in the springs or creeks near it, but they never again camped on Skeleton Ridge. This perhaps was because of the bloody fight there, but more likely it was because a trail from Camp Verde to McDowell soon threaded the pass between the ridge and Pine Mountain, and the spring in the gap became a soldiers' campsite. Near it have been found the remains of old military packsaddles and other gear, according to Blackburn. With so much white travel, the Indians would not dare resume occupation of the ridge. Thus, with the 1873 fight—if one occurred on this promontory—ended forever Yavapai occupation of Skeleton Ridge, or anyone else's permanent residence there. An occasional cowboy or other wanderer may climb it out of curiosity(we found an empty whiskey bottle of recent date up there), but there is otherwise nothing to attract people. Skeleton Ridge is just that: a skeleton from a period in the past when it was populated and useful, but now a curiosity, of interest only to the historian.

BIBLIOGRAPHY

1. For details of this offensive, see Dan L. Thrapp, *The Conquest of Apacheria*, Norman: University of Oklahoma Press, 1967, pp. 119-143.

2. George Crook, *Annual Report*, 1873.

3. *General George Crook: His Autobiography*, ed. and annotated by Martin F. Schmitt, Norman: University of Oklahoma Press, 1960, pp. 177-178.

4. *Chronological List of Actions, &c., with Indians, from January 1, 1866, to January, 1891*, Washington: Adjutant General's Office, 1891, p. 31.

5. *Prescott* [Arizona] *Miner*, April 5, 1873.

6. Ralph Hedrick Ogle, *Federal Control of the Western Apaches, 1848-1886*, Albuquerque: Univ. of New Mexico Press, 1940, p. 116.

7. *Map of Arizona Territory*. Prepared by Authority of Bvt. Major General O. B. Willcox, under the Direction of 1st Lieut. Fred A. Smith, Adjutant 12th Infty., Engineer Officer, D.A., 1879.

8. Ray Brandes, *Frontier Military Posts of Arizona*, Globe, Arizona: Dale Stuart King, 1960, pp. 46-47.

9. Will C. Barnes, *Arizona Place Names*, Tucson: University of Arizona, General Bulletin No. 2, 1935, 1st ed., p. 410.

10. Dan L. Thrapp, *Al Sieber, Chief of Scouts*, Norman: University of Oklahoma Press, 1964, p. 125ff.

Cibicu,
an Apache Interpretation

by Eve Ball from interviews with Ace Daklugie

THE NARRATOR of "Cibicu, an Apache Interpretation" is Ace Daklugie, son of the Nednhi Apache chief, Juh. He was born near Fort Bowie, Arizona [he thinks], in 1874; his mother Ishton, *The Woman*, was a full sister of Geronimo. Because no records were then kept he did not know his exact age.

His Apache name, Daklugie, means *Forces His Way Through the Thick of the Struggle,* and was given to him after participation in a skirmish which he refused to discuss. He was with his parents, sometimes on the warpath, until after his mother was killed by Mexican cavalry, and after his father drowned in the Rio Aros. From that time he either accompanied Geronimo, or lived with Mangus, the son of Mangas Coloradas.

Daklugie was among those who escaped in the battle of "The Arroyo," in Chihuahua, when attacked by Colonel Lorenzo Garcia's troops of Mexican infantry. He went with Mangus when the Apaches were followed by U.S. troops into the Sierra Madre, and when on that occasion many of the Indians surrendered. But perhaps his most dangerous feat took place when he went alone into the camp of the U.S. cavalry to arrange for the surrender of Mangus and that little handful left of his band. He said that Mangus was never captured by anybody.

In 1886, Mangus' band and a few stragglers were entrained at Holbrook, Arizona, for transporting to Florida. Daklugie was one of 131 Apaches selected to attend Carlisle, the famous school for Indians out of Harrisburg, Pennsylvania. There he was given a Christian name, Asa, which he disliked exceedingly and so asked his friends to call him Ace. He was also presented with a birth date.

During the ten years' attendance at Carlisle, the Apaches were moved about—first to Mt. Vernon Barracks, Alabama, and then to Fort Sill, Oklahoma. When Daklugie returned to his people it was to the reservation near Lawton, given to them by the Comanches, Kiowas, and Kiowa-Apaches. Within a few months Daklugie was made superintendent in charge of the cattle belonging to the Apaches.

That year, 1898, he married Ramona, daughter of Chief Chihuahua, who had also been at Carlisle.

He became the confidant and interpreter for his uncle, Geronimo. And when that leader decided to give his memoirs to S. M. Barrett, Ace Daklugie interpreted his uncle's life for the book, *Geronimo's Story of His Life*. He accompanied Geronimo on many trips, including that to the World's Fair at St. Louis. Dressed in beaded buckskin with eagle plumes dangling from his helmet to his heels, he and his uncle led the inaugural parade of Theodore Roosevelt.

Daklugie volunteered for service in the company of cavalry enlisted on the reservation near Fort Sill; he also volunteered for service as guide on several occasions. He held several honorable discharges from the Army and drew a pension from the government. His discharge papers commended him on his ability, dependability, and horsemanship.

He and his brother-in-law, Eugene Chihuahua, were largely responsible for securing the release of the prisoners of war who had been held twenty-seven years. The death of Geronimo, combined with the military's need for their reservation to serve as terrain for the newly organized School of Fire at Fort Sill, Oklahoma, encouraged the two to make an attempt to secure a reservation of their own, preferably in Arizona. When the governor of Arizona vetoed that hope, Ace went to the Mescalero Apache Reservation in New Mexico and interviewed the Agent, James A. Carroll. With his approval Daklugie went to the three chiefs who assured him that he and his would be welcome provided they could obtain the consent of the authorities in Washington. Undaunted, Daklugie went to the Secretary of the Interior, the Commissioner of Indian Affairs, and appeared before the Senate of the United States. Miraculously, it seemed to him, he obtained the consent of those involved.

Meanwhile Eugene Chihuahua made an attempt to secure the consent of the Apaches at Fort Sill to the move. Eugene was opposed by some, primarily dissenters among the Warm Springs band. Finally it was decided that those who wished might go to New Mexico, and the rest would be given 160 acres of land as a homestead near Lawton.

In 1912 the two brought the rest to Mescalero, New Mexico.

Well educated and very intelligent, Daklugie disapproved of the manner of life on the reservation. He demanded and obtained a village for the Chiricahua, some thirty miles from the agency at Mescalero. Because of the deer in the high mountains their village was called White Tail.

Daklugie served the reservation in several capacities, the longest as Chairman of the Tribal Council. Under his wise and unselfish administration many beneficial projects were accomplished. After his refusal to serve again, he, nonetheless, was continually called upon as the wise patriarch, to solve their problems.

After the death of his wife, Daklugie never again entered their home. He lived with his granddaughter, Evangeline Kazhe, and often visited his two daughters, Maude Geronimo and Lydia Shanta.

Daklugie died April 14, 1955, and was buried at the White Tail cemetery beside Ramona.

❧◡☙

The Battle of Cibicu occurred on August 30, 1881, some forty-five miles northwest of Fort Apache, on the Whiteriver Reservation in Arizona. The Apache medicine-man Noche-del-klinne had drawn under his influence many of those Apaches who lived on the reservation. The military, attempting to break up the medicine-man's power, and to return the Apaches to their control, went to the site of the Apache encampments. With the army were Apache scouts who had enlisted in the service. At Cibicu Creek, in a series of tragic events, both Indians and troopers were killed. The scouts, at a crucial moment and amidst the confusion, aided their people.

Interpretations given of the events of that day, and the several days following around Fort Apache have been almost all military or civilian accounts. Daklugie, present during part of the conflicts, gives his account as an Apache interpretation.

❧◡☙

"After they turned cannon loose on us at Apache Pass," said Ace Daklugie, "my people knew that the Apaches were doomed. That was long before I was born but my father, Juh, the Nednhi chief, was there. Mangas Coloradas, Cochise, Victorio, Nana, and many other great leaders joined forces to stop that army coming in from the west.[1] The Indians were sure of stopping the soldiers' attempt to reach the water until they fired wagons at them.[2]

"They knew from that time that the *Indah* (white people) outnumbered them by tremendous odds, and that they had better weapons, new and terrible ones. The soldiers had an unlimited supply of food, blankets, clothing, and ammunition furnished them. The Indians had to rustle everything they got. Guns would last a long time, but bullets were hard to get. Each one had to be used effectively. Renewing the supply presented a constant challenge; and of all the Apache warriors, Nana, old and lame, was most successful in staging ammunition raids. But, of course, he had The Power[3] over rattlesnakes and ammunition trains.[4]

Ace Daklugie. Photograph given to Mrs. Eve Ball by the daughter of Ace, Maude Daklugie Geronimo. Photo taken in 1910.

Left: Alchisay, White Mountain or Coyotero Apache chieftain. Photo taken in 1886 when he worked with the U.S. Army. Above: Victorio, a Mimbreño Apache who died in combat in the mountains of Mexico at the hands of Mexican troopers. Arizona Pioneers' Historical Society photo.

"My people feared much more than the manpower and terrible weapons of the white man the insatiable greed he had for gold. You think we are superstitious about it because Ussen (God) forbade our digging in the earth for it. Gold is the symbol of the sun, as the sun is for Ussen, and sacred to him.[5] It is the Whites who are the superstitious ones. You love gold so much that you picture your Happy Place as paved with it.[6] My father knew of places where he could pick up great quantities of gold, but he didn't want the useless stuff. And that was not forbidden. But the Whites would risk their lives for it.

"Long before I was born [1874, he thinks] my people began calling the white robbers Indah. That word does not mean "white people"; literally it means The Living. We termed ourselves *Indeh*, The Dead. The wise old chiefs knew that the hordes of invaders would eventually exterminate us and take our country. They knew, too, that the time was short. Hence, we were already The Dead. How many of the Nednhi are there living today? George Martine and I. We have children, yes. But I married a Chiricahua (Ramona Chihuahua) and Martine a Warm Springs (Lillian Mangus). According to our way of reckoning, our children belong to the tribes of the mothers. White Eyes do not realize what part this love of gold played in bringing about our extermination.[7]

"We were The Dead; we are still The Dead. Today we are hopeless. But in the days of Juh and Geronimo my people, knowing what was in store for them, were determined that so long as one warrior had one arrow he would fire it in defense of his tribe.[8]

"Your officers called both the Nednhi and Warm Springs Apaches Chiricahua, but they were not. Only the bands of Cochise and Chihuahua were true Chiricahua. Because the three tribes visited each other and sometimes united temporarily the Whites said that. They were mistaken as they were about many other things. My father's band, the Nednhi, lived in Mexico on the border of Chihuahua and Sonora. The Chihenne (Warm Springs) had their own land. The name means Red People. They were called that not because of the color of their skins, but because their distinguishing mark was a band of red clay drawn from ear to ear across their faces. In [pictures in some] books the bands look white; that is how you tell a Chihenne.

"I do not know of any Chiricahua or Nednhi who was unwilling to fight for his people except two brothers who were not banished, but so disliked that they went to live with the Mescaleros.[9] But there were a few among the Chihenne who were brave warriors, and hoped to save the lives of their people by submitting to life on reservations. Loco and a few of his followers did that. There was no compulsory military service among the Apaches. But Victorio! He was the most fortunate of all the chiefs because he died defending his people. He is the only one of the great Apache chiefs to have that honor. Mangas Coloradas was so eager to make peace with the enemy that he went alone into their camp and was treacherously murdered.[10]

"My father, Juh, boasted that though our enemies, both Mexican and Anglo, could kill us, that they could not enslave an Apache. Our men would die before they would burrow into the mountains for gold. For the Whites Ussen had made the pick and shovel; for the Indian, the bow and arrow, the spear and shield.[11] Though some Apache captives did work for a time as vaqueros on the haciendas, they did it only because it afforded them an opportunity to escape.[12]

"But very few of our men were ever captured. When you read of an attack on a ranchería,[13] and the capture or killing of 37, you can be sure that the number reported killed or captured were women and children.[14] I've read those books. I know what they say. The soldiers didn't capture Geronimo at Ojo Caliente (Warm Springs). And that young agent John Clum didn't capture him, either. Nobody ever captured Geronimo.[15] And nobody ever captured Mangus. Mangus sent me to the soldiers' camp to arrange for his surrender. He wasn't captured.

"The Whites thought that we had no religion, but in that they were mistaken. Before the Apache had contact with civilization and Christianity he was a much better man morally than he is today. We believed in Ussen, Creator of Life. Each morning at dawn we prayed to Him. I still pray to Him. Many of our ceremonial dances are prayers. The Ghost Dance was a prayer,[16] one for which the united efforts of the Apaches was needed.

"In 1881 most of the Apaches were on the San Carlos Reservation. It was in early summer that my father learned that the Medicine Man [Noche-del-klinne] was teaching those who went to him the dance. It was not performed as most of ours are, in a circle about a fire. The participants formed concentric circles with the Medicine Man in the center.[17] Those who could get passes [to leave the reservation] attended it and when they returned reported it to their chiefs. More and more people went, many without passes.[18] The agent sent word for the Prophet, as many of the white people called him, to come in and report to him, but Noche-del-klinne did not. Tiffany was the worst agent, I think, that the Apaches ever had, and they hated him largely because he sold the food the government furnished for them, and tried to starve them to death.[19] Though he and Colonel Eugene A. Carr at Fort Apache were not on good terms, the officers had orders to furnish assistance if requested to do so by the agent.[20] Carr, too, summoned the Medicine Man to the fort but he did not come.[21] Then Carr sent Sam Bowman, an interpreter, out to spy on the Indians. Bowman was very much alarmed and talked of getting out of the service; he thought the rites meant trouble.

Above: Chihuahua, who killed Captain
Sterling at San Carlos, Arizona, April 19,
1882. Above right: Geronimo, most publicized
of the Apaches, shown here in a cavalry
dress blouse of the period 1885. The photo
was taken at Mt. Vernon Barracks, in
Alabama, in 1889. Right: Sanchez, Apache
who killed Captain Hentig during the
Battle of Cibicu. Photos courtesy Arizona
Pioneers' Historical Society.

128

"Carr, too, became alarmed and decided to go out with a big force to arrest Noche-del-klinne.[22]

"At first my father paid little attention to reports that came to him of the dances; but when great numbers of people went he began to suspect that the Medicine Man might be able to influence the braves against fighting. He knew that Loco would favor nonresistance; he knew, too, that under attack Loco would fight. And among Loco's band were a few like Betzinez that would oppose war.[23] He did not anticipate that his Nednhi would be swayed to becoming disloyal to him, for he knew their dependability. But when he learned that Chihuahua, Nana, Kaytennae and more of the real fighting men of the tribe had gone to the gatherings, he thought it time to investigate.

"The camp had been moved from Carrizo Creek west to the Cibicu, about forty-five miles northwest of Fort Apache. It was there that our family, with that of Geronimo, camped on the stream, not far from the lodge and brush arbor of Noche-del-klinne. Naiche, chief of the Chiricahua who had gone to San Carlos after the death of Cochise, had gone ahead of us and was with Nana and Kaytennae. About two-thirds of the band had refused to go and had elected my father as their chief. Juh, Geronimo, and Naiche were good friends.

"At first none of the war-like bands joined in the Ghost Dance. They watched and listened. They were impressed by the Medicine Man and believed in his sincerity, but not until after Juh and my uncle talked with Nana did they accept his teachings. That old fire-eater [Nana] told them that he and his *segundo* Kaytennae had felt as Juh did until after joining the dance. After performing until almost dawn Noche-del-klinne had terminated the rites. With a few he started up an incline in the misty light. Before reaching the crest he stopped and lifted his arms in prayer. Dimly those with him saw the bodies of three great chiefs, Mangas Coloradas, Cochise, and Victorio rise slowly into sight. When their bodies had emerged from the earth and were visible to their knees they began to sink slowly back. Nana said that he had seen this, and the word of Nana could not be questioned.

"Juh and Geronimo were greatly impressed by this account. Both had previously held war dances to incite their followers to fighting pitch, but that was easily done. There was no compulsory military service among my people. When their chief danced around their fire and called his men once, according to rank, it was rarely that one failed to join his leader. Getting them to fight was very simple; but talking an Apache out of it is a very different undertaking.

"Shortly before Geronimo died he told me that he had never understood why he and Juh could have been influenced to follow the teachings of Noche-del-klinne. But at that time they were convinced that the Apaches should leave revenge to Ussen.

"Sergeant Mose, a scout from Fort Apache, came out to Cibicu to warn the Medicine Man that troops were coming to arrest him. The Apaches knew that because Colonel [Eugene Asa] Carr's orders had not been obeyed they might expect reprisals. And when a scout (for the Apaches) reported the coming of troops, Sanchez, grandfather of Kaywaykla, with others rode out to meet them and learn the size of the forces. Noche-del-klinne sat quietly in his brush arbor awaiting the cavalry. When told that he was under arrest he agreed quietly to go in, but asked for three or four days' time so that he might heal a sick man. Colonel Carr said that he must go immediately, and the Medicine Man sent his son for his horse. His wife prepared food and brought it to him.

"Colonel Carr, with, I think, more than half of his army, started back toward the fort, but left two officers, one a young lieutenant (Thomas Cruse) in charge of the scouts,[24] to bring in the poor, thin, frail aged man.

"The first section of the troops got out of sight before the second started. I watched from the hillside with other children. We saw the Medicine Man eating, and heard the scouts urging him to hurry. He finished his meal and left, surrounded by the scouts. Even then I knew how our men disliked those who were enlisted with the soldiers.

"As they rode off, many warriors followed them. Geronimo, Juh, Naiche, and others rode along to see that no harm came to Noche-del-klinne. I stayed in camp with my mother as did other children. What happened after the troops got out of sight I learned from others who witnessed the killing of the Medicine Man. When the second group reached the first they had camped for the night and put up tents for the officers. The Apaches did not go very close till they saw the Prophet in a sort of barricade made with the stuff they carried. When an officer ordered the Indians to leave they didn't like it, but did nothing except watch.

"Suddenly a shot was fired; then many. My father did not know who fired first; but once it started the warriors got into the fight. Some were killed on both sides. Apaches don't have the mania for counting things that White Eyes do. Our wounded we took care of, and our dead we buried, but we didn't bother to count the enemy's dead. They weren't worth counting. On both sides there were dead and wounded. While the shooting went on Lozen [sister of Victorio] and Sanchez [uncle of Kaywaykla] swooped down on the horses, and drove a bunch off. They wanted more than mounts, especially the ammunition mules, for they had not yet been unloaded. They got one or two; I have heard the story told both ways. But I know that we got a good supply of ammunition.

"Noche-del-klinne was hit. An officer and some enlisted men were killed, and others wounded. Kanseah told me that the Medicine Man's wife got there and attempted to reach her husband. She was shot; so was his son.[25] When the wounded Prophet got up on hands and knees and tried to crawl to his wife a soldier killed him with an axe.[26]

"The bugle was blown, but Juh did not think the soldiers would spend the night in camp. Enough warriors stayed to make sure that they would not return to attack our ranchería. That is something an Apache does not do, for he who kills in darkness must walk in darkness (be blind) through eternity.[27]

"The troops travelled by night, but the Apaches did not follow them to the fort.

"My father learned later that the commanding officer reported that Fort Apache was attacked the next day.[28] If so it was not done by any from our camp. Any sniper could have fired into the fort, for it was not walled. Of all the forts the only one I ever saw with a wall was Fort Cummings. I know it had one because I climbed it, Frank Mangus and I, one night and robbed it.[29]

"We did know that in the fall some of the Apache scouts were court-martialed for mutiny. They were tried and some sent to Alca-

White Mountain Apache Scouts who participated in the Battle of Cibicu. Arizona Pioneers' Historical Society photo dated 1880.

traz. That's where they put Kaytennae later. And three were sentenced to be hanged, Dandy Jim, Dead Shot, and Skippy.[30] Somebody higher than Colonel Carr must have ordered that courts-martial. I never knew an Indian who attended it, but from my experience as a scout at Fort Sill, after I returned from Carlisle, I doubt that any but officers testified. And would any judge have taken the word of any enlisted man? I doubt it. Those officers, Carr and Cruse, must have needed an alibi badly to have placed the blame for firing the first shots on the scouts.

"Many years later I learned this: General Willcox ordered an investigation of the actions of Carr and Cruse. That was an indication that he was not satisfied that they had acted wisely. They were in the field to prevent trouble, not start it. The mutiny of Cruse's scouts reflected upon his ability as an officer. The Apaches knew that the officers had difficulty in maintaining discipline, and that there were many, many deserters among the enlisted men. The commander of that division undoubtedly knew that, too. Did that influence the judge who tried the scouts and the jury on that case to return a verdict of the officers' being guilty of nothing more serious than an error in judgment?[31] I do not know.

"General George Crook, who had left things in good condition when he left Arizona for the northwest, was returned. He, too, must have been dissatisfied, for he immediately began meeting with the Indians to get their side of the story. Captain Bourke said, '... there was a coincidence of sentiment among all people whose opinion was worthy of consultation, that the blame did not rest with the Indians; ... No one had heard the Apaches' story, and no one seemed to care whether they had a story or not.'

"Cruse, himself, tells of his dread of meeting with the General, and his relief when he got off without as severe a reprimand as he expected.[32] Did even Crook feel the necessity of upholding Cruse and Carr?

"And Bourke, in his book, gives a copy of the report of the Federal Grand Jury of Arizona addressed 'To the Honorable Wilson Hoover, District Judge,' in which it gives the truth concerning conditions on the reservation and the conduct of Agent Tiffany which led to the break of the Apaches from it. He said that 'to the credit of Hon. Carl Schurz —then Secretary of the Interior ... the heads of the Commissioner of Indian Affairs, the Inspector-General of the Indian Bureau, and the agent at San Carlos fell into the basket.'[33] That is the only instance within the knowledge of the Apaches of an agent's having been dismissed. The thieves were usually 'permitted to resign.'[34]

"Crook, though our enemy, was respected by my people. To an Apache no human relationship not founded on respect is of any value.

"I enlisted as a scout at Fort Sill and am receiving a pension for my military service. I learned something of military procedures. As books came out on the campaigns against the Apaches I bought and read them. I learned of officers who got promotions, some to becoming brigadier generals, who gave honest and accurate accounts of their experiences in various conflicts. Some were even sympathetic with the Indians. But some used their books to twist and distort the truth of their contemptible actions to secure promotions and the respect of the white people. Among these I classify Carr, Cruse, and Forsyth. They may have been able to deceive their commanding officers but the Indians know of what they were guilty and have only contempt for them.

"We will never forget what Carr and Cruse did at Cibicu."

NOTES

1. This was the Battle of Apache Pass in 1862, in which the California column was involved. For one version of this and other events of this period see John C. Cremony, *Life Among the Apaches*, New York: Macmillan Company, 1938.

2. The use of cannon by the army led the Apache to believe that the soldiers had fired "wagon wheels" at them according to Cremony, *Life Among the Apaches*, pp. 136-140.

3. The Power is, even for Apaches, difficult to explain. It was usually acquired during the four-day fast and vigil made by the adolescent boy preparatory to going on the first of his four required raids as an apprentice to a warrior. But, it was also obtained by other means. Apaches will not talk much about The Power.

4. Jasper Kanseah, now dead, was a nephew of Geronimo—his youngest warrior and the last to die. This information he gave to me during many interviews at his home at White Tail on the Mescalero Apache Reservation, and in my home at Ruidoso. Other information on these points came from interviews lasting over a period of seven years with James Kaywaykla, nephew of Victorio and narrator in my forthcoming book, *In the Days of Victorio*, to be released shortly by the University of Arizona Press. Kaywaykla died a few years ago.

5. Kaywaykla, interviews.

6. Dan L. Thrapp, *The Conquest of Apachería*, Norman: Univ. of Oklahoma Press, 1967, p. 24.

7. Thrapp, *The Conquest...*, p. 24.

8. From numerous interviews at Mescalero, New Mexico, and in my home with Eugene Chihuahua, son of the Chiricahua chief of that name. Chihuahua, too, has died. The interviews with Kanseah and Kaywaykla also provided data.

9. The Chinos.

10. Ray Brandes, unpublished manuscript on the life of Mangas Coloradas.

11. Interviews with Kaywaykla.

12. Interviews with Kanseah, and with Carlos Chavez in the capitol building in the City of Chihuahua. Señor Chavez was working on a book concerning the depredations of the Apaches.

13. Term meaning village.

14. I have interviewed more than sixty Apaches, including the oldest living and they are unanimous in this statement.

15. The old Apaches were unanimous in saying that nobody ever captured Geromino. Some of them were present at the "melodramatic scene" at Ojo Caliente, and deny that it ever occurred as told by Clum especially in "Geronimo," *Arizona Historical Review* Vol. 1 (2), pp. 14-49 (1928), (3), pp. 13-35; the series also appeared in the *New Mexico Historical Review*, Vol. 3, pp. 1-40, 121-144, 217-264 (1928).

16. See David Humphreys Miller, *The Ghost Dance*, New York: Duell, Sloan and Pearce, 1959.

17. James Mooney, "The Ghost Dance Religion and the Sioux Outbreak of 1890," Bureau of American Ethnology *14th Annual Report, 1892-1893*, Pt. II., Washington, 1896.

18. Thrapp, *The Conquest...*, p. 220.

19. Interviews with Chihuahua and Kaywaykla.

20. Thrapp, *The Conquest...*, pp. 220-221.

21. Thrapp, *The Conquest...*, p. 221.

22. Dan Thrapp in *The Conquest...*, p. 221, gives from the military record the number as 117 men, including 5 officers, 79 soldiers, 23 scouts, a guide, an interpreter, a pack train of 6 men, and 9 civilians. For other viewpoints on the events at Cibicu, both military and civilian see John P. Clum, "Apache Misrule, a Bungling Indian Agent Sets the Military Arm in Motion," *Arizona Historical Review*, Vol. 4 (I) April 1931, pp. 57-68; (II) July 1931, pp. 52-64; (III), October 1931, pp. 64-71. Another version at odds with Clum is by Col. Cornelius C. Smith, "The Army and the Apache, an Open Letter," *Arizona Historical Review*, Vol. 4 (IV), Jan. 1932, pp. 62-70.

23. Betzinez was opposed to fighting. Regardless of the title of his book, *I Fought With Geronimo* (with Sturtevant Nye), Harrisburg: The Stackpole Company, 1959, the Apaches say that Jason Betzinez did not fight with anybody.

24. Thomas Cruse, *Apache Days and After*, Caldwell: Idaho, the Caxton Press, 1944.

25. Cruse, *Apache Days....*

26. Interviews with Kanseah. W. L. Carter in *From Yorktown to Santiago With the 6th U.S. Cavalry*. Baltimore, 1900, gives another version of the number of troopers involved, and the number on both sides who were killed and wounded. Edmund C. Hentig was the officer killed in the action at Cibicu.

27. Interviews with Kaywaykla.

28. Thrapp, *The Conquest...*, pp. 226-228.

29. Interviews with Kaywaykla.

30. They were hanged at Fort Grant, Arizona, March 3, 1882.

31. John G. Bourke, *On the Border with Crook*, New York: Charles Scribner's Sons, 1891.

32. Cruse, *Apache Days....*

33. Bourke, *On the Border...*, pp. 438-440.

34. Interviews with Kaywaykla.

William Babcock Hazen: Curmudgeon or Crusader?

by William Reed

Perhaps the two most controversial figures of the United States Army during the post-Civil War period were Generals George Armstrong Custer[1] and William Babcock Hazen. The more flamboyant Custer, who went on to gain dubious fame at the Battle of the Little Big Horn, was better known to the general public; he was not by any means better known within the ranks of the United States Army.

General Hazen, when not at war for the army, had a lifelong penchant for starting wars with, within, or about the army. His contemporaries described him variously as "critical," "outspoken," "belligerent," and "contentious," and concluded that ". . . no one in the service had a more unfortunate faculty for involving himself in controversies . . . it has not been easy in all cases to determine to what traits of character his difficulties were chargeable."[2] Many historians agree with this unflattering appraisal, one going so far as to suggest that Hazen ". . . might well have been called 'an old curmudgeon' had that phrase then been in common use."[3]

A review of the military record of Hazen does suggest to the casual observer that "conflict" was his major pastime. If so, he was well born to such a pursuit. The Hazen family, descended from Edward Hazen who immigrated to the Massachusetts Bay Colony in the seventeenth century, had a long record of military service. One ancestor, Moses Hazen, fought with distinction both in the French and Indian War and the American Revolutionary War. Retired in 1781 as a brigadier-general,

Moses and his two brothers, who also held commands in the army, settled in Vermont on land granted to them for their services. It was in West Hartford, Windsor County, Vermont, that William Babcock Hazen was born on September 30, 1830.[4]

At an early age Hazen moved with his parents to Hiram, Ohio, where he grew to manhood. He received an appointment to the U.S. Military Academy at West Point in 1851 and, following mediocre record at that institution, graduated twenty-eighth out of a class of thirty-four in 1855. As a second lieutenant of infantry, Hazen served at Fort Lane, Fort Yamhill and other posts in the Oregon Territory until 1858, at which time he was transferred to the Southwest.[5] He quickly established a reputation as a hard-driving and competent combat officer against the Apache and Kickapoo Indians on the Nueces River and in the Fort Davis area, although to this time little detail has been recorded concerning this early portion of his career.

The *Army and Navy Journal,* May 11, 1869, carried an interesting testimonial to the assiduous care with which Hazen customarily carried out his military assignments. While serving in the Oregon territory, he was assigned collateral duties as post commissary and quartermaster. This was an inevitable responsibility of most young officers, and one which, as inevitably, resulted in personal bookkeeping errors and a resultant stoppage of pay. It was said of Lieutenant Hazen that he was the only officer to perform that duty when young in the service and to have no stoppages against him.

Lieutenant Hazen, while with the 8th Infantry, was seriously wounded by Comanche Indians November 3, 1859, and was sent home on sick leave. This was an incident of mixed blessing. His command was captured by Confederate forces a short time after his transfer, and

William B. Hazen.
Photo from the Brady Collections in
the U.S. National Archives.

Hazen fretted away the next fifteen months on the inactive list while recuperating from his wounds. He remained convinced that had he remained with his command he might somehow have averted the catastrophe of their capture.

Hazen returned to active duty on February 21, 1861, as assistant professor of infantry tactics at West Point. He was promoted to first lieutenant in April and—belatedly for gallantry in the field—to captain about six weeks later.

It was at this point in his career that he and Custer first met; the manner of their introduction precipitated a lifelong feud between the two men. Custer graduated from the Academy at West Point at the very bottom of his class in June, 1861, after setting something of a record in the accumulation of demerits. Five days after graduation Custer was placed in arrest and court martialed under charges preferred by Captain Hazen for failing to stop a fight between two cadets. He escaped with a reprimand, partly as a result of a favorable recommendation from Hazen but—apparently unaware of this fact—he harbored an ill-disguised animosity for Hazen from that time forward.

Both Hazen and Custer went on to gain honors in the American Civil War. Hazen was granted leave of absence from the army to organize and command the Forty-first Ohio Volunteers. His service during the war was in the Western theatre. Custer served with the Army of the Potomac. Both men emerged with the rank of Major-General, and both reverted to the rank of captain at the end of hostilities. With the reorganization of the army in 1866, Custer was appointed lieutenant-colonel of the newly-created Seventh Cavalry. Hazen was named colonel of the Thirty-eighth Infantry about the same time, though he continued for awhile to serve as acting Inspector General in the Department of the

The Barracks at Fort Davis, 1873. This post functioned from September 1854 to June 1891. While stationed at Fort Davis in 1858, the young lieutenant Hazen wrote the report contained herein. U.S. National Archives photo.

Platte. In August of 1866, Hazen was sent to inspect the forts along the Bozeman Road and the upper Missouri River. His report was highly critical, and from this point on he began to develop an unfortunate and persistent reputation as a "grouch" by nature, prone to attack any issue, and possessed with a proclivity for "unwarranted criticism of his superiors."[6]

In 1872 Hazen wrote a report attacking graft in the trading post at Fort Sill, Oklahoma. Subsequent investigation implicated persons high in the government, including the incumbent Secretary of War, William Belknap. Shortly afterwards Hazen was abruptly ordered transferred to Fort Buford, North Dakota; a transfer which many felt was an act of personal vengeance by the Secretary of War.[7] While there he wrote a series of scathing denunciations of the attempts by the promoters of the Northern Pacific Railroad Company to induce settlers into the territory by false advertising. In a letter to the *New York Tribune*, published February 27, 1874, he stated that:

> For two years I have been an observer of the effort upon the part of the Northern Pacific Railroad Company to make the world believe this section to be a valuable agricultural area, and, with many others I have kept silent although knowing the falsity of their representation . . . this country will not produce the fruits and cereals of the East . . . and can in no way be artificially irrigated, and will not, in our day and generation, sell for one penny an acre, except through fraud or ignorance. . . .[8]

Hazen's letter prompted an immediate reaction, both in support of and antagonistic to his views, from persons all over the country. His major critic was Custer. Custer has been accused of almost single-handedly causing the gold rush into the Black Hills of Dakota in the Fall of 1874. Some suspected him of attempting to revive the fortunes of the Northern Pacific Railroad; if so, this would explain his antagonism.[9] The consensus of historical opinion is that Hazen was writing in a vindictive mood—as the result of his "banishment,"—rather than in a spirit of public concern as he avowed. Among other evidence is a document, only recently discovered among the records of the Adjutant General's Office, Washington, D.C., which sheds a new light on the debate. It tends to support the minority opinion that the viewpoint of Hazen was neither impromptu nor vindictive in nature, but in fact stemmed from a deep-seated skepticism and an uncompromising honesty which throughout his life prompted him to "crusade" for causes in which he believed regardless of popular opinion to the contrary.

The following excerpt from the aforementioned document is in the form of a field report by Hazen of a campaign into the Guadalupe Mountains, against a marauding Apache band while, as a young lieutenant, he was stationed at Fort Davis, Texas, in 1858:

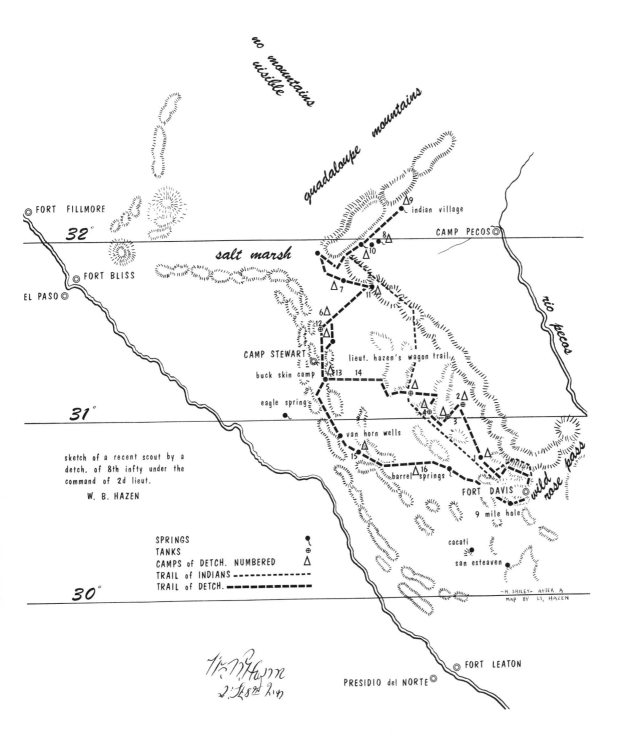

no mountains visible

guadaloupe mountains

FORT FILLMORE

32°

salt marsh

CAMP PECOS

△9 indian village

8△

△10

FORT BLISS

rio pecos

EL PASO

△7

6△

⊕12

△11

CAMP STEWART

lieut. hazen's wagon trail

buck skin camp

△13   14

5

2△

eagle spring

△

⊕

△

31°

3

van horn wells

△

△

sketch of a recent scout by a
detch. of 8th infty under the
command of 2d lieut.

W. B. HAZEN

15

16△

△

barrel springs

wild rose pass

FORT DAVIS

9 mile hole

cacati

SPRINGS
TANKS
CAMPS of DETCH. NUMBERED
TRAIL of INDIANS
TRAIL of DETCH.

●
⊕
△

▪▪▪▪▪▪▪▪▪▪

san esteaven

30°

-H. SHILEY- AFTER A
MAP BY LI. HAZEN

FORT LEATON

PRESIDIO del NORTE

Campaign in the Guadalupe
Mountains, 1858

I took up the march the morning of the 12th... after going about ten miles, we found ourselves in the immediate vicinity of their camp... I therefore... picketed the pack animals... and proceeded at once to attack the Camp....There were several horses in Camp. The women and children were instantly packed upon these, and started up a bold and precipitous mountain. Their men running also with great rapidity. We pressed them so closely that they were compelled to abandon their horses and the few valuables they had endeavored to take with them, among which were several rifles. Firing was kept up during this time by the men, and returned by the Indians when they had made a good safe distance between them and us. I have therefore no killed or wounded to report. It being excessively hot, and the men ...exhausted, the pursuit was abandoned for a time....The camp was now entered. It consisted of fifteen lodges. The surprise had been so complete that they had succeeded in carrying nothing away. In several lodges their breakfast was still cooking on the fire. We found large quantities of Indian property of all kinds, consisting of prepared food, finely dressed skins and peltries, dresses of all kinds, camp furniture and horse gear, not only of their own rude construction, but much procured from Civilized people.

Also arms and ammunition in considerable quantities, about fifty scalps, and large piles of various articles too numerous to mention, the accumulation of years. A few of the lightest of these were preserved by the men, the remainder were burned with their lodges.

I again started up the mountain, and after reaching a convenient position firing was commenced, but it being impossible to get within even tolerable range, I again descended to prepare for the night.

The effect of the shot during the day is not known. No bodies were found. A Squaw was captured in the afternoon and twenty-two animals, "horses and mules."

I now moved the Command about three miles out from the mountain and encamped. The number of Indians at this point is not accurately known. It is safe to estimate from six to ten in each lodge, of these not more than one in eight are fighting men.

I am satisfied that this is the only band that inhabits these mountains, and is but a branch of the Muscalaro [sic] Apaches living further north.

At evening I again returned to the Indian Camp accompanied by the guide and three mounted. We there discovered five Indians and nine animals. Making a rapid dash upon them, we killed one (so reported to me, although I did not see him after he fell) and captured seven of the animals. We now returned to Camp for the night, during which the Indians came down the mountain and proceeded up the Country. They had with them three animals. Our horses being entirely unfit for pursuit, after thoroughly scouring the country on foot, I commenced our return on the evening of the 13th, and after making fifteen miles encamped for the night. During the night the Squaw taken prisoner effected her escape, being at the time tied hand and foot, and under the charge of a sentinel.

It had been my intention to take up the old trail and follow it to its termination, but in doing so I saw the certain loss of all our horses, besides the twenty-nine animals captured, none being in condition for such a trip. These Indians would also be apprised of our approach, and anything like a surprise; the only successful Indian attack, out of the question.

I speedily determined upon returning, leaving the unfinished portion of the Scout for another time, when there should be more water and better grass.

The men were all dismounted, and many of the saddles packed on mules, but it made little difference in the endurance of the horse. One gave out today, the 14th, and was left behind. The two left going up, were recovered today, but the strength gained in three or four days only enabled them to keep along a couple more.

We made twenty miles today, encamped near a small pool of rain water, which was all required for immediate wants, and none was left for filling the barrels. We now had eighteen miles to go before reaching the first Salt Spring, and as some delay was made in the morning, by sending back for the animals that had given out, the march had to be made in the heat of the day. This, the 15th, proved the severest day of the whole trip, and I think the severest I ever saw. Our route lay across a level sand prairie, which with a vertical sun soon became scorching hot. So much so as to heat the soles of the shoes to a painful degree. The metal of the guns became so heated that it could not be touched by the hand. Several of the men discharged their pieces, fearing they would be discharged by the excessive heat. The little water that was in the canteens became too hot to be drunk. The slight breezes that would occasionally pass over the plain, were nothing less than siroccoes, it was necessary to hold one's breath til they subsided. Several of the men drank their urine, which only increased their terrible thirst. Two of them wandered away from the trail, and were afterwards brought in by the guide. The salt water when reached, was drunk in large quantities by both men and animals. The latter were much weakened by it. We were compelled however to encamp for the night, as the nearest water in the direction of our course was at Buckskin Camp, twenty miles distant.

This night a melancholy occurrence took place in camp by which two lives were lost. At about 2 O'Clock in the morning of the 16th as the 3d relief was posted, one of the sentinals [sic] of the 2d relief was missed from his post, but as it was quite dark, and all of the men greatly fatigued from the march of the day, it was supposed he had gone immediately to his bed on seeing the relief approaching. Nothing more was thought of it and the circumstance was not reported to me.

It appears however, that he had gone about twenty paces outside of his post and had gone to sleep in a bunch of grass before being relieved. When the 3d relief had been posted about an hour, one of the sentinals hearing a slight rustling in the grass, looked in the direction and discovered what he supposed to be an Indian crawling upon him. Seeing further that he had a gun in his hand, and was about raising it, and knowing that there was strict orders for no one to go out side of camp without informing the guard, he supposed it to be an Indian in the act of shooting him. He immediately fired, probably without challenging, killing him instantly.

He at the same time cried out Indians, thoroughly alarming Camp. One of the others sentinals Pvt. Michael Hyer of Co. C 8th Infy. now taking fright, abandoned his post, running into camp, and screaming at the top of his voice, and more hideously than any Indian I ever heard, he also discharged his piece, probably at random, but apparently towards camp. Several pieces were leveled upon him, he being taken for an Indian, and one discharged, killing him also. Some animals having been hit by stray shots now flitted through Camp at great speed, completing the confusion, and giving it every feature of a real attack. I soon succeeded in restoring order, when the nature of the alarm was quite perceptible.

The first man killed was Pvt. Michael Kellett of Co. D 8th Infy. The bodies were buried in the best manner possible, having no spades, and we were soon under march, reaching fresh water a little past noon. Three horses failed today and were left behind. I determined to rest a day here, hoping that the remainder of the horses would gather strength sufficiently to take them back to the post, and also get up those left behind during the day. Two of them were brought in on the evening of the 17th, but were only able to keep along a few miles next day.

We were early on our way the morning of the 18th, striking for the Fort Davis and El Paso road at Van Horns Wells, twenty miles distant. This we reached about 1 P.M. and remained til evening, then came on fifteen miles, and halted for the night.

My object in getting on the road as soon as possible was, that in case if it became necessary to abandon more animals, there would be a greater probability of recovering them.

Making an early start next morning, we reached Fort Davis by two days easy marching the 19th & 20th. The Command is all in good health, but many are nearly destitute of clothing.

By refferance [sic] to the sketch, my rout, [sic] places of stopping and other points can be seen. Much of it lies through mountains. This became necessary in following the trail, striking water, and passing from point to point. *With regard to the Country passed over, I do not hesitate to pronounce it perfectly worthless for agricultural purposes, with one or two trifling exceptions. Whatever else it may be valuable for is not visable [sic] to one passing over it. That about the Guadaloupe Mountains abounds in the finest building stone of several varieties, lime and salt. But from its situation this must remain valueless.* (Italics are mine)

Of the twelve American horses taken out, it was with the greatest difficulty and constant attention that three were brought back. I think I am warranted in pronouncing American horses, of a large size, that have always been fed with grain, with regular water, of little service for traversing the mountains and prairies of Texas where they can get neither, and at a season of the year when grass is scanty and indifferent. The poorest mule stood the trip much better than the best horse, while even ordinary ones [mules] were ready to start upon a similar expedition.

With regard to the men of the Command, I am gratified to express much satisfaction at the manner in which a few performed their duties. Sergt. W. S. Irving of Co. D 8th Infy., Corpl. Francis Croal and Pvts. Charles Setzer, John Tucker and Charles Sheppard of Co. F. 8th Infy. showed themselves at all times ready, prompt, and efficient in the performance of any duty either assigned or suggested. With a few exceptions, the remainder of the men were of little service at any time, except to fill details, the duties of which they failed to execute. While in the Indian Country, they were much frightened, ready to fire at any time, on any thing, and it was with peril that I could visit the sentinels at night.

There may be some excuse in the fact of their being nearly all recruits, their first experience in an Indian country, and the fatigues of the march, but I think I never saw so worthless a set of men thrown together before in my life.

The two Mexicans who accompanied me as guides were of invaluable service. The necessity of a few such men on every Scout among Indians cannot be too highly estimated. They were indefatigable in their exertions to secure the stock, and but for them much of it might not have been secured. And in its final disposition I must recommend that they be allowed a horse each. This I promised them. One of them volunteered for the expedition, the other is the regular guide of the Post.

I had understood that there were orders in this Mil. Dpt. that all captured property should be sold for the benefit of the enlisted men of the Command that captured them. I find that no orders of the kind are on record at this post, and agreeable to your orders have turned the captured animals over to the Qr. M. [sic] of this post. His receipt is herewith appended, marked "B." [The receipts referred to were not taken. So directed by the Commanding Officer.] But as I have been assured from many sources that such orders are in force, I cannot refrain from remonstrating against their constant service for the benefit of the government, as they are now nearly all broken down, and out of condition, until directions are received respecting them.

In case it be decided that they are the property of the Captors, it is of course made so as a reward for services. I must therefore recommend that the Non. C. Offrs. and Pvts. before mentioned be permitted to each choose a horse, or mule, in the order in which they are named, since they performed nearly all the laborious duties of the Scout, packing, herding, driving, caring for the animals &C besides performing much valuable service at the time of the attack, while the others were sacking the camp. And that the remainder be sold for the benefit of the remainder of the Command.

I am very Respectfully
Your obdt. Servt.

W. B. Hazen
2nd Lt. 8th Infy.
Comdt. Dtch.

To Lt. W. Mc.E. Dye
1st Lt. & Adjt. 8th Infy.[10]

The language of this report reveals a number of interesting facets concerning the character of William Babcock Hazen. First, he was a man of dogged determination. Second, he was a strict disciplinarian who demanded a great deal from his men and as much or more of himself. Third, he was strongly opinionated. Of special importance to the argumentation of this paper is the reference by Hazen in the above document to the fact that—in terms of his boyhood farming experience in Ohio—he considered the Guadalupe Mountains of Texas of no agricultural value. This has a familiar ring. The convictions of the young lieutenant of twenty-eight in 1858, sound much like the convictions of the forty-four-year-old Major-General in 1874. Another piece of evidence that tends to support the contention that Hazen's 1874 criticism of the Dakotas was born of honest conviction rather than in a spirit of "sour grapes," is the following excerpt from his report concerning the earlier mentioned inspection tour of the forts along the Bozeman Road in 1866:

> At a point...near old Fort Kearney, the soil becomes thin and weak and the atmosphere dry and continues so all the way to the Rocky Mountains, and west of them in Montana, Idaho and Utah, so far as I have seen.
>
> The country has little value....It will in time be settled by a scanty pastoral population. No amount of railroad schemes of colonization or government encouragement can ever make more of it.[11]

The uncompromising and opinionated character of General Hazen —a trait which made him numerous enemies—is further exemplified in the following statements in the same report:

> I am confident that our troops are too inactive....I would place no troops in mining regions, as miners are better Indian fighters than soldiers, are numerous, and always well armed and organized for defence....The ideal Indian of the popular mind is found only in poetry and Cooper's novels. The Indian who now inhabits the plains is a dirty beggar and thief, who murders the the weak and unprotected, but never attacks an armed foe.... The white man owes the Indian nothing.[12]

It is obvious that Hazen bore no love for Indians. He did, however, have a strong sense of honesty and fair-play. Two years after expressing the foregoing sentiment concerning Indians, and while serving as the Superintendent of the Southern Indian District, Hazen personally intervened to prevent what he believed to be a proposed massacre of friendly Kiowa Indians along the Washita River by Custer.[13] By this action he incurred the wrath of his superior, General Philip Sheridan,[14] and added further "fuel to the fire" in his ongoing feud with Custer. General Sheridan, commenting on the above episode in 1872, avowed that,

> Had it not been for Colonel Hazen, who represented that these Indians were friendly when I followed their trail without missing it for a moment from the 'battle' of the 'Washita' until I overtook them, the Texas front would be in a better condition than now....[15]

Regardless of who was "right" in this particular controversy, the passage of time brings to light a much clearer picture of Hazen the "curmudgeon." Hard, uncompromising, as tough on himself as he was on others, William Babcock Hazen never faltered in the fifty-seven years of his life in his "crusade" against incompetency and dishonesty. In 1885, two years before his death, he was court-martialed for public criticism of Secretary of War Robert Todd Lincoln.[16] Hazen criticized Lincoln for failing to take his recommended action in relieving members of a stranded Arctic expedition to Lady Franklin Bay in 1883. It was Hazen's belief that indecision and inactivity by Lincoln was directly responsible for the fact that, when relief finally arrived, only seven members of the twenty-five man expedition remained alive.[17] Hazen voiced his criticism of Lincoln in a personal letter, which was returned to him by Lincoln with a warning to keep it quiet. Instead, Hazen published in the *Washington Evening Star* of March 2, 1885, a statement that he had written such a letter, and revealed much of the contents thereof.

Hindsight, and the discovery of additional documentation relating to the career of this remarkable "curmudgeon," reveals that General William Babcock Hazen was right about a number of things for which he was criticized by his contemporaries. Hazen was a conscientious professional soldier who refused to compromise his convictions for the sake of expediency. He remained convinced until his death that "... the iron hand which is just but always firm can alone make soldiers that can be relied upon."[20] This admonition, written by General Hazen in the twilight of his career, is reminiscent of the advice of another "crusader," Walt Whitman. He put it this way: "Trust thyself! Every heart vibrates to that iron string!"

General William B. Hazen.
Photo from the Brady
Collections in the
U.S. National Archives.

146

1. General George Armstrong Custer figured prominently in the career of Hazen. Both men were often in the forefront of a major public controversy, but Custer was by nature the more flamboyant of the two. Well known for his bravado and volatile temperament, Custer seemed throughout his tempestuous career to be more than willing to engage in any confrontation that would bring his name before the American public. For a comprehensive treatment of Custer, see Jay Monaghan, *Custer*, Boston: Little, Brown and Co., 1943.

2. *Army and Navy Journal*, January 22, 1887, as reprinted in *The 1887 Annual Reunion of the Association of Graduates Office*, New York: U.S. Military Academy, 1887, p. 39.

3. Edgar I. Stewart (comp.). *Penny-an-Acre Empire*. Norman, Univ. of Oklahoma Press, p. 252.

4. Dumas Malone (ed.), *Dictionary of American Biography*. New York: Charles Scribner's Sons, 1938, vol. 8, pp. 477-479. The article in this publication about Hazen was written by Frederic Logan Paxon. A brief sketch in the *Army and Navy Journal* of April 19, 1879, describes Hazen as "short, thick-set, with a typical French military cut of countenance."

5. Stewart, *Penny-an-Acre . . .*, pp. 3-4; Malone, *Dictionary . . .*, p. 478. The details of Hazen's academic record at West Point were furnished by U.S. Military Academy Assistant Archivist Kenneth W. Rapp.

6. The *New York Times*, January 17, 1887 where the obituary summation of General Hazen's life, like most sources of that period, agrees with the opinion that Hazen's ". . . temperament was disputatious and aggressive." The writer of a pamphlet article, *The 1887 Annual Reunion . . .* which previously appeared in the January 22, 1887 edition of the *Army and Navy Journal*, tried first to be non-committal by stating that,

> In the case of an officer so well known as General Hazen, it may
> be safely left for each one to form a personal judgment as to his
> character.

Yet three sentences later, as an example of the emotional intensity which Hazen characteristically generated in people with whom he came in contact, the writer found it impossible to maintain his objectivity. Referring to the last post of duty held by General Hazen, the writer stated emphatically that, "He was clearly out of place in the Signal Bureau, which required a man of different temperament."

7. Custer, in testifying before the Clymer Committee in 1876, declared Hazen, ". . . for daring to make a communication relative to the Fort Sill business, had been 'exiled' to Fort Buford. . . ." See Stewart, *Penny-an-Acre . . .*, p. 16; also Stewart, *Custer's Luck*, Norman: Univ. of Oklahoma Press, 1955, p. 131. As quoted in the *New York Times*, March 6, 1876, the *Cincinnati Commercial* declared that it was Hazen's testimony before a congressional investigating committee in 1872 that led to his transfer . . . to Fort Buford.

8. This is an excerpt from the letter of Hazen's which caused a national furor. It was printed and reprinted in major newspapers throughout the country, and precipitated a letter and newspaper debate between Custer and Hazen—and dozens of other prominent personalities—over a period of years.

9. George A. Custer, "Order Book," ms., Yale Western Americana Collection. Printed in 43rd Congress, 2nd Session, *Senate Ex. Doc. 32*, 1875, pp. 1-9, as cited by William H. Goetzman, *Exploration and Empire*, New York: Alfred A. Knopf, 1966, pp. 420-421.

10. Records of the Adjutant General's Office, U.S. National Archives, microfilm series 567, roll 580, pp. 0536-0549.

11. "Inspection by Generals Rusling and Hazen," 39th Congress, 2nd Session, *House Ex. Doc. 45.* Although not in the title, this was the "Tour of Inspection from the Missouri to the Pacific in 1866," as cited by Stewart in *Penny-an-Acre...*, p. 8.

12. "Inspection by Generals Rusling and Hazen," pp. 4-5.

13. A full account of this incident may be found in Stewart, *Penny-an-Acre...*, pp. 10-13.

14. Philip Henry Sheridan, born March 6, 1831, distinguished himself as a brilliant troop commander during the American Civil War from which he emerged a major-general. At the time of the incident along the Washita River involving Hazen, Sheridan was commander in charge of military operations in the department of the Missouri. On June 1, 1888, two months before his death, Congress bestowed upon him the highest military rank, that of General in the regular army. See Dumas Malone, *Dictionary...*, vol. 17, pp. 79-81, for the article written by Charles Dudley Rhodes.

15. *Army and Navy Journal,* June 29, 1872, as cited by Stewart, in *Penny-an-Acre....*

16. Robert Todd Lincoln, born August 1, 1843, served an uneventful term as Secretary of War from 1880 to 1884. His management of the relief of the Greely Expedition to the Arctic during the years 1882-1883, evoked criticism not only from Hazen — who was serving at the time as Chief Signal Officer — but from Greely and others as well. Lincoln died in 1926 at the age of 83. See Malone, *Dictionary...*, vol. 11, pp. 266-267, for the sketch by Frederic Logan Paxon.

17. As Chief Signal Officer, Hazen was directly responsible to the Secretary of War for expeditions to the Arctic. He felt a strong sense of personal responsibility for the failure to relieve Lieutenant Greely and his party at Lady Franklin Bay in 1883. After the failure of a Naval vessel, the *Proteus,* to reach the stranded party during the summer of 1883, Hazen urged Lincoln to authorize the dispatch of another vessel. Lincoln vacillated, on the grounds that it was too late in the year to risk another ship and crew in the winter ice packs. In his annual report as Chief Signal Officer in 1884, Hazen commented:

> ...this bureau did all in its power to have other ships sent at once...but was unsuccessful, after having been assured that it would be done. It is now almost certain that had any of these steps had been taken loss of life and disaster would have been averted....

See, *Annual Report of Chief Signal Officer, 1884,* U.S. GPO, Washington, D.C.

18. *New York Herald,* April 18, 1885, as cited in Malone, *Dictionary...*, p. 480.

19. Malone, *Dictionary...*, p. 480; the article by Frederic Logan Paxon.

20. William Babcock Hazen, *A Narrative of Military Service,* Boston: Ticknor and Company, 1885. This work contains excerpts from the service record of Hazen concerning similar campaigns to that described in this article.

The Congressional Medal of Honor During the Indian Wars

by James Robert Moriarty III

THE AMERICAN CITIZEN who possesses the Medal of Honor is the holder of the highest military award for valor that can be given to an individual by the United States of America. The man who wears the symbol walks with that privileged group from all nations who have received their country's highest decoration. He shares the company of the few heroes who have been honored by similar awards.

A reputation for superior military prowess is difficult to obtain in the course of modern warfare, but it was always within reach of the stoutest warrior in times past.[1]

Yet, prior to the American Civil War, few Americans had given much thought to the armed forces during times of peace.

During the winter of 1861 through 1862, a number of men in our nation's capitol began to concern themselves with the necessity for recognizing the deeds of American soldiers, sailors, and marines who were distinguishing themselves in the defense of the Union.[2]

For the first time since the Revolutionary War, the American citizen began to realize the importance of his military forces. Those who looked back in order to determine what honors had been given to servicemen during the short history of our nation found that George Washington stood alone in recognizing this need. He had been the only major figure up to that time who had actively concerned himself about providing a decoration to honor our military heroes.

General Washington's precedent for rewarding men for military deeds created the Purple Heart on August 7, 1782. The decoration was for "singular meritorious action." Three men had been awarded this decoration by 1783, and according to the records no others were given.[3]

There had been certain "certificates of merit" authorized during 1847 for soldiers, but without provision for a medal.[4] Later Congress awarded holders of these certificates extra pay of two dollars per month. The "brevet" system of promotions had been in operation throughout our military history, but this system like many others, had fallen victim to political abuses and the honor of "brevet rank" had grown meaningless by 1861.

Senator James W. Grimes of Iowa, who was Chairman of the Senate Naval Committee during the year 1861, introduced a bill to create a medal for the navy. After passing both Houses of Congress, President Abraham Lincoln approved the bill on December 21, 1861, which established a Medal of Honor for enlisted men of the Navy and Marine Corps. This was the first decoration formally authorized by the American government to be worn as a badge of honor by our military forces.

On February 17, 1862, Senator Henry Wilson of Massachusetts (U. S. Grant's Vice President, 1873-1877), introduced a resolution providing for "Medals of Honor to enlisted men of the army and voluntary forces who shall have distinguished themselves by their gallantry in action and other soldierlike qualities." This became law on July 12, 1862, with Lincoln's approval.

An amendment of March 3, 1863, extended the provision to include officers as well as enlisted men, with provisions made retroactive to the beginning of the Civil War. This legislation stood as the basis for the Army Medal of Honor until July 9, 1918, when it was superseded by a completely revised statute. The necessity for the revision came about because of a series of misunderstandings and misinterpretations for the use of our country's highest medal.

In 1869, M. H. Beaumont, who published a magazine titled *The Soldier's Friend*, wrote from New York to the War Department stating that he had been repeatedly requested to publish the names of all the Medal of Honor recipients. The abuses as well as the confusion relating to who had earned and who had not earned the Medal of Honor, led Mr. Beaumont to write to the War Department. He said that there were some persons using the medal for the purpose of soliciting charity, and in addition, there were others he knew of who had obtained the decoration surreptitiously.

The increasing number of applications for the medal by ex-soldiers, after the Civil War, added to the confusion. An organization was created on April 23, 1890, whose purpose was to perpetuate the ideals of the medal. The Medal of Honor Legion was first organized as a local society; on August 14, 1890, it became a national organization. In direct response to the efforts of members of the Society, Secretary of War Russell A. Alger, on June 26, 1897, announced that paragraph 177 of the Army Regulations had been revised at the direction of President McKinley, and that new regulations henceforth would define the award of the Medal of Honor. The War Department now had an authoritative and comprehensive system for awarding the medal.

An Act of Congress approved on April 24, 1904, made it mandatory that all claims for the medal be accompanied by official documents describing the deed. At this time the design of the Army Medal of Honor was changed.[5] Originally the design for the Medal had been the same for the Army and Navy excepting that the Army medal, instead of being attached to its ribbon by an anchor, was attached by means of

The Congressional Medal of Honor issued to Sergeant John Mott, Company "F," 3rd U.S. Cavalry, for heroism in action against the Apaches during the Battle of the Whetstone Mountains, May 5, 1877. Photo courtesy History Division, Los Angeles County Museum of Natural History.

the American Eagle standing on a crossed cannon and cannon balls. The formal description was "in bas-relief, on the star, the Union held a shield in her right hand against an attacker, who crouched to the left, holding forked-tongued serpents which struck at the shield." In the left hand of the Union was held the fasces, the ancient Roman symbol of unified authority, an axe bound in staves of wood. This is still a common symbol on many of our ten cent pieces. The thirty-four stars which encircle these figures represented the number of states at the time the medal was designed.

The reverse of the medal bore a blank for the name of the awardee and the date and place of his deed. This design remained the standard design for the Army and Navy from the time it was struck on November 17, 1862, by the firm of William Wilson and Son, in Philadelphia, until April 24, 1904, when the Army Medal of Honor design was changed.

On April 27, 1916, the United States Congress approved an Act which provided for the creation of a Medal of Honor Roll upon which the names of the discharged medal recipients who had earned the medal in combat and who had attained the age of sixty-five years were to be recorded.

The passage of this final act marked the successful culmination of the twenty-six-year effort by the members of the Legion of the Medal of Honor to obtain for the medal and its recipients the high status that it now holds.

Between October 16, 1916, and January 17, 1917, all of the 2,625 Medals of Honor which had been awarded up to that time were reconsidered by a select board of citizens. The deliberations of the board were completed on February 15, 1917. Nine hundred and eleven names were stricken from the original list.[6]

Eight hundred and sixty-four of these names were involved in one group. In this instance the Medal of Honor had been given to all members of a single army regiment, the 27th Maine Volunteer Infantry. In June of 1863, it appears that enlistments were running low in this regiment, and as an inducement to keep the regiment on active duty during a critical period (the defense of Washington), President Lincoln authorized Medals of Honor for any of its members who volunteered for extended duty, but through some clerical error, not only the volunteers received the medal, but also the balance of the regiment who had chosen to go home in spite of the President's offer. Of the remaining forty-seven scattered cases, the board felt that the medal had not properly been awarded for distinguished services as defined in the Act of June 3, 1916. Among the forty-seven who lost their medals was one William F. Cody, far better known as Buffalo Bill.

In the final report, the board indicated that in the majority of the cases where the medal had been issued prior to 1916, the decoration had been earned by the recipient. The highest standard for distinguished conduct in combat had been attained in these cases and there could be no question as to the propriety of the award.

The first Medal of Honor as a signal of bravery, was awarded to Assistant Surgeon Bernard John Dowling Irwin,[7] for his role in an 1861 Arizona Indian War action. The Irish-born officer was certified for:

> distinguished gallantry in action against hostile Chiricahua Indians near Apache Pass 13 and 14 February 1861, while serving as assistant surgeon voluntarily taking command of troops and attacking and defeating a marauding party of hostile Apaches encountered en route to the assistance of a body of troops engaged with Indians at Apache Pass.

The last Medal of Honor awarded for the period considered as that of the Indian Wars was given to Oscar Burkhard, born in Germany, a private in the Hospital Corps. His citation read:

> During a belated uprising of Chippewa Indians, Oscar Burkhard courageously risked his life in rescuing wounded comrades under heavy fire and is cited for bravery in action against Indians at Leech Lake, 5 October, 1898.[8]

Those operations of the United States Army which took place between March 25, 1865, and December 31, 1891, are for official purposes, the period of the Indian Campaigns. There were at least 1,067 separate actions within thirteen different campaigns.[9]

The Campaign on the Northern Plains which extended from 1862 through 1875, was conducted primarily against the Sioux and the Northern Cheyennes. The Little Big Horn Expedition (1876-1877) brought the destruction of elements of the 7th Cavalry under George Armstrong Custer, but was just one part of the continuing campaigns in the Northern Plains.[10]

The Nez Percé Campaign of 1877 was conducted against the southern branch of the Nez Percé led by Chief Joseph. The 1st Cavalry was sent to compel them to return to the reservation, but Chief Joseph chose to resist. This great Indian warrior engaged eleven separate commands of the army in thirteen battles and skirmishes in a period of less than eleven weeks. He was, however, finally forced to surrender on October 4, 1877, to Colonel Nelson A. Miles.[11]

The Bannock and Sheepeater Campaigns of 1878 and 1879, were actions against the Bannock, Piute, and other Indian tribes of the Southern Idaho region who threatened rebellion partly because of their dissatisfaction with land allotments. Elements of the 2nd, 5th, 12th, and 21st Infantry, the 4th Artillery, and the 1st and 2nd Cavalry were brought into the field against these tribes.[12] The campaign was conducted vigorously, and by the end of September 1879, judged to be complete.

The Ute Campaign of 1879-1880, took elements of the 2nd and 5th Cavalry, as well as the 4th Infantry, out of Fort Steel, Wyoming, into the Milk River country, Colorado, where on the 29th of September 1879, they were attacked and besieged by three to four hundred Indian warriors. From late in 1878 until early September 1879, frequent reports had come to General John Pope, Commanding the Department of the Missouri, that the White River Utes had started several extensive fires in the mountains west of Hot Sulfur Springs, Colorado, and had created other disturbances. These had prompted the sending of his troops to the Milk River country.

On September 26, the command held a conference at Bear Creek with the Indians. Arrangements were made for Major Thomas T. Thornburgh to meet with several chiefs on the morning of the 30th. For a

Left: Brigadier General Benjamin John Dowling Irwin, Surgeon, U.S.A., who was awarded the first Medal of Honor during the Indian Wars, for bravery at Apache Pass, Arizona, in 1861. Above: Private Oscar Burkhard, "Sgt. First Class, Hospital Corps, U.S.A., 120 N. James Street, Rome, New York." Cited for bravery in action against hostile Indians at Leech Lake, Minnesota, on 5 October 1898, he was the recipient of the Congressional Medal of Honor. Smithsonian Institution, Military History Division photo.

time it looked as though the difficulties would be settled. Before this time the troops under Thornburgh had reached the Milk River. He left Troop "D" to continue the march along the road with wagons while he and the rest of the troops turned off the road and took a trail leading to his left. He had scarcely gone a mile when he suddenly came upon a large force of Indians.

Not knowing what to expect, the Major dismounted, deployed his men and endeavored to open conversation with the Indians. His efforts drew a volley of rifle fire and a violent engagement began. Outnumbered, the troopers chose to walk and to lead their horses while firing. They meant to make their way back to the wagons at Milk River. The Indians, however, broke the skirmish line and managed to get between the wagons and the troopers. Holding a high knoll they commanded the line of Thornburgh's retreat. Captain John Scott Payne picked twenty men, led a desperate charge and routed the Indians, opening the way to retreat; Payne was wounded on this, the 29th of September, 1879.

Troop "F" of the 5th Cavalry had covered the left flank with a party of two non-coms, one trumpeter and seven men. The company commander ordered these troops to mount and charge. Thornburgh came up in time to countermand this order, and told the men to keep the position of defense covering the retreat. This position on the left was defended with utmost bravery until the troops were ordered to withdraw to the wagon train.

The position was desperate, but the men fought with unflinching courage. On the same day his fellow officer Payne was wounded, Thornburgh was killed within 500 yards of the wagons with one shot from a hostile rifle. Most of the men made the road and established an elliptical defense using the bodies of the dead horses and overturned wagons. While completely surrounded the small force found themselves reasonably well sheltered by the debris.[13]

They were 200 yards from the river, however, and as there were large numbers of casualties, the need for water became a serious problem.

On the morning of October 2, 1879, a small group of cavalrymen, under the command of Captain Francis Safford Dodge, fought their way into the little fortification. With them was Sergeant Henry Johnson of Troop "D," 9th U.S. Cavalry. Johnson had been born a slave in Virginia on June 11, 1850. Now this veteran trooper in the service of his country, would voluntarily leave a sheltered position and under heavy fire, at very close range, carry out his duties as sergeant of the guard. He made the rounds of the fire pits in direct exposure to the enemy in order that he might instruct his guards. On the next night, in a desperate action, arming himself with two pistols and all the canteens he could carry, this black sergeant literally fought his way the two hundred yards to the river. Filling all the canteens, he managed to bring the water back to the wounded.

This desperate situation was relieved by the arrival of troops, including elements of the 4th, 6th, 7th, 15th, 16th, and 19th Infantry Regiments supported by 3rd, 5th, and 9th Cavalry Regiments. The entire Ute Campaign was completed in November 1880 and there are no more heroic deeds performed by men in any regiment in the U.S. Army than the list of Medal of Honor winners from the 9th Cavalry, the United States Army's "Buffalo Soldiers." The veteran soldier Sergeant Henry Johnson is a primary example of the gallant men who fought under the Regimental Standard of the Ninth; Captain Dodge also received a Medal of Honor for his actions at Milk River.

Following the rush to Pike's Peak region in 1858-1859, and the movements of tribes in Colorado and nearby areas, white-Indian conflicts kept the country in a turmoil. On November 29, 1864, Colonel J. M. Chivington organized a punitive expedition of volunteer units and in a surprise attack killed several hundred Cheyennes and Arapahoes on Sand Creek, in the villages of Black Kettle and White Antelope.

The Medicine Lodge Treaty signed in 1867, was an attempt by Congress to negotiate with the Southwest Plains Indians. It provided reservations for the Kiowas and Comanches between the Red and Washita Rivers. It provided an area south of the Arkansas River for the Southern Cheyennes and the Arapahoes.[14] The Indians, however, did not adhere to the terms and soon, Major-General Philip Sheridan, commanding the Department of the Missouri, took the field with his troops in campaigns against the Comanches, Cheyennes, and other tribes between 1867 and 1875.

The Indian Campaigns of the Pacific Coast began in 1840, and extended through 1873.[15] That phase of the coastal campaigns known as the Modoc Campaign occurred in 1872-1873. With usual ineptitude, the Bureau of Indian Affairs placed the Modoc, a small and restless tribe, on a reservation with the Klamaths, their traditional enemies. The situation became intolerable and the majority of the Modocs, led by a chief known as Captain Jack, jumped the reserve.

Elements of the 1st Cavalry chased them and after a brief skirmish fought on November 29, 1872, Captain Jack was able to get away with about 120 warriors. Armed with weapons and ample supplies he retreated to a naturally fortified area in the lava beds east of Mount Shasta.

On 17 January 1873, Colonel Alvan Cullom Gillem (who had been brevetted five times for gallantry and meritorious service during the Civil War), with a detachment of some 400 men, half of them regulars from the 1st Cavalry and the 21st Infantry attacked the Modoc positions. The troops, however, made no progress in the almost impossible terrain and suffered a loss of ten killed and twenty-eight wounded.

By the spring of 1873, Brigadier-General Edward Richard Sprigg Canby, Commander of the Department of the Pacific (brevetted five times for gallantry and meritorious services during the Civil War), collected 1,000 men, elements of the 1st Cavalry, the 12th and 21st Infantry Regiments, and the 4th Artillery to besiege the Modocs in their fortified area. The Indian Bureau failed at negotiations, but Canby and three civilian commissioners arranged a parlay with an equal number of Modocs on April 11th. In violation of the truce, the Indians attacked the peacemakers. Captain Jack killed Canby; others were killed and wounded; the siege immediately resumed.

Canby was replaced by Brigadier-General Jefferson Columbus Davis (brevetted five times during the Civil War), who arrived in May, moved his men into the lava beds, and began harassing the Indians night and day with mortar and rifle fire. With the source of water cut off, the Indians were finally forced into the open and all were captured on June 1, 1873. Captain Jack and two others hanged; the rest of the tribe were removed to the Indian Territory. These actions ended the California Indian Campaigns.[16]

During the Modoc Campaigns, however, some very distinguished service records were built including that of Major John Green of the 1st U. S. Cavalry so honored with the Medal of Honor. Green was born in Germany on November 20, 1825, and like many of the immigrants to this nation entered the service of the Army. He had enlisted during the Mexican War and was brevetted twice during the Civil War. He eventually achieved the rank of Brigadier-General.

At the time of the award, Green served as Commanding Officer, 1st U.S. Cavalry with the rank of major at Fort Klamath.

In the Fall of 1872, the Modoc Indian troubles had reached a dangerous stage. The Indian agent demanded that they be forced to comply with his wishes and quickly return to the reservation assigned to them. The natives defied him. The next step was an appeal, by the agent, in the name of the Central Office in Washington, to the C.O., Fort Klamath, to furnish a force sufficient to compel the Modocs to return to Camp Yainak. Green, forced to comply, detailed Captain James Jackson of the 1st Cavalry with a force of thirty men for this purpose. Jackson had also been brevetted twice for gallant service, would receive a brevet for his gallantry in the ensuing conflict with the Modocs, would later be brevetted for gallant service in Idaho in 1877, and would be granted the Medal of Honor for distinguished gallantry in action at Camp Meadows, Idaho, on August 20, 1877! Jackson left Fort Klamath on November 28, 1872, in a move which opened the Modoc War.[17]

The Modoc Indians selected as their stronghold a stretch of country known as the Lava Beds south of Tule Lake, a most inaccessible region. The lava beds comprised an intricate net of gorges, crests, and crevices amply supplied with water from Tule Lake and covering a surface area of four by seven miles. A major expedition was started against the hostiles toward the middle of January 1873.

The fight that ensued, when the soldiers came up to the impregnable position the Indians held, was desperate. Between forty and fifty men were killed.

While on this occasion many deeds of valor on the part of the troops came to light, the most conspicuous person during the fight was Major John Green. He had received a brevet promotion for action at Mount Turnbull, Arizona, in 1869, and would, in addition to the brevet promotion for the coming Modoc action be awarded the Medal of Honor. His conduct on 17 January 1873, won the admiration of all who observed him.

Green, commanding a line of skirmishers on the battle ground, found the terrain of such peculiar formation that an unbroken line of

Major John Green, Medal of Honor winner, with group of officers. U.S. National Archives photograph.

skirmishers would, after a few minutes of advance, find itself split into small detachments cut off from one another by impassable crevices and exposed to sudden flanking fire from an unseen enemy. Extreme caution was necessary if the advancing men hoped to avoid disaster. The rank and file who felt their enemy constantly slipping away from their front never saw more than a half dozen Indians at a time and so were unable to bring any punishment to bear.

The Indians on the other hand, inflicted steadily increasing casualties on the erratic skirmish line. The entire forward movement bogged down as the soldiers began to lose heart as well as confidence. When the line was formally organized again and preparations to advance brought to a point of execution, some of the men in the line near Major Green appeared none too eager to execute the order to move forward. In fairness it must be pointed out they had sustained severe losses without any visible counter effect upon the enemy, also they were now in a position that was reasonably sheltered.

Major Green observing this at once stepped forward and calmly walked up and down in full view of the enemy. This demonstration of fearless courage in the face of possible death stiffened his men and brought them into the advance.

During the entire engagement, Green exposed himself with a recklessness and ready courage that impressed all his men. Under fire he was the example of the superior man who inspired the soldier to disdain death and danger, and to devote full energy to the fulfillment of his duty. In the long period of warfare which followed, and during the last days of desperate fighting and pursuing, it was again Major Green who proved the model soldier. His courage, zeal, instruction, and intelligence impressed his men more than any other officer with the idea of absolute fearlessness during the campaign. Self-protection and shelter were ever secondary in his mind to the accomplishment of the objective he had in view. He richly deserved his Medal of Honor.

The Apache Campaigns of 1871 through 1886 were undertaken by Brigadier-General George Crook after he became Commander of the Department of Arizona in 1871. In a series of winter campaigns using small detachments, he pacified the area by 1874. In later years dissatisfaction with the Indian Bureau's policy[18] of frequent removal, brought dissident elements led by Chato, Victorio, and Geronimo off the reservations and they raided settlements along both sides of the border. Victorio was killed by Mexican troops in 1880, but Chato and Geronimo remained at large until May 1883, when they surrendered to General Crook who led elements of the 6th Cavalry. Geronimo later caused additional troubles and then negotiated with Crook late in March 1886.[19] Geronimo did not surrender; he and part of his band escaped.[20]

Not until September 1886, when Lieutenant Charles B. Gatewood negotiated the formal surrender, could Geronimo and his band be removed to Florida, and later to the Fort Sill military reservation.

In the campaigns against the Apache Indians, several times the Indians were brought to bay and forced to fight.[21] One of the major forays took place in the Battle of the Piñito mountains of Sonora on 3 May 1886. Again the "Buffalo Soldiers" of the 10th U.S. Cavalry were in the field.

On April 27, 1886, Geronimo crossed the border into the United States and raided through the Santa Cruz Valley in Arizona. During these raids, he butchered a rancher's wife, Mrs. Peck, and one of her children, captured the husband, and carried off the thirteen-year-old daughter as captives. News of the raid reached the captain commanding Company "K" of the 10th Cavalry. Captain Thomas Coverly Lebo picked up the Indians' trail and began tracking them. For more than 200 miles the troopers followed, and at last the Indians turned to fight on a rocky slope in the Piñito Mountains thirty miles south of the border in the State of Sonora.

Lebo dismounted Company "K" and forming skirmish lines advanced up the slope. They were halted by a veritable curtain of fire which killed Private Hollis and severely wounded a veteran trooper, Corporal Scott.

Forced to withdraw downslope and take cover, it was discovered that Corporal Scott had been left behind. A short-range rifle duel followed this discovery and Scott lay exposed between the two parties unable to crawl to safety. Recognizing the desperate position his noncommissioned officer was in, and with complete disregard for his own personal safety, a young lieutenant, marvelously named Powhatan H. Clarke,[22] dashed out from behind a sheltered position directly into the fire of the Apaches. He reached the corporal, miraculously picked him up, and dashed back to the safety of his own line. This act, performed on 3 May 1886, was performed well in advance of his own troopers who were themselves so busily engaged in keeping the hostiles at bay that many of them had not noticed the absence of their comrade. Young Lieutenant Clarke's intrepid daring and the exceptional courage that he displayed by dashing among the Indians, firing as he advanced and killing several of them before he reached the place where the corporal lay, surely prevented the man's death. But, this had not been Clarke's first such deed for he had been breveted for gallant service in actions against hostile Indians near the Salt River in Arizona on March 2, 1870.

Irwin, the immigrant Irish surgeon; Johnson, the former slave; Green, the German immigrant; Oscar Burkhard, the German immigrant, and Powhatan Clarke — Americans all, who served their nation with the highest credits of manhood.

Such American soldiers have distinguished themselves on battlefields all over the world and few knew them as well as General Douglas MacArthur, who in the last days of his own life paid the soldiers a great tribute. With a depth of understanding and an experience in these matters that has been equaled by few men in our time, the general said:

> ...This award is not intended primarily to honor a personality, but to symbolize a great moral code — the code of conduct and chivalry of those who guard this beloved land of culture and ancient descent. That is the meaning of this medallion. For all eyes and for all time, it is an expression of the epic of the American soldier.... I do not know the dignity of their birth, but I do know the glory of their death. They died unquestioningly, uncomplaining, with faith in their hearts, and on their lips the hope that we would go on to victory. Always for — duty — honor — country; always their blood and sweat and tears as we sought the way and the light and the truth....[23]

Photo taken from painting of Lt. Powhatan Clarke, who was awarded the Congressional Medal of Honor for heroism in the Piñito Mountains, Sonora, Mexico, 3 May 1886. Smithsonian Institution, Military Division photo.

Trans-Mississippi West Indian Campaigns 1865-1891

Statistics, Congressional Medals of Honor

Arizona:

Apaches & Arizona campaigns, no place	72
Apache Pass	1
Agua Fria River	3
Apache Creek	1
Big Dry Wash	1
Big Dry Fork	1
Camp Hualpai	1
Cibicu	3
Clear Creek	1
Date Creek	1
Davidson Canyon	1
Chiricahua Mountains	32
Fort Apache	1
Hells Canyon	3
Picacho Mountain	2
Lyry Creek	3
Red Creek	3
San Carlos	2
Santa Maria Mountains	3
Seneca	5
Simon Valley	1
Sunset Pass	1
Sycamore Canyon	1
Tonto Creek	1
Turret Mountain	5
Whetstone Mountains	7
	156

California/Oregon:

Lava Beds	2

Colorado:

Milk River	11
White River Agency	1
	12

Indian Territory:

Gageby Creek	1

Idaho:

Camas Meadows	4
Clearwater	1
White Bird Canyon	2
	7

Kansas and Nebraska 1

Kansas:

Fort Dodge	1
Plum Creek	1
Republican River	2
Sappa Creek	8
	12

Mexico:
Piñito Mountains   1
Santa Cruz Mountains   1
Sierra Madre Mountains   1
   3

Minnesota:
Leech Lake   1

Montana:
Big Hole   6
Bear Paw Mountain   10
Cedar Creek   30
Little Big Horn   27
Little Muddy   3
Mixpah Creek   1
O'Fallons Creek   2
Powder River   2
Pumpkin Creek   1
Rosebud River   4
Slim Buttes   1
Sioux   4
Wolf Mountain   3
   94

Nebraska:
Gilmans Ranch   1
Fort Hartsuff   4
Little Blue   5
Loupe Fork   3
Spring Creek   1
   14

New Mexico:
Carrizo Canyon   2
Cuchillo Negro Mountains   4
Florida Mountains   1
Fort Selden   5
Horseshoe Canyon   2
Las Animas Canyon   3
New Mexico   1
   18

No place cited   2

South Dakota:
Fort Kearny to Fort Smith   1
Slim Buttes   1
White River   6
White Clay Creek   3
Wounded Knee Creek   18
   29

Texas:

Brazos River	1
Colorado Valley	1
Fort Griffin	1
Kickapoo Springs	1
Pecos River	3
Muchague Valley	1
Red River	14
Staked Plains	5
Washita River	17
Wichita River	18
	62

Utah:

Cienega Springs	1

Wyoming:

Bluff Station	1
Elkhorn Creek	1
Powder River	2
	4
	419

Issuance of Medals of Honor by
BIRTHPLACES OF RECIPIENTS

Arizona	4	Tennessee	5
Arkansas	2	Texas	4
California	1	Vermont	1
Connecticut	4	Virginia	7
District of Columbia	2	West Virginia	1
Florida	1	Wisconsin	4
Georgia	1		
Illinois	10	Australia	1
Indiana	8	Bavaria	3
Iowa	3	Canada	5
Kentucky	11	Denmark	1
Louisiana	4	England	11
Maine	8	France	3
Maryland	16	Germany	31
Massachusetts	21	Ireland	76
Michigan	8	Mexico	1
Minnesota	1	New Brunswick	1
Missouri	7	Newfoundland	1
Nebraska	1	Prince Edward Isle	1
New Hampshire	5	Prussia	3
New Jersey	7	Scotland	6
New York	42	South Wales	1
North Carolina	3	Sweden	2
Ohio	25	Switzerland	4
Pennsylvania	38	West Indies	1
Rhode Island	2	No place given	9
South Carolina	1		

Year	Count	Year	Count
1861	1	1878	0
1862	0	1879	17
1863	0	1880	3
1864	0	1881	9
1865	1	1882	5
1866	0	1883	0
1867	1	1884	0
1868	44	1885	0
1868-9	8	1886	4
1869	57	1887	0
1870	26	1888	0
1871	6	1889	2
1871-3	1	1890	27
1872	21	1891	7
1872-3	19	1892	0
1872-4	1	1893	0
1873	15	1894	0
1874	28	1895	0
1875	13	1896	0
1876	41	1897	0
1876-7	31	1898	1
1877	30		

NOTES

1. For a discussion of ideas and beliefs about warfare see James R. Moriarty, "Ritual Combat, A Comparison of the Aztec 'War of Flowers' and the Medieval 'Melee'," *Katunob*, Vol. VII, No. 1, March 1969, pp. 25-36. (Issued January 1970)

2. "Medal of Honor Recipients, 1863-1963," prepared for the Subcommittee on Veterans' Affairs of the Committee on Labor and Public Welfare, *Sen. Ex. Docs.*, 88th Congress, 2nd Session, 1963-1964, pp. 13-17.

3. See *The Army Almanac*, Harrisburg, Pa.: The Stackpole Company, 1959, pp. 305-306.

4. "Certificates of Merit and Medal of Honor," *House Ex. Docs.*, 52nd Cong., 1891-1892, 1st Session, Vol. 1, p. 313. (in 38 vols.)

5. *Insignia and Decorations of the United States Armed Forces*, Washington, D.C.: The National Geographic Society, 1944, p. 21.

6. J. W. Bunkley, *Military and Naval Recognition Book*, New York: D. Van Nostrand Company, Inc., 1942, pp. 172-178.

7. Two recent articles detail the incident at Apache Pass. That by Robert M. Utley, "The Bascom Affair: A Reconstruction," *Arizona and the West*, Vol. 3, no. 1, 1961, pp. 59-68, and that by Benjamin Sacks, "New Evidence on the Bascom Affair," in the same journal, Vol. 4, no. 3, 1962, pp. 261-278.

8. See "Medal of Honor Recipients . . .," pp. 50, 627, 621; and Joseph L. Schott, *Above and Beyond: The Story of the Congressional Medal of Honor*, New York: G. P. Putnam's Sons, 1963, p. 64.

9. "Defining 'Indian War,'" in *House* (Public) *Reports*, 63rd Cong., 2nd. Sess. Dec. 1, 1913-Oct. 24, 1914, vol. 3, Washington, G.P.O., 1914, p. 6 (House Report #1084).

10. Mari Sandoz, *Crazy Horse: The Strange Man of the Oglalas, A Biography*, Omaha: Univ. of Nebraska Press, 1961, pp. 302-317. See also Laurence Greene, *America Goes to Press*, New York: The Bobbs-Merrill Co., 1936, pp. 231-237, and Robert M. Utley, *The Last Days of the Sioux Nation*, New Haven: Yale Univ. Press, 1963, pp. 31-33, 49.

11. Edward H. Spicer, *The Buffalo Hunters Give In: A Short History of the Indians of the United States*, New York: Van Nostrand Reinhold Co., 1969, pp. 82-87.

12. John A. Gorman, *The Western Horse*, Danville: The Interstate Printers and Publishers, Inc., 1967, pp. 147-253.

13. Frank Gilbert Roe, *The Indian and the Horse*, Norman: Univ. Oklahoma Press, 1955, pp. 175-188.

14. Wilcomb E. Washburn, editor, *The Indian and the White Man*, Garden City: Doubleday and Co., 1964, pp. 101-131; and Allan Nevins, *The Gateway to History*, Garden City: Doubleday and Co., Inc., 1962, pp. 295-299.

15. William H. Goetzmann, *Army Exploration in the American West, 1803-1863*, New Haven: Yale Univ. Press, 1959, pp. 3-21; James M. Merrill, *Spurs to Glory*, Rand McNally and Co., 1966, pp. 56, 65-75; *The Army Almanac*, pp. 708-709.

16. *The Army Almanac*, pp. 700-709.

17. Potomac Corral of the Westerners, *Great Western Indian Fights*, Omaha: Univ. of Nebraska Press, 1960, pp. 189-191.

18. "Indian Outbreak in Arizona," in Index to the *House Ex. Docs.*, 47th Cong., 1st Sess. (1881-1882), Vol. 2, War, No. 1, Pt. 2, Vol. 1, pp. 120-121. Washington, G.P.O., 1882, in 26 Vols. See also Keith H. Basso, *The Cibecue Apache*, New York: Holt, Rinehart and Winston, 1970, p. 8.

19. Major-General John K. Herr and Edward S. Wallace, *Story of the U.S. Cavalry*, Boston: Little, Brown and Co., 1953, pp. 201-210; Merrill, *Spurs to Glory*, pp. 180, 200, 229-241.

20. *Great Western Indian Fights*, pp. 255-256.

21. *The Army Almanac*, pp. 707-708.

22. William H. Leckie, *The Buffalo Soldiers*, Norman: Univ. of Oklahoma Press, 1967, pp. 243-244; Francis B. Heitman, *Historical Register & Dictionary of the United States Army . . .*, Washington, G.P.O., 1903, reprinted Urbana, Univ. of Illinois Press, 1965, 2 Vols.; *House Ex. Docs.*, 49th Cong., 2nd Sess., 1886-1887, Vol. 1, pp. 166-167. (28 vols.)

23. General Douglas MacArthur, "Farewell Address to the June Graduating Class at West Point, 1964."

Background to Battle: Circumstances Relating to Death on the Gila, 1857

by Greta S. Ezell and Paul H. Ezell

IN JUNE OF 1857, on an arid plain beside the middle Gila River of central Arizona, the Yuma Indians of the Colorado River and the "Maricopa" Indians of the Gila met in the final battle of a family quarrel of several centuries duration. Neither group fought alone; each was reinforced with such allies that almost all of the Yuman-speaking people ever associated with Arizona were involved. Only the Cocopa living at the delta of the Colorado River to the southwest and the Walapai-Havasupai to the far north beyond the Bill Williams River were completely uninvolved.

Through at least four centuries a system of enmities and alliances had developed in Arizona and southern California with the Yuman-speaking people as the basic participants and the Colorado River as the pivot point. Central to one side in mid-nineteenth century were the Yuma and Mohave of the Colorado River and the Yavapai of upland Arizona, with peripheral allies (not necessarily linguistically related) extending toward New Mexico in the east, into desert California on the west, and into the Sonoran gulf coast to the south. In opposition to this combination were the Maricopa of the Gila River and the Cocopa of the Colorado, with linguistically related allies and/or friends stretching across southern California to the Pacific Ocean on the west and Piman-speaking allies to the east on the Gila. The Yuman-speaking Walapai-Havasupai, although friends of the Maricopa and enemies of their opposition, were cut off from much association or cooperation with them by Yavapai control of the intervening country.

Between these two systems there had been for at least four centuries a continuing series of conflicts, sometimes involving only one member on each side, sometimes with two or more allies on either side; but the disruptive element was the conflict between the Yuma and the Maricopa. Only this one developed beyond the normal Yuman pattern of limited warfare for (in effect) fun, exercise, and kudos to a level of intensity that could only result in the elimination of one side or the other.

June 1857 was the time, and the triangular area encompassed by the eastern foothills of the Sierra Estrella and the Gila River in central Arizona was the place, where that conflict was resolved. Why it did take place then and there and, furthermore, resulted not in the elimination of one or the other side, but virtually of both, can only be understood by exploration of some of the ethnographic and historical background of the peoples involved.

When Columbus set foot on Hispaniola he became the southern anchor of a chain reaction which stretched through three-and-a-half centuries and a third of a continent to its northern terminus in mid-nineteenth century Arizona. The intervening links were forged by an almost equal mixture of the Spanish occupiers of Mexico as bearers of Hispanic culture, and the Indians of southern California and Arizona as bearers of Yuman culture. When the Spaniards first began their conquest of Mexico, the Yuman groups were just beginning the last territorial adjustments in their occupation of their territory.

Well before the discovery of the New World, Yuman-speaking groups were occupying a wide sweep of what was to become the American Southwest. It stretched from the Pacific coast in the region of the present international boundary eastward through the mountains, across the southern portion of the then less arid south-central valley of California to the Colorado River and beyond into the western portion of the elevated area of Arizona north of the Gila River. That river and the territory south of it was inhabited by Piman-speaking groups who were the northern outliers of a linguistic family which extended south along the coast and in the mountains even into the central valley of Mexico.

While most of the Piman people were farming-oriented, this was especially so along the middle stretches of the Gila River and of the Salt River just north of it where there had arisen a series of large communities of sedentary farmers who were beginning to push out ambassadors and colonists into the areas beyond their immediate control. Some of these contacts were westward with the Yuman groups on the Colorado River. Basically the Yuman people, from the Pacific coast to central

Arizona, were oriented toward hunting and gathering for subsistence rather than to farming; only those on the river were ever to develop any reliable agriculture. Even this, however, would be based upon the annual flooding of the river with its consequent soaking of the adjacent lowlands, rather than on any deliberate watering of the arable land.

Whether or not the people still living at that time around the inland sea of the central California valley would have developed agriculture of any kind will probably never be known, for soon a widespread and long-lasting drought affected all of the area. Not only were the flourishing communities along the Gila and Salt Rivers drastically reduced in size by lack of produce and internal conflict as a result thereof, the increasing aridity in the areas away from the rivers caused an influx to them of other Piman-speaking peoples from the less-watered areas. Along the Gila the two Piman-speaking groups arrived at a system of peaceful coexistence, the newcomers and the remaining members of the original inhabitants sharing the areal resources as an amalgamated whole (today known as the Gila River Pimas), with belligerence directed outward and utilized basically as a means of territorial defense. In the mountains of California and Arizona the Yuman-speaking peoples (principally the Kamiai—Diegueño—of the Californias and the Walapai-Havasupai and Yavapai of Arizona) tightened their belts and waited out the drouth around the scattered remaining sources of water.

For the Colorado River the results were more dramatic. The river was already occupied along most of its reach by a series of culturally related groups (Mohave, Halchidhoma, Kohuana, Halyikwamai and Cocopa), each sharing to more or less degree a strong sense of nationality and an enthusiasm for belligerence, whether in the form of raiding or more formal battle. As the drouth continued over the decades, the inland sea, no longer replenished by local rain and periodic overflow from the Colorado, became more saline as it diminished in size, and the people remaining on its shores were forced into the surrounding territory. This movement brought to the Colorado River one last group, the Yuma, which also manifested the characteristics of nationalism and belligerence, apparently to as great an extent as the Mohaves, the most war-oriented of the groups already on the river. The Yumas successfully laid claim to the Halchidhoma territory, forcing some of them northward to a position closer to the Mohave, and first one portion, the Opa, and then another, the Cocomaricopa, eastward to a renewal of the old association with the Pimas of the Gila River. The Opa occupied the big bend of the Gila just west of its junction with the Salt and downriver to the Painted Rocks Mountains, the Cocomaricopa westward from there to below Agua Caliente.

Thus was established the aboriginal population distribution found by the Spaniards when they finally reached the limits of their northern expansion at the end of the seventeenth century.

In the beginning, the Spaniards had established themselves in the New World by force alone, a rather surprising accomplishment for such a relatively small group of men, but as they achieved a secure base of operations in central Mexico, they expanded northward by an adroit combination of politics and force, religion and welfare. From a relatively pacified area (with a small military force in residence, a functioning mission altering the aboriginal culture to conform to Hispanic ideals, and settlers moving in to occupy the "empty" land), an advance party of one or two priests and a handful of soldiers moved northward into new territory seeking centers of aboriginal populations near arable land. When a satisfactory location was found, a mission was established and crops planted. The Indians were gathered to it by curiosity, generous handouts of supplies, manipulations of inter-group jealousies and only the minimum amount of force necessary to maintain Hispanic dominance. As soon as possible, even before all groups were entirely converted, a new northward extension was instigated. If the unconverted remained recalcitrant, a larger military group was brought into the "pacified" area to enforce the peace.

For a century and a half this policy was applied to a third of the continent before it lost its effectiveness. Distance from the source of decisions and supplies, exhaustion of the readily available gold resources, and the vagaries of European politics combined to reduce the availability of the final element of the policy—sufficient force. When the Yaqui and Seri Indians of Sonora and the Apache of Arizona and New Mexico refused to be readily converted, military force was not forthcoming to achieve the necessary pacification. Rather, a new objective of containment of the already occupied territory was substituted for one of expansion, and the Spanish forces dug in at approximately the present international border, with a line of presidios established to restrain the unsubdued Indians in the interior and fend off the worst of the Apache attacks from the northeast. To the north the frontier settlements depended upon the goodwill and fighting ability of the Pimas and allied Opas and Cocomaricopas to protect them from the Yavapais and Apaches beyond; to the northwest they depended upon distance and diplomacy to assure that the Yuman tribes of the Colorado did not frustrate their desire to achieve communication with California by an overland route.

In general, this dual policy was successful. Only with the Yumas themselves, sitting astride the only feasible route (down the Gila and across the Colorado) for large groups to travel to California did it fail. The Havasupai-Walapai and the Yavapai friends of the Yuma were

never directly affected by, nor did they themselves affect, the Spaniards.
The Cocopa (friends of the Halchidhoma, enemies of the Yuma) to the
south and the Mohave (friends of the Yuma) to the north were too far
off the desired route to be much influenced by the Spaniards; the Halyi-
kwamai-Kohuana and the Halchidhoma (on one side and the other of
their mutual enemy, the Yuma) were less far from the route but still
not directly involved. The Halchidhoma, through their relatives on the
Gila (Opa and Cocomaricopa) were friendly to the Spaniards; and the
Pima were tolerant of all, so long as the integrity of their territory was
not under attack.

Without permanently occupying an acre of land, the Spaniards introduced into this relatively stable situation of location, alliances and
enmities, four factors which planted and fertilized the seeds of drastic
changes which in the end resulted in the virtual destruction of the
Yuma, Halyikwamai, Kohuana, Halchidhoma, Cocomaricopa and Opa.
At the time of Spanish contact, each of these groups numbered from
two to three thousand in population, about one-third of which were
warriors. By mid-nineteenth century (150 years later) the Yuma population had been reduced by more than half and the other groups combined (then known as the "Maricopa") had dwindled to some two

Pasqual, principal
leader of the Quechans
from 1854-1887. U.S.
National Archives
photo.

thousand. On the other hand, the Pimas—only peripherally involved in the Yuman family quarrels—had increased by at least a third despite continuous though sporadic raiding attacks by both Yavapai and Apache.

Two of the factors introduced by the Spaniards were matters of deliberate policy. Concerned with the unreliability of water transportation to California, the northwest frontier area seemed to the authorities to be a logical location for a land route. Time and again the Spaniards probed to the west-northwest; first to see if a land connection existed, then to determine if it were feasible for the use of settlers in the quantity needed to secure California from Russian encroachment from the north. The second factor of deliberate policy was partly to obtain this route and partly to secure the northwestern frontier despite the increasingly inadequate supplies of men and goods. This involved a combination of honors and gifts to individual tribes as well as hopefully self-perpetuating treaties of peace among them and with the Spaniards and later the Mexicans. Neither of the policies was successful. The road to California was never established as a safe, reliable route; rather the Hispanic probing simply increased the Yumas' uneasiness at the Hispanic presence. The gifts, honors, and treaties did not buy them friendship or peace on the frontier; the treaties among the Indians were soon broken, and the gifts and honors created competition among the various groups for them as they became symbolic evidence of dominance in the power situation.

Of the two factors inadvertently introduced into the situation by the Spaniards, one had its first impact well before first Hispanic contact. The Indians had no pre-established immunities to the new diseases which spread well in front of the advance of the Spaniards. Their communication from group to group was insured by the far-traveling characteristics of at least some individuals of each group. No reliable estimate can be given on the pre-contact effect of European diseases, but it can be stated that in post-contact times it continued to be devastating in some cases as new generations were born without immunity. The trauma (both physical and emotional) resulting from the death tolls among some groups must have been disrupting.

The second inadvertent factor (a dual one) can be seen more clearly. An accepted element of Hispanic culture was the presence among them of involuntary servitude. Scattered throughout reports from the frontier are references to "servants" and "slaves" with frequent identification of these as belonging to groups from beyond the settled frontier. Among the pre-Hispanic Indians of the Gila and Colorado rivers there were occasional instances of small children or young

girls growing up among groups not of their birth, but the basic pattern
was not to take captives. Warfare was almost entirely a matter of vengeance, with death to the enemy the object of the battle. The second element of this dual factor came through the introduction of horse flesh into the frontier area.

To both the Pimans and Yumans, horses represented transportation and prestige; in addition, to the Yumans they represented food. When the Spaniards began buying slaves from the frontier Indians, frequently in exchange for horses, a new economic incentive was added to the general Yuman predilection for warfare. Soon an active trade in slaves developed which provided the impetus both for increased raids for saleable bodies and captured horses, and for retaliatory war. As with the belligerent forays by the Yuman groups on the Gila against those of the Colorado, the Pima took little part in the slave trade, although they did purchase horses in exchange for their produce. Their main concern was protection and care of their farm lands and its product; they were involved in the Yuman wars primarily in giving assistance when Gila River villages were attacked.

The individual raids between the Yuman groups were probably not too destructive, since at least some of them included as few as two warriors in the attacking party. Of greater impact was the increase in full-scale battle with as many as 200 warriors involved on each side. When inter-group tension became unbearable, some "brave one" (not normally the society's chief, who seldom went to war) would dream of victory in war, for all success or failure in all aspects of Yuman life was determined by dreams. With as many companions as accepted his dream as true, and a shaman both to make periodic forecasts concerning the probabilities of success and to cure those who were wounded, he set off on the eight-day trip to the homeland of the enemy. In addition to packets of food, canteens of water, and knives, some of the group carried feather-decorated lances, some bows and arrows, some shields and large-headed clubs with sharply pointed handles; a very few carried the short pikes which signified they would never retreat. With a long easy lope in sharp contrast to their normal slouching gait, the tall warriors covered the miles to their destination. Although the Yuma traditionally never rode horses in the martial trips up the Gila, they did use them against other groups, and the Mohave and Gila River groups frequently used them in all aspects of their warfare. Each night they danced and sang of success in war and how anxious they were to reach the enemy. Each night the shaman smoked to test again for omens good or bad. Even should the results be ominous they went forward the next day—if they were to be killed, they would die with honor, but they might, instead, take a scalp and return home with even more honor.

On the last night they were too close to the enemy to sing; rather they prepared for the morning's action. Weapons were checked and bow guards laced on by the archers; breechcloths were re-arranged, sandals re-tied; their long ropes of hair were bound up on their heads with ribbons and sashes, and eagle down and hawk feathers tied firmly in place; faces were striped with red, black or white paint; ear and nose pendants inserted and beads re-draped. Before dawn they moved, hoping to surprise the enemy but ready for formal battle if such were to be. Usually they did surprise and kill a few, but the alarm was spread and they were soon faced with a full force of the enemy drawn up in lines of defense, clubmen in front, bowmen behind. Forming their own line, they sent forward their champions to challenge the foe, first to verbal battle relating to the courage and manhood of the enemy, then to physical combat.

As one champion fell another took his place; and another; and another, until with a cry the two lines of clubmen swept forward to stab and smash their way into the enemy lines as the bowmen shot into the melee. Only those who fought through to the other side could

Antonio Azul, Pima Indian. Photo by Alexander Gardner, in Washington, D.C., 1872. Smithsonian Institution National Anthropological Archives photo.

return home to carry the tales of bravery and sorrow. In early times it was feasible to scalp the fallen enemy and cremate dead companions, but as war intensified to where numerous sweeps through the lines were made these customs were gradually abandoned, for fewer and fewer were left to carry them out when the battle was done.

❧

The early seeds of destruction sown by the Spaniards grew slowly. The first effects of the Spanish-introduced diseases were not associated by the Indians with the Spaniards; illness was considered to be caused primarily by wrong dreaming, secondarily by malevolent action on the part of some shaman. Those who survived the first epidemics developed immunities and, thereafter, only new infants were affected. For three-quarters of a century the Gila and Colorado rivers were largely ignored by the Spaniards as they concentrated on establishing their control over upper Sonora—building missions, gathering nearby Indians to within sound of the bells, bringing in colonists to exploit the mines, the land, and the labor. When Indians from beyond the frontier made the long trip over arid lands to the mission centers, they were given attention and gifts according to their rank, and saw for themselves the quality of life in the frontier settlements. Being closer to the principal towns and directly related to the native inhabitants there, the Pimas (and through them their Opa and Cocomaricopa allies) had most contact with the Spaniards, but the people of the Colorado also made trips to the Spanish settlements. During this period the fever for California was not yet burning high in Spanish blood and the Colorado Indians were generally ignored; only the Halchidhoma, while visiting their relatives on the Gila, had much status in Spanish eyes. But the long-standing quarrels on the Colorado continued with the additional impetus of the slave trade.

Suddenly California did become important. To protect her claims to the Pacific coast, Spain in 1769 sent missionaries and soldiers up the peninsula and by sea to San Diego and Monterey to counter the Russian threat from the north. But the land trip was arduous and the sea trip dangerous, and more people were needed to reach farther north to San Francisco Bay. So there was refurbished the dream of a land route from Sonora—down the Gila and across the Colorado, in by the back door. As keepers of that door the Yumas became important and were consequently wooed. Gifts and honors were showered upon the men who were accepted by the Spaniards as leaders of the nation; much attention and effort was applied to achieve permanent peace among the groups on the two rivers.

To ensure that the door stayed open priests, colonists, and soldiers were established in 1780 in Yuma territory as a base for further pacification of the entire river. At first the Spaniards, both civilian and military, were welcomed because they represented an immediate source of goods and honors as well as a means of direct access to the slave markets and seats of authority in the interior — the Yuma became the only group on the two rivers to have priests of their own. But their satisfaction soon faded as it became apparent that this also meant Spanish control of themselves, their land, and their relations with their neighbors. When colonists and livestock on their way to California damaged fields and depleted their food supplies, the Yumas decided they would be better off without the additional honor and killed most of the resident Spaniards, civilian and military alike, and took the remainder captive. Punitive expeditions from both California and Sonora were exercises in futility even though the latter were enthusiastically joined by Halchidhoma, Cocomaricopa, and Pima allies from Tubutama in Sonora.

Between skirmishes, some of the captured Spaniards were traded for goods and the few captive Indians, but then the Yumas simply faded away, leaving the Spaniards nothing upon which to vent their wrath but a few easily replaceable huts. The Spaniards returned home to west and south as affairs closer to the centers of population claimed their attention, leaving the Yumas once more to build their villages and nurse a justifiable conviction that the Halchidhoma and Cocomaricopa not only were not their friends but were also liable to become intolerably powerful as a result of their alliance with the Spaniards.

For four decades more the Indians of the two rivers were relatively free of direct Spanish interference in their internecine relationships. Spain's position as a world power was deteriorating; Sonora was beset in the lowlands by intransigent natives and from the northeastern mountains by Apaches and their allies; California was concentrating on solidifying control of the coast. But direct interference was not necessary to maintain impact. The feed-back of slave raid, vengeance raid with some capture, return vengeance raid, continued to operate to such an extent that the Halyikwamai and Kohuana moved north of the Yuma to occupy space next to the larger Halchidhoma group (thus placing these three tribes between the allied Yuma and Mohave and leaving no barrier between the Yuma and their Cocopa enemies to the south) and a few "Indians from the Colorado" made attempts to migrate into the mission areas of the coast but were discouraged by the authorities there as tending to be disruptive of Spanish control. All of the groups on the rivers continued the long-established pattern of visiting both the California and Sonoran settlements, maintaining their contacts with Indian allies and learning at firsthand the functioning of the Spanish power structure.

On the Gila, the Opa and Cocomaricopa withdrew somewhat upstream, removing themselves slightly further from the Yuma. The more easterly Opa now occupied the north bank of the Gila as far east as Gila Butte, some twenty-five miles upstream from its junction with the Salt River. This placed them on the eastern side of the Sierra Estrella and off the established flow of east-west travel which moved south of the Estrellas and directly between the western terminus of the bend of the Gila (near modern Gila Bend) and Pima Butte, rather than following the Gila River on its big curve north of the Estrellas. This move was the first of a series of related events which resulted in the modern term of "Maricopa."

From the time of the first Hispanic contacts there had been two Yuman-speaking groups on the lower Gila—the Opa upstream to the east and the Cocomaricopa downstream. When detailing trips to the river the Spanish reports identified both groups. Reports written inland, however, away from the river sometimes only noted the Cocomaricopa and all records of Gila River Yumans visiting the interior settlements identified the Indians as Comomaricopa. During the entire Mexican period all Yuman speakers on the Gila were labeled Cocomaricopas with no recognition being given to the mixed ethnic origins of the individual there. Presumably the Opa were less given to traveling and less aggressive than the Cocomaricopas; they had, indeed, been the first portion of the Halchidhoma to leave the Colorado when Yuma pressure began to build there.

Unlike the Cocomaricopa (who recall today the move from their former location west of Sierra Estrella and reject the Piman appellation Cocomaricopa for their own Yuman name of Kaveltcadom), the Opa, although still the largest element among the Gila River Yumans, have no memory of any other location for themselves and accept for themselves the Pima-based, American-imposed term of "Maricopa." When they moved out of the mainstream of traffic, their name disappeared into oblivion, although they themselves and their new location were to be the magnet toward which all future Yuman movement was to flow.

Mexico's achievement of independence from Spain had little immediate effect on the Indians of the two rivers; they had never been "controlled" in any sense of the word, and the personnel with whom they had contact in Sonora and California did not appreciably change. It did create, however, a situation which was to increase the pressures on the rivers. The circumstances of the political instability and relative poverty of the central government demanded that Sonora and California rely more upon their own resources and encouraged them, as the farthest removed from the seat of authority, to consider cooperation between them as at least a partial answer to some of their problems.

On the frontier the first sign of this increased cooperation was the establishment of the Cocomaricopa Mail in 1821. Official correspondence for at least a half dozen years was carried from interior Sonora to villages on the Gila River, west along its course to Agua Caliente, northwest to the Halchidhoma on the Colorado and across desert and mountainous California to the coastal settlements, over a road long before established, the couriers being Cocomaricopas and Halchidhomas. During this same period a Baja California priest traveled to Sonora and returned there with a military escort by way of the Cocopa in the delta area. The military escort delayed on the coast for a time but finally returned to Sonora by way of the Cocomaricopa road, being met at Agua Caliente by a group of soldiers from Sonora. All of these larger events bypassed the Yumas and enhanced the Cocomaricopa and Halchidhoma in Mexican eyes, although the Yuma were visited by parties of soldiers from both California and Sonora.

Although these actions were only intended to secure for the Mexicans a choice of routes to California, the Yumas presumably felt threatened by them, and the appearance of American trappers on the lower Gila and Colorado by way of Cocomaricopa territory did little to reassure the Yuma. Beginning in 1827 the Yumas increased their pressure against the Halchidhoma, with the active cooperation of the Mohave, so effectively that by 1829 all of the remaining Halchidhoma had left the Colorado, most of them going to Caborca in upper Sonora to stay with Piman friends while maintaining communication with their relatives on the Gila.

In 1833 there was instituted on the Gila River a custom which makes possible a more accurate account of Gila-Colorado conflict, or at least the more serious aspects of it. In that year several calendar rods were begun, whereby each year meaningful marks were made upon a record stick so that in the future the rod-keeper could recall with accuracy any significant events for that period. One of the events so recorded for the first year was a Yuma raid upon the Gila River group. Having attacked the "Maricopas" successfully, the Yumas were attempting to make off with captured women when they were in turn attacked by the Pimas and nearly all Yumas were killed.

As increasing numbers of Sonorans and Californians began to use the Colorado route through Yuma territory and more American trappers moved through and around the area, the restlessness of the Yumas was increased by communication from California of discontent with the mission situation resulting in minor uprisings of the unmissionized Indians and individual desertions of the neophytes. Although few Colorado Indians actively participated in the California disturbances, numerous deserters reached the river with tales of the unpleasant aspects of Mexican rule, and frequent requests were made for assistance in the revolts.

Shortly after 1835, three events contributed to the creation of the modern "Maricopa." A plague in Sonora killed many of the Halchidhoma there and the few surviving left to join the Opas on the Gila, settling in the upstream area just west of Gila Butte. Shortly thereafter the tattered remnants of the Halyikawamai and Kohuana, weary of being both buffeted and controlled by the Yuma and Mohave on each side of them, left the Colorado for the comparative safety of the Gila where they were allowed to occupy some of the downstream portion of Opa land near Gila Crossing. At about the same time the Cocomaricopa abandoned their former land downstream; they, too, joined the Opa on the north bank of the Gila between Gila Butte and Gila Crossing, adding their population to the group already sharing their name by default. This brought together in one area the five ethnic elements of which the modern "Maricopa" are composed.

Possibly this gathering in one area of the groups created pressures,

Studio portrait of Maricopa Indian probably taken at Yuma, Arizona. Arizona Historical Foundation photo.

for in 1841 the Cocomaricopas from the Gila Crossing area sent a war party to the Colorado. Though they killed many Yumas, most of the Cocomaricopas were killed (but the one Pima who accompanied them survived). In retaliation the Yuma came to the Gila in 1842, again in 1843, and once more in 1844. Each time death took its toll on each of the two groups, for these were not hit-and-run raids but formal battles with warning messages, champions, and battle lines. On all three occasions the Pimas responded to aid their allies in defense of their homeland.

In 1846 the first official Americans reached the Gila. General Stephen Watts Kearny was taking through to California some 100 dragoons of the Army of the West, with accompanying horses, howitzers and baggage; a month later Captain Philip St. George Cooke followed with some 350 volunteers of the Mormon Battalion. Both parties were received with enthusiasm in the Gila villages. At the Colorado they met no Indians, but Kearny did meet a party of Mexicans taking a large horse herd to Sonora. Although these particular groups had only momentary impact on the two rivers, the almost continuous presence of Americans from this time forward was to apply unremitting pressure on the Yumas. Had they not occupied the area of the only feasible ford of the Colorado River they might have been left in comparative peace as were the Cocopa and Mohave.

In the reports of these Americans is seen the last event in the creation of the modern "Maricopa," the first appearance in the literature of the name in its present form, although a variation (Coco Maricopa) was to continue in use for some time. Through attrition, amalgamation and elision five previously independent nations became one, and that one would henceforth be identified by a label which none had ever claimed as its own.

In October 1848 a party of Maricopa warriors travelled toward the Colorado for a joint effort with the Cocopa against the Yumas. Their timing was unfortunate, however, for before the Cocopa arrived they were discovered by the Yuma and at least thirty warriors and Chief Antoine were killed while the Yumas escaped with minimum casualties. When the Cocopa appeared six days later, they too suffered disproportionate losses from an already alerted Yuma force. Although on their return the Maricopa informed Captain Graham's force (then on its way to California) that they were preparing for revenge, it apparently was delayed until the next year when in October they attacked the people of a village on the east bank of the Colorado and killed most of the defending force. A few escaped to the west bank where they sought, but were refused, safety in the American camp there. This encampment had been set up for the convenience of the Mexican-United States

Boundary Commission then attempting to define the particulars of the northern boundary of Mexico as called for by the Treaty of Guadalupe Hidalgo ending the war with Mexico.

Although it was in existence for only three months, the Boundary Commission camp with its complement of soldiers represented the forerunner of a larger and more permanent military force soon to be established there. It also set the pattern for Yuma-American contact for the future—the Yuma were to be tolerated so long as they behaved and did not disturb the Americans. Gold had been discovered in California and there was even then beginning to enter the area the forerunners of the thousands who travelled the southern route to California, all of them by necessity forced to use that ford on the Colorado. This was too valuable a piece of property to be left in the hands of "uncivilized" Indians, and they soon lost it. First to move in was a small band of adventurers who took over not only their ford but also their provisions and their women. The Yumas promptly killed them; but to no avail. More gentlemanly personnel reestablished the ferry, protected by a force of the United States Army which gradually increased in size as it extended its control over more and more of Yuma life.

If the Yuma had hoped that this, too, would be a temporary thing, they were soon disillusioned. When they struck out at the Maricopa in 1850 or 1851, it was easily seen that there was no American military oppression on the Gila. When they paused to taunt the stunned Maricopa, a Pima force routed them, and hounded the survivors through the thickets. Back on the Colorado they could only see increasingly a future filled to the horizon with waves of white men taking over their land—more Boundary Commission personnel, increased numbers of soldiers, well protected railroad survey teams, a steamer beginning regular trips up their Colorado, a city founded on their land, an imposed peace with the Cocopa—year after year, with no relief in sight.

Possibly the catalyst was a combination of an increase in the number of soldiers at Fort Yuma and the intelligence that Maricopa and Pima warriors were fighting with the United States Army against the Apaches; perhaps the Maricopas would now come against them backed by American might, just as they had with Spanish backing some seventy-five years before. In any case, they once more broke the peace with the Cocopa and then turned their attention eastward to forge the last link in the chain that had its beginning far to the south and long ago.

A dying chief predicted from his death bed that a campaign against their mortal enemies would result in their complete overthrow; and a warrior from downstream of the ferry verified this in a dream. Up the river through the villages, beyond to the Mohaves and eastward to the Yavapais went the message: "Come and bring your friends. Join us some days hence, and we will gain honors while we humble the Maricopa." Secure in the knowledge that their call would be answered, they completed preparations and began the long trip with eagerness. But the chief at the ferry was visited by a contrary dream and persuaded all but a few of his fighters not to go. Never mind, one hundred Yumas were enough alone, and soon they would be joined by Mohaves in numbers and Yavapais untold. Up the river they traveled tirelessly until they met the Mohaves 200 strong, then eastward into Yavapai country, skirting the bases of the mountains breaking the flat plains. Seven days they pressed forward from the river; then cautiously for Maricopa country was near. Here came the Yavapais to meet them, down out of the mountains on their best horses, ready this time to do battle rather than raid. Across the Agua Fria they swarmed, then south to cross the Salt well before dawn. Softly now, soon they would be there. Now! in among the first houses, smashing, stabbing, closing in to overcome. Let those in the distance go; they will only bring more for us to scalp. But first let us eat; we have come a long way and the Maricopas have hospitably prepared breakfast. Do they know that we are laughing at them, women that they all are, only fit to cook breakfast for men?

The Maricopas knew. But they had to bide their time awaiting reinforcements. Word had been sent to the Maricopas farther upstream and to the Pimas beyond, but it took time for a warrior properly to prepare himself—paint just so, weapons tested—but soon they were on

Yuma Indians. A photo taken by E. A. Bonine in his studio at Yuma, Arizona, about 1880. Arizona Historical Foundation photograph.

their way. When the sun was high they were ready, only to be met by a reinvigorated, well-fed enemy, tired of finding only empty houses to burn. As the smoke climbed straight up into the endless sky, champions voiced their insults and casually disposed of their opponents. Desperately the Maricopas hurled themselves against their foes only to fall back outnumbered. Higher the smoke climbed, and higher, until its message of urgency was broadcast afar. And the mounted Pimas came with a rush.

At the first shock the Yavapais scattered, daunted by the shift in fortune. Some few stayed to watch from a hill, but most did not delay. Two-thirds of the Mohave retreated, turning back on the long road home.

The Maricopa and Pima pressed forward, forcing the Yuma and loyal Mohave across the Gila and into the plain in the shadow of the Estrellas. Here there was the room to make good use of the horse, and nowhere were thickets for fainthearted to hide. Desperate, the invaders rallied their manpower, taking advantage of a mound on the plain; clubs forward, lances over, they made their last stand. Now was the chance for Maricopa triumph, revenge for the damage previously done. Inward they drove at the defensive circle, deeper and deeper, to meet in the end. Over the plain the horsemen now scattered, clubbing to death those not on the mound.

Silence descended slowly on the plain, then was shattered by mourning Maricopa women as they identified their own dead. Yuma

Above: Maricopa Indian, photo taken by Hartwell in studio in Phoenix, Arizona, about 1880. Arizona Collections photo, Arizona State University.
Left: Yuma Indians in studio photo by E. A. Bonine about 1880. Photo courtesy Arizona Historical Foundation.

and Mohave mourning would come later as the very few who survived made their way home. Left untouched on the slowly darkening plain, the invading dead would never be allowed into the afterworld, for there were none to burn them. But many cremation fires would burn on the Gila for the Maricopa dead.

Never again would the Maricopa be compelled to defend themselves, nor to go forth to avenge their dead. Battered and bruised, reduced in number as they were, yet they were now free to cultivate their chosen land in peace and face the future as best they might.

NOTES

It would be a pointless exercise to list the sources for the histories of Spain, Mexico, and the United States of which the "Battle On the Gila" formed a part. Beyond them, the following have been drawn upon for the geographically immediate developments which culminated in 1857, in the cremation fires of the Maricopa.

Lowell J. Bean and William M. Mason, *Diaries and Accounts of the Romero Expeditions in Arizona and California, 1823-1826,* Palm Springs: Desert Museum, 1962.

George W. Beattie, "Reopening the Anza Road," *Pacific Historical Review,* vol. II, 1933, pp. 52-71.

Herbert E. Bolton (ed.), *Kino's Historical Memoir, Pimería Alta...1683-1711,* Cleveland: Arthur H. Clark Co., 1919. 2 vols. Republished in 1 vol., Univ. of California Press, 1948.

_____, *Anza's California Expeditions,* Berkeley: Univ. of California Press, 1930, 5 vols.

Henry F. Dobyns, Paul H. Ezell, Alden W. Jones and Greta S. Ezell, "Thematic Changes in Yuman Warfare," in V. F. Ray (ed.), *Cultural Stability and Cultural Change,* Proceedings of Ann. Meeting, Am. Ethnological Soc., 1957, pp. 46-71.

Henry F. Dobyns (ed.), *Hepah California! The Journal of Cave Johnson Couts...1848-1849,* Tucson: Arizona Pioneers' Historical Society, 1961.

Henry F. Dobyns, Paul H. and Greta S. Ezell, "Death of a Society," American Anthropological Association *Memoir 90,* 1961.

William H. Emory, "Notes of a Military Reconnaisance from Fort Leavenworth...to San Diego," in 30th Cong., 1st Sess., *Sen. Ex. Doc.* No. 7, Washington, 1848. Reprinted with introduction and notes by Ross Calvin as *Lieutenant Emory Reports,* University of New Mexico Press, 1951.

Paul H. Ezell, "The Cocomaricopa Mail," *Brand Book Number One,* The San Diego Corral of the Westerners, 1968, pp. 28-34.

_____, "The Hispanic Acculturation of the Gila River Pimas," American Anthropological Association *Memoir 90,* 1961.

_____, "The Maricopas: An Identification from Documentary Sources," *Anthropological Papers*, No. 6, Univ. of Arizona Press, Tucson, 1963.

Jack D. Forbes, *Warriors of the Colorado: The Yumas of the Quechan Nation and Their Neighbors*, Norman: Univ. of Oklahoma Press, 1965.

E. W. Gifford, "The Cocopa," Univ. of Calif. *Publications* in American Archaeology and Ethnology, XXXI, 1933, pp. 257-334.

Abraham K. Johnston, "Journal of...," in Emory, *Notes of a Mil. Reconn.*, pp. 567-614.

Harry J. Karns (Transl.), *Unknown Arizona and Sonora, 1693-1701, by Juan M. Manje*, Tucson: Arizona Silhouettes, 1954.

A. L. Kroeber, "Handbook of the Indians of California," *Bulletin* of the Bureau of American Ethnology, LXXVIII, 1925.

Malcolm J. Rogers, "An Outline of Yuman Prehistory," *Southwestern Journal of Anthropology*, vol. 1, no. 2, pp. 157-198.

Gerónimo de Zarate Salmeron, "Relaciones de todas las cosas que en el Nuevo Mexico se han visto y sabido...desde el año 1538 hasta el de 1626," *Documentos para la historia de México*. Third Series.

Amiel W. Whipple, "Journal of an Expedition from San Diego, California, to the Rio Colorado,...1849," in 31st Cong., 2nd Sess., *Sen. Ex. Doc.* No. 19, Washington, 1851. Reprinted with introduction, notes and bibliography by E. I. Edwards as *The Whipple Report*, Los Angeles: Westernlore Press, 1961.

Sources containing specific references to the battle are:

J. Ross Browne, *Adventures in the Apache Country: A Tour Through Arizona and Sonora, with Notes on the Silver Region of Nevada*, Harper, 1869.

John C. Cremony, *Life Among the Apaches*, San Francisco, A. Roman Co., 1868; Facsimile reprint Tucson: Arizona Silhouettes, 1951.

E. W. Gifford, "Yuma Dreams and Omens," *Journal of American Folklore*, XXXIX, 1926, pp. 58-69.

_____, "Northeastern and Western Yavapai," University of California *Publications* in American Archaeology and Ethnology, XXXIV, 1936, pp. 247-354.

Joseph C. Ives, "Report Upon the Colorado River of the West, Explored in 1857 and 1858," in 36th Cong., 1st Sess., *House Exec. Doc. 90*, 1861.

A. L. Kroeber, "Earth Tongue, A Mohave," in *American Indian Life*, edited by E. C. Parsons, New York, 1925, pp. 189-202, 243.

Sylvester Mowry, "Indians of Arizona," in 35th Cong., 1st Sess., Ex. Doc. 2, vol. 2, Part I, Washington, 1857, a letter to Hon. T. W. Denver, Commissioner of Indian Affairs, pp. 584-593.

Frank Russell, "The Pima Indians," *Annual Report* Bureau of American Ethnology, XXVII, 1908, pp. 3-390.

Leslie Spier, *Yuman Tribes of the Gila River*, Chicago: Univ. of Chicago Press, 1940.

George Webb, *A Pima Remembers*, Tucson: Univ. of Arizona Press, 1959.

A Select Bibliography of Articles on Military & Indian Conflicts on the American Frontier

by Harry A. Shiley

Anonymous, "The Indian Massacres and War of 1862," *Harper's Monthly Magazine*, Vol. 27, pp. 1-24, 1863.

_____, "Three Noted Chiefs of the Sioux: Sitting Bull, John Grass and Chief Gall," *Harper's Weekly Magazine*, Vol. 34, pp. 995-996, Dec. 20, 1890.

_____, "The Mexican and Indian Raid of '78," *Quarterly of the Texas State Historical Association*, Vol. 5, pp. 212-251, 1901/02.

_____, "Savage Treachery," *Nebraska History Magazine*, Vol. 22, pp. 119-122, 1941.

_____, "Some Causes of Indian Wars," *Nebraska History Magazine*, Vol. 22, pp. 103-105, 1941.

_____, "Battles and Skirmishes in Wyoming Territory—1853-1882," *Annals of Wyoming*, Vol. 14, pp. 240-242, 1942.

_____, "An Apache's Story of the Indian Wars," *Scenic Southwest*, pp. 1, 3-5, Jan. 1943; pp. 2, 4-5, Feb. 1943.

_____, "Investigations as to Causes of Indian Hostilities West of the Missouri River, 1824," *Annals of Wyoming*, Vol. 15, pp. 198-220, 1943.

_____, "Defending Puget Sound Against the Northern Indians," *Pacific Northwest Quarterly*, Vol. 26, pp. 69-78, 1945.

_____, "Lincoln's Sioux War Order," *Minnesota History*, Vol. 33, pp. 77-79, 1953.

_____, "Seattle's First Taste of Battle, 1856," *Pacific Northwest Quarterly*, Vol. 47(1), pp. 1-8, 1956.

190 _____, "Generals Crook and Miles in Arizona: From the Contemporary Accounts of Fellow Soldiers," *The Smoke Signal, Tucson Corral of the Westerners.* Vol. 15, Spring 1967.

Adams, J., "In the Stronghold of the Piutes," *Overland*, Vol. 22, Series 2, pp. 583-593, Dec. 1893.

Allen, Charles W., "Red Cloud and the U. S. Flag," *Nebraska History Magazine*, Vol. 21, pp. 293-304, 1940.

Allred, B. W., "Massacre of the Dull Knife Band," *Great Western Indian Fights*, Bison Book, University of Nebraska Press, Lincoln, 4th printing, pp. 295-302, 1969.

Anderson, Clinton P., "Canyon De Chelly," see *Great Western Indian Fights*, Bison Book, University of Nebraska Press, Lincoln, 4th printing, pp. 94-101, 1969.

Anderson, Harry, "A Sioux Pictorial Account of General Terry's Council at Fort Walsh, October 17, 1877," *North Dakota History*, Vol. 22, pp. 93-116, 1955.

Anderson, Hattie M. (ed.), "Mining and Indian Fighting in Arizona and New Mexico, 1858-1861," *Panhandle Plains Historical Review*, Vol. 1, pp. 67-115, 1928; Vol. 2, pp. 65-97, 1928.

Andrist, R. K., "Massacre! Minnesota's Sioux Uprising," *American Heritage*, Vol. 13, pp. 8-17, 108-111, April 1962.

Appleman, Roy E., "The Wagon Box Fight," see *Great Western Indian Fights*, Bison Book, University of Nebraska Press, Lincoln, 4th printing, pp. 148-162, 1969.

_____, "The Hayfield Fight," see *Great Western Indian Fights*, Bison Book, University of Nebraska Press, Lincoln, 4th printing, pp. 132-147, 1969.

_____, "The Fetterman Fight," see *Great Western Indian Fights*, Bison Book, University of Nebraska Press, Lincoln, 4th printing, pp. 117-131, 1969.

Arnold, Elliot, "Cochise, Greatest of the Apaches," *Reader's Digest*, Vol. 58, pp. 69-72, April 1951.

Arnold, Lt. Col. Frazer, "Ghost Dance and Wounded Knee," *Cavalry Journal*, Vol. 43, pp. 18-20, 1943.

Athearn, Robert G. (ed.), "Major Hough's March into Southern Ute Country, 1879," *Colorado Magazine*, Vol. 25, pp. 97-109, 1948.

_____, "The Fort Buford 'Massacre'," *Mississippi Valley Historical Review*, Vol. 41, pp. 675-684, 1955.

_____, "Colorado and the Indian War of 1868," *Colorado Magazine*, Vol. 33, pp. 42-51, 1956.

_____, "War Paint Against Brass: The Army and the Plains Indians," *Montana Magazine of History*, Vol. 6, pp. 11-22, 1956.

Ayers, John, "A Soldier's Experience in New Mexico," *New Mexico Historical Review*, Vol. 24, pp. 259-266, 1949.

Bagley, Clarence B., "Our First Indian War," *Washington Historical Quarterly*, Vol. 1, pp. 34-49, Oct. 1907.

_____, "Attitude of the Hudson's Bay Company During the Indian War of 1855-1856," *Washington Historical Quarterly*, Vol. 8, pp. 291-307, 1917.

Bailey, Paul D., "The Navajo Wars," *Arizoniana: the Journal of Arizona History*, Vol. 2, No. 2, pp. 3-12, Summer, 1961.

Baird, G. W., "General Miles' Indian Campaigns," *Century Magazine*, Vol. 42 (ns 20), pp. 351-370, July 1891.

Ball, Eve (with Jasper Kanseah), "The Last of Geronimo's Warriors," *New Mexico Magazine*, Vol. 33, pp. 17, 42-43, June 1955.

Ball, Eve, "The Apache Scouts: A Chiricahua Appraisal," *Arizona and the West*, Vol. 7, pp. 315-328, 1965.

Barnes, Will Croft, "The Apaches' Last Stand in Arizona, The Battle of the Big Dry Wash," *Arizona Historical Review*, Vol. 3(4), pp. 36-59, 1930/31.

_____, "The Battle of Cibecue," *Arizona Highways*, pp. 7, 18-20, March 1936.

Barney, James M., "The Cochise Indian War in Arizona," *Sheriff Magazine*, pp. 29ff., March 1954.

_____, "The Hassaympa Ambuscade," *Arizona Highways*, pp. 11, 18-21, Oct. 1955.

Barsness, John and William Dickinson, "Minute Men of Montana," *Montana*, Vol. 10(2), pp. 2-9, 1960.

Bearss, Edwin C., "Fort Smith as the Agency for the Western Choctaws," *Arkansas Historical Quarterly*, Vol. 27(1), pp. 40-58, 1968.

Bell, J. N., "Massacre of Wounded Knee," *Coronet*, Vol. 40, pp. 78-80, June 1956.

Bellah, J. W., "Thirty-nine Days to Glory," *Holiday*, Vol. 26, pp. 68-69, 124-128, Sept. 1959.

Bender, A. B., "The Soldier in the Far West, 1848-1860," *Pacific Historical Review*, Vol. 8, pp. 159-178, 1939.

Benedict, J. W., "Diary of a Campaign Against the Comanches," *Southwestern Historical Quarterly*, Vol. 32, pp. 300-310, 1928/29.

Benjamin, Peggy H., "The Last of Captain Jack," *Montana*, Vol. 10(2), pp. 22-31, 1960.

Bennett, Burton Estelle, "Volunteer Soldiers of New Mexico and Their Conflicts with the Indians in 1862 and 1863," *Old Santa Fe*, Vol. 1, No. 4, pp. 386-419, April 1914.

Benson, Major H. D., "The Geronimo Campaign," *Army and Navy Journal*, pp. 1240-1248, July 3, 1909.

Berthrong, Donald J., "John Beach and the Removal of the Sauk and Fox from Iowa," *Iowa Journal of History and Politics*, Vol. 54, pp. 313-334, 1956.

Bigler, David L., "The Crisis at Fort Limhi, 1858," *Utah Historical Quarterly*, Vol. 35(2), pp. 121-136, 1967.

Bischoff, William N., "The Yakima Campaign of 1856," *Mid-America*, Vol. 31, pp. 163-169, 1949.

192   Blegen, Theodore C. (ed.), "Armistice and War on the Minnesota Frontier: Sioux and Chippeways, by Ezekiel G. Gear," *Minnesota History*, Vol. 24, pp. 11-25, 1943.

Blount, Bertha, "The Apache in the Southwest, 1846-1886," *Southwestern Historical Quarterly*, Vol. 23, pp. 20-38, 1919/20.

Bourke, John G., "The Indian Messiah," *Nation*, pp. 439-440, Dec. 4, 1890.

_____, "General Crook in the Indian Country," *The Century Magazine*, Vol. 40, No. 5, pp. 643-660, March 1891.

Brandes, Ray, "The Scalp Business on the Border, 1837-1850," *The Smoke Signal, Tucson Corral of the Westerners*, No. 6, pp. 1-3, Fall 1962.

Brinckerhoff, Sidney B., "Camp Date Creek, Arizona Territory: Infantry Outpost in the Yavapai Wars, 1867-1873," *The Smoke Signal, Tucson Corral of the Westerners*, No. 10, Fall 1964.

Brininstool, E. A., "How 'Crazy Horse' Died," *Nebraska History Magazine*, Vol. 12, pp. 4-78, 1929.

Brooks, Juanita, "Indian Relations on the Mormon Frontier," *Utah Historical Quarterly*, Vol. 12, pp. 1-48, 1944.

Brown, D. Alexander, "The Ghost Dance and Battle of Wounded Knee," *American History Illustrated*, Vol. 1(8), pp. 4-16, 1966.

Brown, J. Henry, "The Biggest Little War in American History," *Oregon Historical Quarterly*, Vol. 50, pp. 98-121, 1949.

Brown, Mark H., and W. R. Felton, "L. A. Huffman, Brady of the West," *Montana Magazine of History*, Vol. 6(1), pp. 29-37, 1956.

Browning, D. M., "Indian Disturbances in 'Jackson Hole' Country, Wyoming, 1895," *Annals of Wyoming*, Vol. 16, pp. 5-33, 1944-46.

Burkey, Elmer R., "The Thornburgh Battle with the Utes on Milk Creek," *Colorado Magazine*, Vol. 13, pp. 90-110, 1936.

Burns, Robert Ignatius, S.J., "A Jesuit in the War Against the Northern Indians," *Records of the American Catholic Historical Society of Philadelphia*, Vol. 61, pp. 9-54, 1950.

Byrne, P. E., "The Custer Myth," *North Dakota Historical Quarterly*, Vol. 6, pp. 187-200, 1931/32.

Call, Ambrose A., "Indians Repelled in Kossuth," *Annals of Iowa*, Vol. 31, pp. 81-90, 1951-53.

Campbell, W. S., "The Cheyenne Dog Soldiers," *Chronicles of Oklahoma*, Vol. 1, pp. 90-97, 1921.

Cargill, Andrew Hays, "The Camp Grant Massacre," *Arizona Historical Review*, Vol. 7(3), pp. 73-79, 1936.

Carr, Camillo Casatti Cadmus, "The Days of the Empire — Arizona, 1866-1869," *Journal of the United States Cavalry Association*, pp. 3-22, March 1899.

Carroll, John Alexander, "Echoes from the Little Bighorn," *The Smoke Signal, Tucson Corral of the Westerners*, No. 2 (reprinted 1967), Fall 1960.

Chacon, Major Rafael, "Campaign Against Utes and Apaches in Southern Colorado, 1855," *Colorado Magazine*, Vol. 11, No. 3, pp. 108-112, May 1934.

Christiansen, Paige W., "The Apache Barrier," *Rocky Mountain Social Science Journal*, Vol. 3(2), pp. 93-108, 1966.

Clark, Dan E., "Frontier Defense in Iowa, 1850-1865," *Iowa Journal of History and Politics*, Vol. 16, pp. 315-386, 1918.

Clarke, Powhatan, "A Hot Trail," *Cosmopolitan*, p. 706, Oct. 1894.

Clum, John P., "Apache Misrule—A Bungling Agent Sets the Military Arm in Motion," *New Mexico Historical Review*, Vol. 5, pp. 138-153, 221-239, 1930; also in *Arizona Historical Review*, Vol. 4 (1), pp. 56-68; (2) pp. 52-64; (3) pp. 64-71, 1931.

_____, "Geronimo," *Arizona Historical Review*, Vol. 1 (2), pp. 14-49, 1928; (3) pp. 13-35; also in *New Mexico Historical Review*, Vol. 3, pp. 1-40, 121-144, 217-264, 1928.

_____, "Victorio, Chief of the Warm Spring Apaches," *Arizona Historical Review*, Vol. 2 (4), pp. 74-90, 1929/30.

_____, "Es-kim-in-zin," *New Mexico Historical Review*, Vol. 3, pp. 399-420, Oct. 1928; Vol. 4, No. 1, pp. 1-26, Jan. 1929.

_____, "The San Carlos Apache Police," *New Mexico Historical Review*, Vol. 4, pp. 203-219, 1929; Vol. 5, pp. 67-97, Jan. 1930; also in *Arizona Historical Review*, Vol. 3 (2), pp. 12-25, 1930/31; (3) pp. 21-43.

Coad, Mark M., "Story of Indian Fighting in 1864," *Nebraska History Magazine*, Vol. 6, pp. 102-108, 1923.

Coburn, Wallace David (as told the author by Maj. Will A. Logan), "The Battle of the Little Big Horn," *Montana*, Vol. 6(3), pp. 28-41, 1956.

Coffman, Edward M., "Army Life on the Frontier, 1865-1898," *Military Affairs*, Vol. 20(4), pp. 193-201, 1956.

Colby, Brig. Gen. L. W., "The Sioux Indian War of 1890-1891," *Transactions and Reports of the Nebraska State Historical Society*, Vol. 3, pp. 144-190, 1892.

_____, "Wanagi Olowan Kin (The Ghost Songs of the Dakotas)," *Proceedings and Collections of the Nebraska State Historical Society*, Vol. 1, 2d ser., pp. 131-150, 1895.

Compton, Lawrence V., "The First Battle of Adobe Walls," see *Great Western Indian Fights*, Bison Book, University of Nebraska Press, Lincoln, 4th printing, pp. 102-107, 1969.

Cook, J. H., "Art of Fighting Indians," *American Mercury*, Vol. 23, pp. 170-179, June 1931.

Cornish, D. T., "Ute Indian Trouble in Colorado," *Colorado Magazine*, Vol. 25, pp. 220-232, Sept. 1948.

194 Covington, James Warren (ed.), "Ute Scalp Dance in Denver," *Colorado Magazine*, Vol. 30, pp. 119-124, 1953.

_____, "Federal Relations with the Colorado Utes, 1861-1865," *Colorado Magazine*, Vol. 28, pp. 257-266, 1951.

_____, "Causes of the Dull Knife Raid, 1878," *Chronicles of Oklahoma*, Vol. 26, pp. 13-22, 1948.

Cox, John E., "Soldiering in Dakota Territory in the Seventies, A Communication," *North Dakota Historical Quarterly*, Vol. 6, pp. 63-81, 1931/32.

Cressman, L. S., "Lower Columbia Indian Weapons," *Oregon Historical Quarterly*, Vol. 49, pp. 297-298, 1948.

Crimmins, Martin L. (ed.), "Colonel Robert E. Lee's Report on Indian Combats in Texas," *Southwestern Historical Quarterly*, Vol. 39, pp. 21-32, 1935/36.

Cubage, Annie Rosser, "Engagement at Cabin Creek, Indian Territory, July 1st and 2nd, 1863," *Chronicles of Oklahoma*, Vol. 10, pp. 44-51, 1932.

Cullens, J., "Custer's Last Stand," *Army Quarterly and Defense Journal* (Great Britain), Vol. 90(1), pp. 104-109, 1965.

Daly, H. W., "The Geronimo Campaign," *Arizona Historical Review*, Vol. 3(2), pp. 26-44, 1930/31.

Daniell, Forrest, "Texas Pioneer Surveyors and Indians," *Southwestern Historical Quarterly*, Vol. 60(4), pp. 501-506, 1956/57.

Davis, H. L., "Last Indian Outbreak, 1906," *American Mercury*, Vol. 30, pp. 50-57, Sept. 1933.

D'Elia, Donald J., "The Argument Over Civilian or Military Indian Control, 1865-1880," *Historian*, Vol. 24(2), pp. 207-225, 1962.

Deming, E. W., "Custer's Last Stand; Indians' Version," *Literary Digest*, Vol. 90, pp. 36-40, July 10, 1926.

Dempsey, Hugh A., "Cypress Hills Massacre," *Montana Magazine of History*, Vol. 3, pp. 1-9, Autumn 1953.

De Rudio, C., "Incident in the Little Big Horn Fight," *Harper's Weekly*, Vol. 41, pp. 949-950, Sept. 25, 1897.

Deutsch, Herman J., "Indian and White in the Inland Empire," *Pacific Northwest Quarterly*, Vol. 47(2), pp. 44-51, 1956.

Dillon, Richard H., "Costs of the Modoc War," *California Historical Society Quarterly*, Vol. 28, pp. 161-164, 1949.

Dodd, Jack, "The Soldiers Have Theirs: Four Lakes and Spokane Plains," see *Great Western Indian Fights*, Bison Book, University of Nebraska Press, Lincoln, 4th printing, pp. 61-72, 1969.

_____, "The Indians Have an Inning: To-Hoto-Nim-Me," see *Great Western Indian Fights*, Bison Book, University of Nebraska Press, Lincoln, 4th printing, pp. 50-60, 1969.

Dougherty, Capt. W. E., "The Recent Messiah Craze," *Journal of the Military Service Institution of the United States*, Vol. 12, pp. 576-578, 1891.

Dunn, William Edward, "Apache Relations in Texas, 1718-1750," *Quarterly of the Texas State Historical Association*, Vol. 14, pp. 198-274, 1910/11.

Dykes, J. C., "The Battle of Palo Duro Canyon," see *Great Western Indian Fights*, Bison Book, University of Nebraska Press, Lincoln, 4th printing, pp. 214-220, 1969.

_____, "The Second Battle of Adobe Walls," see *Great Western Indian Fights*, Bison Book, University of Nebraska Press, Lincoln, 4th printing, pp. 203-213, 1969.

Eastman, Elaine Goodale, "The Ghost Dance War and Wounded Knee Massacre of 1890-91," *Nebraska History Magazine*, Vol. 26, pp. 26-42, 1945.

Eaton, George O., "A String for the Bow: An Incident of the Apache Wars," *Winners of the West*, Vol. 15, No. 3, Sept. 1938.

Ediger, Theodore A., and Vinnie Hoffman, "Some Reminiscences of the Battle of the Washita: Moving Behind's Story of the Battle of Washita," *Chronicles of Oklahoma*, Vol. 33, pp. 137-141, 1955.

Elliott, T. C., "Steptoe Butte and Steptoe Battle-field," *Washington Historical Quarterly*, Vol. 18, pp. 243-253, 1927.

Emerson, Arthur W., "The Battle of Pyramid Lake," see *Great Western Indian Fights*, Bison Book, University of Nebraska Press, Lincoln, 4th printing, pp. 73-81, 1969.

Ermatinger, Frank, "Earliest Expedition Against Puget Sound Indians," *Washington Historical Quarterly*, Vol. 1, pp. 16-29, Jan. 1907.

Ewers, John C., "Primitive American Commandos," *Hobbies*, Vol. 49, pp. 110-113, Jan. 1945.

_____, "The Indian Wars of the West," see *Great Western Indian Fights*, Bison Book, University of Nebraska Press, Lincoln, 4th printing, pp. 19-25, 1969.

Farley, Alan W., "An Indian Captivity and Its Legal Aftermath," *Kansas Historical Quarterly*, Vol. 21, pp. 247-256, 1954.

Fechet, Maj. E. G., "The True Story of the Death of Sitting Bull," *Proceedings and Collections of the Nebraska State Historical Society*, 2d ser. 2, pp. 179-189, 1898.

Fensten, Joseph J., "Indian Removal," *Chronicles of Oklahoma*, Vol. 11, pp. 1073-1083, 1933.

Fiebeger, Col. Gustave Joseph, "General Crook's Campaign in Old Mexico, in 1883," *Proceedings of the Annual Meeting of the Order of Indian Wars of the U.S. held February 20, 1936*, pp. 22-32.

Finley, Mrs. James A., "The Messiah Superstition," *Journal of American Folk-Lore*, Vol. 4, pp. 66-68, 1891.

Fisher, O. Clark, "Battle of Bandera Pass," see *Great Western Indian Fights*, Bison Book, University of Nebraska Press, Lincoln, 4th printing, pp. 41-45, 1969.

Foreman, Carolyn Thomas (ed.), "The Cherokee War Path," *Chronicles of Oklahoma*, Vol. 9, pp. 233-263, 1931.

Foreman, Grant (ed.), "In Search of the Comanches (The Journal of J. C. Eldredge)," *Panhandle Plains Historical Review*, Vol. 7, pp. 7-41, 1934.

Forsyth, General G. A., "A Frontier Fight," *Harper's Magazine*, Vol. 91, No. 541, pp. 42-62, June 1895.

_____, "Apache Raid," *Harper's Weekly Magazine*, Vol. 43, pp. 43-47, Jan. 14, 1899.

Fountain, Albert, "Lieutenant Fountain's Fight with the Apache Indians at Lillie's Ranch Mogollon Mountains, Dec. 9, 1885, and at Dry Creek, New Mexico, Dec. 19, 1885," *Proceedings of the Annual Meeting and Dinner of the Order of Indian Wars of the U.S.*, pp. 33-41, Jan. 19, 1928.

Freeman, Charles R., "The Battle of Honey Springs," *Chronicles of Oklahoma*, Vol. 13, pp. 154-168, 1935.

Freeman, Winfield, "The Battle of the Arickaree," *Kansas Historical Collections*, Vol. 6, pp. 346-367, 1910.

Frink, Maurice M., "Died Here Innocent," *Outing*, pp. 549-554, Feb. 1915.

Frost, Lawrence, "Battle of the Washita," see *Great Western Indian Fights*, Bison Book, University of Nebraska Press, Lincoln, 4th printing, pp. 175-181, 1969.

Fry, J. B., "Comments by General Fry on the Custer Battle," *Century Magazine*, Vol. 43 (ns 21), pp. 385-387, Jan. 1892.

Gardner, Hamilton, "Philip St. George Cooke and the Apache, 1854," *New Mexico Historical Review*, Vol. 28, pp. 115-132, 1953.

Gatewood, Lieutenant Charles B., "Lieut. Charles B. Gatewood, 6th U.S. Cavalry, and the Surrender of Geronimo," *Arizona Historical Review*, Vol. 4(1), pp. 29-44, 1931/32.

Gibbon, Brig. Gen. John, "Transfer of Indian Bureau to War Department," *American Catholic Quarterly Review*, Vol. 19, pp. 244-259, 1894.

_____, "Adventures of American Army and Navy Officers; The Battle of the Big Hole," *Harper's Weekly Magazine*, Vol. 39, pp. 1215-1216, 1235-1236, Dec. 21, 1895.

Gibbs, Josiah F., "Gunnison Massacre, 1853 — Millard County, Utah — Indian Mareer's Version of the Tragedy, 1894," *Utah Historical Quarterly*, Vol. 1, pp. 67-75, 1928.

_____, "Black Hawk's Last Raid, 1866," *Utah Historical Quarterly*, Vol. 4, pp. 99-108, 1931.

Glenn, Robert A., "The Osage War," *Missouri Historical Review*, Vol. 14, pp. 201-210, 1919/20.

Gluek, Alvin C., Jr., "The Sioux Uprising: A Problem in International Relations," *Minnesota History*, Vol. 34, pp. 317-324, 1955.

Godfrey, Major E. S., "Custer's Last Battle," *Century Magazine*, Vol. 43 (ns 21), pp. 358-384, Jan. 1892.

_____, "Cavalry Fire Discipline," *Journal of the Military Service Institution of the United States*, Vol. 19, p. 259, 1896.

Goodwin, Grenville (ed.), "Experiences of an Indian Scout, Excerpts from the Life of John Rope, an 'Old Timer' of the White Mountain Apaches," *Arizona Historical Review*, Vol. 7(1), pp. 31-68; (2) pp. 31-73, 1936.

Graham, W. A., "Custer Myth," *American Heritage*, Vol. 5, No. 4, pp. 30-35, June 1954.

Gray, John S., "Custer Throws a Boomerang," *Montana*, Vol. 11(2), pp. 2-12, 1961.

Green, Lt. L. D., "The Army and the Indian," *Harper's Weekly Magazine*, Vol. 38, p. 471, May 19, 1894.

Gregg, T. B., "Four Indian Horsemen Who Set the Pace for Custer," *Outlook*, Vol. 138, pp. 727-728, Dec. 31, 1924.

Gresham, Lt. John C., "The Story of Wounded Knee," *Harper's Weekly Magazine*, Vol. 35, pp. 106-107, Feb. 7, 1891.

Guthrie, John, "The Fetterman Massacre," *Annals of Wyoming*, Vol. 9, pp. 714-718, 1932/35.

Gwyther, George (M.D.), "Our Scout to Black Canyon," *Overland Monthly*, Vol. 10, pp. 123-124, Feb. 1873.

Hafen, LeRoy R., "The Fort Pueblo Massacre and the Punitive Expedition Against the Utes," *Colorado Magazine*, Vol. 4, pp. 49-58, 1927.

Hagemann, E. R., "Scout Out from Camp McDowell," *Arizoniana, the Journal of Arizona History*, Vol. 5, No. 3, pp. 29-47, Fall 1964.

Hagerty, Leroy W., "Indian Raids Along the Platte and Little Blue Rivers, 1864-1865," *Nebraska History Magazine*, Vol. 28, pp. 176-186, 239-260, 1947.

Haines, Francis (ed.), "Letters of an Army Captain on the Sioux Campaign of 1879-1880," *Pacific Northwest Quarterly*, Vol. 39, pp. 39-64, 1948.

Harrison, Lowell H., "Indians vs. Buffalo Hunters at Adobe Walls," *American History Illustrated*, Vol. 2(1), pp. 18-27, 1967.

Harrison, Michael, "Chief Charlot's Battle with Bureaucracy," *Montana*, Vol. 10(4), pp. 27-33, 1960.

Hastings, James R., "The Tragedy at Camp Grant in 1871," *Arizona and the West*, Vol. 1 (2), pp. 146-160, Summer 1959.

Hawthorne, Lt. Harry L., "The Sioux Campaign of 1890-91," *Journal of the Military Service of the United States*, Vol. 19, pp. 185-187, 1896.

Hayter, Earl W., "The Ponca Removal," *North Dakota Historical Quarterly*, Vol. 6, pp. 262-275, 1931/32.

Hembree, Waman C., "Yakima Indian War Diary," *Washington Historical Quarterly*, Vol. 16, pp. 273-283, 1925.

Henderson, Harry McCorry, "The Surveyors Fight," *Southwestern Historical Quarterly*, Vol. 56, pp. 25-35, 1952.

198 Henry, G. V., "Adventures of American Army and Navy Officers; Wounded in an Indian Fight," *Harper's Weekly Magazine*, Vol. 39, p. 627, July 1895.

Herriott, F. I., "The Aftermath of the Spirit Lake Massacre—March 8-15, 1857," *Annals of Iowa*, Vol. 18, pp. 434-470, 482-517, 597-631, 1931/33.

Holden, W. C., "Frontier Defense, 1846-1860," *West Texas Historical Association Year Book*, Vol. 6, 1930.

Hopkins, Richard C., "Kit Carson and the Navajo Expedition," *Montana*, Vol. 18(2), pp. 52-61, 1968.

Howard, Oliver O., "The True Story of the Wallowa Campaign," *North American Review*, Vol. 129, pp. 53-64, 1879.

_____, "Indian War Papers—Causes of the Piute and Bannock War," *Overland Monthly*, Vol. 9, pp. 492-498, 1887.

Howay, F. W., "Indian Attacks Upon Maritime Traders of the North-West Coast, 1785-1805," *Canadian Historical Review*, Vol. 6, pp. 287-309, 1925.

_____, "The Introduction of Intoxicating Liquors Amongst the Indians of the Northwest Coast," *British Columbia Historical Quarterly*, Vol. 6, pp. 157-169, 1942.

Hull, Myra E. (ed.), "Soldiering on the High Plains, the Diary of Lewis Byrum Hull, 1864-1866," *Kansas Historical Quarterly*, Vol. 7, pp. 3-53, 1938.

Hurst, John, "The Beecher Island Fight," *Kansas Historical Collections*, Vol. 15, pp. 530-538, 1915.

Hussey, John Adam, and George Walcott Ames, Jr., "California Preparations to Meet the Walla Walla Invasion, 1846," *California Historical Society Quarterly*, Vol. 21, pp. 9-21, 1942.

Hutchins, James S., "Mounted Riflemen: The Real Role of Cavalry in the Indian Wars," see *Probing the American West*, papers from the Santa Fe Conference, Santa Fe, Museum of New Mexico Press, pp. 79-85, 1962.

_____, "Poison in the Pemmican," *Montana*, Vol. 8(3), pp. 8-25, 1958.

_____, "The Fight at Beecher Island," see *Great Western Indian Fights*, Bison Book, University of Nebraska Press, Lincoln, 4th printing, pp. 165-174, 1969.

Irwin, Bernard J. D., "The Chiricahua Apache Indians: A Thrilling Incident in the Early History of Arizona Territory (The Bascom Incident)," *Infantry Journal*, pp. 368-375, April 1928.

James, Rhett S. (ed.), "Brigham Young-Chief Washakie Indian Farm Negotiations, 1854-1857," *Annals of Wyoming*, Vol. 39(2), pp. 245-256, 1967.

Johannsen, Robert W. (ed.), "Edward O. C. Ord on Frontier Defense," *California Historical Society Quarterly*, Vol. 35, pp. 23-27, 1956.

Jones, Okah L., Jr., "The Origins of the Navajo Indian Police, 1872-1873," *Arizona and the West*, Vol. 8(3), pp. 225-238, 1966.

Jones, Robert Huhn, "The Northwestern Frontier and the Impact of the Sioux War, 1862," *Mid-America*, Vol. 41(3), pp. 131-153, 1959.

Josephy, A. M., Jr., "Revolt in the Pueblos," *American Heritage*, Vol. 12, pp. 65-77, June 1961.

_____, "Last Stand of Chief Joseph," *American Heritage*, Vol. 9, pp. 36-43, 78-79, Feb. 1958.

Kelley, W. F., "The Indian Troubles and the Battle of Wounded Knee," *Transactions and Reports of the Nebraska State Historical Society*, Vol. 4, pp. 30-50, 1892.

King, Captain Charles, "Custer's Last Battle," *Harper's Magazine*, Vol. 81, No. 483, pp. 378-387, Aug. 1890.

Kinsley, H. B., "Frank Grouard, Government Scout," *Overland Monthly*, Vol. n.s. 81, pp. 18-19, Aug. 1923.

Knight, Oliver, "A Revised Check List of Indian War Correspondents, 1866-91," *Journalism Quarterly*, Vol. 38(1), pp. 81-82, 1961.

Koch, Lena Clara, "The Federal Indian Policy in Texas, 1845-1860," *Southwestern Historical Quarterly*, Vol. 28, 1924-1925; Vol. 29, 1925-1926.

Leermakers, J. A., "The Battle of the Rosebud," see *Great Western Indian Fights*, Bison Book, University of Nebraska Press, Lincoln, 4th printing, pp. 225-234, 1969.

Lindgren, Raymond E., "A Diary of Kit Carson's Navajo Campaign, 1863-1864," *New Mexico Historical Review*, Vol. 21, pp. 226-247, 1946.

Loomis, Noel M., "The Battle of Wood Lake," see *Great Western Indian Fights*, Bison Book, University of Nebraska Press, Lincoln, 4th printing, pp. 86-93, 1969.

Luce, E. S., "Custer Battlefield," *American Heritage*, Vol. 5, No. 4, pp. 36-43, June 1954.

Lummis, Charles F., "Apache Warrior," *The Kansas Magazine*, pp. 225ff, Sept. 1886.

Lyon, Juana Fraser, "Archie McIntosh, the Scottish Indian Scout," *The Journal of Arizona History*, Vol. 7, No. 3, pp. 103-122, Autumn 1966.

McCann, Lloyd E., "The Grattan Massacre," *Nebraska History Magazine*, Vol. 37, pp. 1-25, 1956.

McClintock, James H., "Fighting Apaches: Narrative of the Fifth Cavalry's Deadly Conflict in the Superstition Mountains," *Sunset Magazine*, Vol. 18, pp. 340-343, Feb. 1907.

McConnell, R. C., "The Custer Expedition of 1876, Participation in by Isaiah Dorman, Negro," *Journal of Negro History*, Vol. 33, pp. 344-352, July 1948.

McElroy, Harold L., "Mercurial Military: A Study of The Central Montana Frontier Army Policy," *Montana Magazine of History*, Vol. 4, pp. 9-23, Fall 1954.

McNickle, D'Arcy, "Indian and European: Indian-White Relations from Discovery to 1887," *Annals of the American Academy of Political and Social Science*, Vol. 311, pp. 1-11, 1957.

Mark, Frederick A., "The Bannack Indian War of 1878," see *Great Western Indian Fights*, Bison Book, University of Nebraska Press, Lincoln, 4th printing, pp. 270-280, 1969.

Marshall, A. D., "Phil Kearney Fort Massacre," *Overland Magazine*, Vol. 61, pp. 228-230, March 1913.

Mattes, Merrill J., The Enigma of Wounded Knee," *Plains Anthropologist*, Vol. 5, pp. 1-11, 1960.

Mattison, Ray H., "The Battle of Massacre Canyon," see *Great Western Indian Fights*, Bison Book, University of Nebraska Press, Lincoln, 4th printing, pp. 185-188, 1969.

_____, "The Military Frontier on the Upper Missouri," *Nebraska History Magazine*, Vol. 37, pp. 159-182, 1956.

Mellor, William J., "The Military Investigation of Colonel John M. Chivington Following the Sand Creek Massacre," *Chronicles of Oklahoma*, Vol. 16, pp. 444-464, 1938.

Merriam, L. C., Jr. (ed.), "The First Oregon Cavalry and the Oregon Central Military Road Survey of 1865," *Oregon Historical Quarterly*, Vol. 60(1), pp. 89-124, 1959.

Merritt, General Wesley, "Three Indian Campaigns," *Harper's New Monthly Magazine*, Vol. 80, pp. 720-737, April 1890.

Metcalf, George, "Tragedy at Wounded Knee," see *Great Indian Fights*, Bison Book, University of Nebraska Press, Lincoln, 4th printing, pp. 307-317, 1969.

Miles, Maj. Gen. Nelson A., "The Future of the Indian Question," *North American Review*, Vol. 152, pp. 1-11, 1891.

_____, "Rounding Up the Red Man," *Cosmopolitan*, Vol. 51, pp. 105-114, June 1911.

_____, "My First Fight on the Plains," *Cosmopolitan*, Vol. 50, pp. 792-802, May 1911.

Morgan, George H., "The Fight at the Big Dry Wash in the Mogollon Mountains, Arizona, July 17, 1882, with Renegade Apache Scouts from the San Carlos Reservation," *Proceedings of the Annual Meeting of the Order of Indian Wars of the U.S. held Feb. 24, 1940*, pp. 21-28.

Morris, T., "Report on Indian War and Treaties," *Washington Historical Quarterly*, Vol. 19, pp. 134-141, 1928.

Morton, L., "End of Formalized Warfare," *American Heritage*, Vol. 6, pp. 12-19+, Aug. 1955.

Muckleroy, Anna, "The Indian Policy of the Republic of Texas," *Southwestern Historical Quarterly*, Vol. 25, 1921-22; Vol. 26, 1922-23.

Nasatir, A. P. (ed.), "The International Significance of the Jones and Immell Massacre and of the Aricara Outbreak in 1823," *Pacific Northwest Quarterly*, Vol. 30, pp. 77-108, 1939.

Neil, William M., "The Territorial Governor as Indian Superintendent in the Trans-Mississippi West," *Mississippi Valley Historical Review*, Vol. 43(2), pp. 213-237, 1956.

Nelson, Harold L., "Military Roads for War and Peace, 1791-1836," *Military Affairs*, Vol. 19(1), pp. 1-14, 1955.

Nesbitt, Paul, "Battle of the Washita," *Chronicles of Oklahoma*, Vol. 3, pp. 3-32, 1925.

Nye, E. L., "Cavalry Horse," *Montana*, Vol. 7(2), pp. 40-45, 1957.

O'Danachair, Caoimhín, (ed.), "A Soldier's Letters Home, 1863-74," *Irish Sword*, Vol. 3(10), pp. 57-64, 1957.

Oliphant, J. Orin (ed.), "Journals of the Indian War of 1855-56," *Washington Historical Quarterly*, Vol. 15, pp. 11-31, 1924.

Opler, Morris E., "The Raid and War-Path Language of the Chiricahua Apache, *American Anthropologist*, Vol. 42, pp. 617-634, Oct.-Dec. 1940.

_____, "A Chiricahua Apache's Account of the Geronimo Campaign of 1886," *New Mexico Historical Review*, Vol. 13, pp. 360-386, 1938.

_____, and Catherine H. Opler, "Mescalero Apache History in the Southwest," *New Mexico Historical Review*, Vol. 25, pp. 1-36, 1950.

Patterson, Bradley H., Jr., "The Pierre's Hole Fight," see *Great Western Indian Fights*, Bison Book, University of Nebraska Press, Lincoln, 4th printing, pp. 30-38, 1969.

Peck, Mrs. W. F., "Black Hawk," *Annals of Iowa*, Vol. 2, pp. 450-464, 1895/97.

Peery, Dan W., "The Kiowa's Defiance," *Chronicles of Oklahoma*, Vol. 13, pp. 30-36, 1935.

Perrine, Fred S., "Military Escorts on the Santa Fe Trail," *New Mexico Historical Review*, Vol. 2, pp. 175-193, 269-304; Vol. 3, pp. 265-300, 1928.

Pipes, Nellie B., "Indian Conditions in 1836-38," *Oregon Historical Quarterly*, Vol. 32, pp. 332-342, 1931.

Pool, William C., "The Battle of Dove Creek," *Southwestern Historical Quarterly*, Vol. 53, pp. 367-385, 1950.

Porter, Kenneth W., "Negroes and Indians on the Texas Frontier, 1834-1874," *Southwestern Historical Quarterly*, Vol. 53, pp. 151-163, 1949.

_____, "Negroes and Indians on the Texas Frontier, 1831-1876," *Journal of Negro History*, Vol. 41(3), pp. 185-214, 1956; (4), pp. 285-310.

Prosch, Thomas W., "The Indian War in Washington Territory," *Quarterly of the Oregon Historical Society*, Vol. 16, pp. 1-23, 1915.

Rankin, M. Wilson, "The Meeker Massacre: From Reminiscences of Frontier Days," *Annals of Wyoming*, Vol. 16, pp. 87-145, 1944.

Redfield, Francis M., "Reminiscences of Francis M. Redfield, Chief Joseph's War," *Pacific Northwest Quarterly*, Vol. 27, pp. 66-77, 1936.

202 Reeve, Frank D., "The Apache Indians in Texas," *The Southwestern Historical Quarterly*, Vol. 1, No. 2, pp. 189-219, 1946.

_____, (ed.), "War and Peace: Two Arizona Diaries," *New Mexico Historical Review*, Vol. 24, pp. 95-129, 1949.

Regan, John H., "The Expulsion of the Cherokees from East Texas," *Quarterly of the Texas State Historical Association*, Vol. 1, pp. 38-46, 1897/98.

Remington, Frederic, "Sioux Outbreak in South Dakota," *Harper's Weekly Magazine*, Vol. 35, pp. 57+, 64-65, Jan. 24, 1891.

_____, "Lieutenant Casey's Last Scout," *Harper's Weekly Magazine*, Vol. 35, pp. 85-89, Jan. 31, 1891.

_____, "The Art of War and Newspaper Men," *Harper's Weekly Magazine*, Vol. 34, p. 947, Dec. 6, 1890.

_____, "Indians as Irregular Cavalry," *Harper's Weekly Magazine*, Vol. 34, pp. 1004-1006, Dec. 27, 1890.

_____, "Massai's Crooked Trail," *Harper's New Monthly Magazine*, Vol. 96, pp. 240-246, Jan. 1898.

Renner, F. G., "Blood on the Lava," see *Great Western Indian Fights*, Bison Book, University of Nebraska Press, Lincoln, 4th printing, pp. 192-199, 1969.

Richardson, Ernest M., "Battle of Lightning Creek," *Montana*, Vol. 10(3), pp. 42-52, 1960.

Richardson, Lt. W. P., "Some Observations Upon the Sioux Campaign of 1890-91," *Journal of the Military Service Institution of the United States*, Vol. 18, pp. 512-531, 1896.

Rickey, Don Jr., "The Enlisted Men of the Indian Wars," *Military Affairs*, Vol. 23(2), pp. 91-96, 1959.

Riddle, Jack P., "Besieged on Milk Creek," see *Great Western Indian Fights*, Bison Book, University of Nebraska Press, Lincoln, 4th printing, pp. 281-291, 1969.

Rinehart, M.R., "To Wyoming; Custer Battle Anniversary," *Saturday Evening Post*, Vol. 199, pp. 16-17, Oct. 2, 1926.

Rinehart, W. V., "War in the Great Northwest," *Washington Historical Quarterly*, Vol. 22, pp. 83-98, 1931.

Rister, C. C., "The Significance of the Jacksboro Indian Affair of 1871," *Southwestern Historical Quarterly*, Vol. 29, pp. 181-200, 1925/26.

Robinson, Frank U., "The Battle of Snake Mountain," *Military Affairs*, Vol. 14, No. 2, pp. 92-98, 1950.

Roddis, Louis H., "The Last Indian Uprising in the United States," *Minnesota History*, Vol. 3, pp. 273-290, 1919/20.

Ronnenberg, H. A., "America's Greatest Mass Execution," *American Mercury*, Vol. 67, pp. 565-571, Nov. 1948.

Rosenberg, M., and D. Rosenberg, "There Are No Indians Left Now But Me," *American Heritage*, Vol. 15, pp. 18-23+, June 1964.

Ross, A. R., "Indian Raids in Colorado, 1875," *Colorado Magazine*, Vol. 24, pp. 258-263, 1947.

Russell, Don, "The Dual on the War Bonnet," *Military Affairs*, Vol. 1, No. 2, pp. 55-69, 1937.

Rutland, Robert (ed.), "The Dragoons in the Iowa Territory, 1845," *Iowa Journal of History and Politics*, Vol. 51, pp. 156-182, 1953.

_____, "A Journal of the First Dragoons in the Iowa Territory, 1844," *Iowa Journal of History and Politics*, Vol. 51, pp. 57-78, 1953.

Sacks, Benjamin, "New Evidence on the Bascom Affair," *Arizona and the West*, Vol. 4, pp. 261-278, 1962.

Salzman, M., Jr., "Geronimo the Napoleon of Indians," The *Journal of Arizona History*, Vol. 8, No. 4, pp. 215-247, Winter 1967. Reprinted from *The Border*, March 1909.

Sandoz, M., "Grisly Epilogue," *American Heritage*, Vol. 17, p. 73, April 1966.

Santee, J. F., "Edward R. S. Canby, Modoc War, 1873," *Oregon Historical Quarterly*, Vol. 33, pp. 70-78, 1932.

Sass, H. R., "Man Who Looked Like Napoleon: Joseph, Chief of a Nez Perce Tribe," *Collier's*, Vol. 106, pp. 23, 60-62, Sept. 21, 1940.

_____, "Warriors' Path; Hundred-Years War of the Iroquois and Cherokees," *Collier's*, Vol. 100, pp. 22-26, July 24, 1937.

Savage, W. Sherman, "The Role of Negro Soldiers in Protecting the Indian Frontier from Intruders," *Journal of Negro History*, Vol. 36, pp. 25-34, 1951.

Schlesinger, Sigmund, "The Beecher Island Fight," *Kansas Historical Collections*, Vol. 15, pp. 538-547, 1919.

Schmitt, Karl, "Wichita-Kiowa Relations and the 1874 Outbreak," *Chronicles of Oklahoma*, Vol. 28, pp. 154-160, 1950.

Scott, Brig. Gen. E. D., "Wounded Knee, a Look at the Record," *Field Artillery Journal*, Vol. 24, pp. 5-24, 1939.

Scott, Winfield, "The Indian War of 1858," *Washington Historical Quarterly*, Vol. 2, pp. 237-240.

Seymour, Charles G., "The Sioux Rebellion, the Final Review," *Harper's Weekly Magazine*, Vol. 35, p. 106, 108-109, Feb. 7, 1891.

Shallenberger, A. C., "The Last Pawnee-Sioux Indian Battle and Buffalo Hunt," *Nebraska History Magazine*, Vol. 16, pp. 132-145, 1935.

Sharp, Paul F., "Massacre at Cypress Hills: A Whoop-up Country Preview," *Montana Magazine of History*, Vol. 4, pp. 26-41, 1954.

Sheldon, Addison E., "After Wounded Knee—A Recollection," *Nebraska History Magazine*, Vol. 22, p. 45, 1941.

Sherman, Caroline B. (ed.), "A Young Army Officer's Experiences in Indian Territory," *Chronicles of Oklahoma*, Vol. 13, pp. 146-153, 1935.

Shields, Alice Mathews, "Army Life on the Wyoming Frontier: Interview Brings Descriptions of Life at the Military Outposts, from a Woman's Experiences," *Annals of Wyoming*, Vol. 13, pp. 331-343, 1941.

Shipp, Lt. W. E., "Captain Crawford's Last Expedition," *The United States Cavalry Association Journal*, pp. 278-300, Oct. 1908.

Shortridge, Wilson P., "Henry Hastings Sibley and the Minnesota Frontier," *Minnesota History*, Vol. 3, pp. 115-125, 1919/20.

Simms, D. Harper, "The Apache Scouts Who Won a War," see *Great Western Indian Fights*, Bison Book, University of Nebraska Press, Lincoln, 4th printing, pp. 257-265, 1969.

_____, "The Incredible Story of the Chiricahua Scouts," *The Westerners Brand Book*, Chicago Corral, Vol. 13, No. 6, Aug. 1956.

Sinclair, F. H., "White Man's Medicine Fight," *Montana*, Vol. 6(3), pp. 1-10, 1956.

Smith, C. C., "Fight at Cibicu," *Arizona Highways*, Vol. 32, pp. 2-5, May 1956.

Smith, D., "Scalp for a Scalp: Sioux and Crow Were Never at Peace," *Scholastic*, Vol. 43, pp. 17-19, Nov. 15, 1943.

Smith, Marian W., "The War Complex of the Plains Indians," *Proceedings of the American Philosophical Society*, Vol. 78, pp. 425-464, 1938.

Smith, Ralph A., "Mexican and Anglo-Saxon Trade in Scalps, Slaves & Livestock, 1835-1841," *West Texas Historical Association Yearbook*, No. 36, pp. 98-115, 1960.

_____, "Apache 'Ranching' Below the Gila, 1841-1845," *Arizoniana: the Journal of Arizona History*, Vol. 3, No. 4, pp. 1-17, Winter 1962.

Smitter, W., "Red Warrior Who Licked Custer," *Coronet*, Vol. 26, pp. 117-120, Aug. 1949.

Sprague, M., "Bloody End of Meeker's Utopia," *American Heritage*, Vol. 8, pp. 36-39, 90-94, Oct. 1957.

Stewart, Edgar I., "Variations on a Minor Theme: Some Controversial Problems of the Custer Fight," *Montana Magazine of History*, Vol. 1, pp. 23-35, July 1951.

_____, "Major Brisbin's Relief of Fort Pease: A Prelude to the Bloody Little Big Horn Massacre," *Montana Magazine of History*, Vol. 6, pp. 23-41, Summer 1956.

_____, "Which Indian Killed Custer?" *Montana Magazine of History*, Vol. 8(3), pp. 26-32, 1958.

_____, (ed.), "I Rode With Custer," *Montana Magazine of History*, Vol. 4, pp. 17-29, Summer 1954.

Sumner, E. V., "Besieged by the Utes," *Century Magazine*, Vol. 42 (ns 20), pp. 837-847, Oct. 1891.

Thrapp, Dan L., "Dan O'Leary, Arizona Scout: A Vignette," *Arizona and the West*, Vol. 7(4), pp. 287-298, 1965.

Titus, Nelson C., "The Last Stand of the Nez Perces," *Washington Historical Quarterly*, Vol. 6, pp. 145-153, 1915.

Traub, Capt. Peter E., "The First Act of the Last Sioux Campaign," *Journal of the United States Cavalry Association*, Vol. 15, pp. 872-879, 1905.

Trickett, Dean, "Civil War in the Indian Territory: 1862," *Chronicles of Oklahoma*, Vol. 19, pp. 55-69, 381-396, 1941.

Tyler, Barbara Ann, "Cochise: Apache War Leader, 1858-1861," *The Journal of Arizona History*, Vol. 6, No. 1, pp. 1-10, Spring 1965.

Utley, Robert M., "The Surrender of Geronimo," *Arizoniana: the Journal of Arizona History*, Vol. 4, No. 1, pp. 1-9, Spring 1963.

_____, "The Battle of the Little Bighorn," see *Great Western Indian Fights*, Bison Book, University of Nebraska Press, Lincoln, 4th printing, pp. 235-253, 1969.

_____, "The Bascom Affair: a reconstruction," *Arizona and the West*, Vol. 3(1), pp. 59-68, 1961.

_____, "The Celebrated Peace Policy of General Grant," *North Dakota History*, Vol. 20, pp. 121-142, 1953.

Vestal, S., "Man Who Killed Custer," *American Heritage*, Vol. 8, pp. 4-9, 90-91, Feb. 1957.

Vigness, David M., "Indian Raids on the Lower Rio Grande, 1836-1837," *Southwestern Historical Quarterly*, Vol. 59(1), pp. 14-23, 1955.

Vincent, John R., "Midwest Indians and Frontier Photography," *Annals of Iowa*, Vol. 38(1), pp. 26-35, 1965.

Walker, Don D., (ed.), "Cowboys, Indians and Cavalry: A Cattleman's Account of the Fights of 1884," *Utah Historical Quarterly*, Vol. 34(3), pp. 255-262, 1966.

Wallace, E. W., "Border Warrior," *American Heritage*, Vol. 9, No. 4, pp. 22-25, 102-103, June 1958.

Wallace, Ernest and Adrian S. Anderson, "R. S. MacKenzie and the Kickapoos: The Raid into Mexico in 1873," *Arizona and the West*, Vol. 7(2), pp. 105-126, 1965.

Watson, Chandler B., "Recollections of the Bannock War," *Oregon Historical Quarterly*, Vol. 68(4), pp. 317-329, 1967.

Watson, Elmo Scott, "The Indian Wars and the Press: 1866-1867," *Journalism Quarterly*, Vol. 317, pp. 301-312, Dec. 1940.

_____, "The Last Indian War, 1890-91—A Study of Newspaper Jingoism," *Journalism Quarterly*, Vol. 20, pp. 205-219, 1943.

Welsh, Herbert, "The Meaning of the Dakota Outbreak," *Scribner's Magazine*, Vol. 9, pp. 429-452, 1891.

Wemett, W. M., "Custer's Expedition to the Black Hills in 1874," *North Dakota Historical Quarterly*, Vol. 6, pp. 292-301, 1931/32.

206 Wick, B. L., "The Struggle for the Half-Breed Tract," *Annals of Iowa*, Vol. 7, pp. 16-29, 1905/07.

Williamson, Daniel R., "Story of Oskay De No Tah, The Flying Fighter," *Arizona Historical Review*, Vol. 3 (3), pp. 78-83, Oct. 1930.

Wilson, G., "The Sioux War," *Nation*, Vol. 52, pp. 29-30, 1891.

Winter, C. F., "Surrender of Poundmaker," *Canadian Magazine*, Vol. M 36, pp. 411-419, March 1911.

Wold, Pauline, "Some Recollections of the Leech Lake Uprising," *Minnesota History*, Vol. 24, pp. 142-148, 1943.

Wood, C. E. S., "Chief Joseph, the Nez Perce," *Century Magazine*, Vol. 28, No. 1, May 1884.

Woodward, Arthur, "Sidelights on Fifty Years of Apache Warfare," *Arizoniana: the Journal of Arizona History*, Vol. 2, No. 3, pp. 3-14, Fall 1961.

Worcester, Donald E., "The Weapons of American Indians," *New Mexico Historical Review*, Vol. 20, pp. 227-238, 1945.

_____, "Spanish Horses Among the Plains Tribes," *Pacific Historical Review*, Vol. 14, pp. 409-417, 1945.

_____, "The Beginnings of the Apache Menace of the Southwest," *New Mexico Historical Review*, Vol. 16, pp. 1-14, 1941.

Worley, Ted R., "Arkansas and the 'Hostile' Indians, 1835-1838," *Arkansas Historical Quarterly*, Vol. 6, pp. 155-164, 1947.

Worman, C. G., "Guns of the 7th Cavalry," *Hobbies*, Vol. 71, pp. 126-127, Nov. 1966.

Wylie, Helen, "On the Warpath," *Palimpsest*, Vol. 9, pp. 75-79, 1928.

Young, Otis E., "The United States Mounted Ranger Battalion, 1832-1833," *Mississippi Valley Historical Review*, Vol. 41, pp. 453-470, 1954.

Zogbaum, Rufus Fairchild, "Jumping an Indian Village," *Outing Magazine*, Vol. 10, No. 2, p. 98ff, Nov. 1896.

Troopers West

has been set
in Aldus and Palatino types
and printed on
Mohawk Superfine Text and
Dorado Dull.
Book designed by
Bob Yeager.